John Whetham Boddam-Whetham

Western Wanderings

A Record of Travel in the Evening Land

John Whetham Boddam-Whetham

Western Wanderings
A Record of Travel in the Evening Land

ISBN/EAN: 9783337190262

Printed in Europe, USA, Canada, Australia, Japan

Cover: Foto ©Andreas Hilbeck / pixelio.de

More available books at **www.hansebooks.com**

NIAGARA FALLS.—Whirlpool Rapids.

WESTERN WANDERINGS

A RECORD OF TRAVEL IN THE EVENING LAND

BY

J. W. BODDAM-WHETHAM

ILLUSTRATED

LONDON
RICHARD BENTLEY AND SON
Publishers in Ordinary to Her Majesty
1874

The following sketches of Wanderings in the Far West are presented to the Public, not so much as having pretensions to literary merit, as possessing, possibly, some degree of interest for those who have never visited the Evening Land; and affording some hints and information to those who may be intending to journey in that direction, and may care to diverge occasionally from the beaten track.

May the truthfulness of the record atone for its defects.

J. W. B.-W.

CONTENTS.

CHAPTER I.
ACROSS THE ATLANTIC.

The poetry of motion—A growl—Rough weather—Fellow-passengers—A new-fashioned honeymoon—Emigrants—Life on the ocean-wave—An arrival—The pilot-boat—The Harbour . . 1

CHAPTER II.
NEW YORK TO NIAGARA.

Civil service—A free country—Street-cars—Hotels—Cookery—Sight-seeing—Billiards—Central Park—Flowers—A naval engagement—The Hudson—A 'Pullman' car—The old lady and her luggage—Susquehanna—An express train—Buffalo City . 7

CHAPTER III.
NIAGARA TO CHICAGO.

The Cataract House—Proffers of assistance—A soliloquy—The Falls—Tolls—A want of caution—Curiosities—An elevator—Birds—Over the Falls—A 'Sleeping-car'—Tobacco-chewing—Snoring—Lake Michigan 20

CHAPTER IV.
CHICAGO TO OMAHA.

Trials—Enterprise—A moving story—Pig-sticking—New version of one of the Labours of Hercules—Hotel life *versus* home life—To the Mississippi—Reserve—Tower—Farmers' Granges—A bad track—Council Bluffs—Baths—The Missouri . . . 32

CHAPTER V.

OMAHA TO SALT LAKE CITY.

Up the Missouri—Snakes—Nebraska—Indians—Prairie—Buffalo—Eating-stations—Prairie dogs—Denver—Redrocks—Indian races—Agates—Indian battle—Sheep mountain—A storm—Echo Cañon—The Devil's Slide—Salt Lake City 47

CHAPTER VI.

SALT LAKE CITY TO VIRGINIA CITY.

Early days—The Tabernacle—A vision—Mormons—Ann Eliza—Brigham Young—Mormon shops—American Fork Cañon—Salt Lake—A pageant—The Theatre—Mormonism—The Great American Desert—Euchre—Tricks that are vain—Nevada—Train-robbers—Americanisms—Reno 72

CHAPTER VII.

VIRGINIA CITY TO STOCKTON.

Politicians—A silver mine—Sutro Tunnel—A commercial crisis—Geysers—Lake Tahoe—Shakespeare—Donner Lake—The old traveller—Two American forces—Cape Horn—Alabaster Cave—Sacramento—Mosquitoes—The pedlar boy—The poor man's carriage—Gold currency—Wages 89

CHAPTER VIII.

STOCKTON TO THE YOSEMITE VALLEY.

Stockton—Dust—Gophers—Quails—Staging—Tarantulas—Hydraulic mining—Mammoth Trees—A curious flower—A theory—Table mountain—Deserted villages—Chinese Camp—Wine—The Siamese Twins—Manzanita—The summit 103

CHAPTER IX.

THE YOSEMITE VALLEY.

The descent—A patient steed—The Valley—The Hotel—A philosopher—Riding astride—The Yosemite Falls—Mirror Lake—A legend—Bridal-veil Fall—Glacier Point and Sentinel Dome—The Nevada and Vernal Falls—A rapid—The Cosmopolitan—Improvements—Impressions—Digger Indians—Departure . . 120

CHAPTER X.

TO SAN FRANCISCO.

Stage jokes—The Golden City—Site—Vegetation—Dust—Overwork—Lone mountain—Seal rocks—Mission Dolores—Bits—Bars—Free lunch—Julep—A character—Architecture—Chinese—High wages—Hoodlums—Chinese facetiæ—Visit to the bad Chinese quarter—Chinese superstitions and troubles . . . 143

CHAPTER XI.

SAN FRANCISCO.

Peculiarities—Quacks—Farallone Islands—Woodward's Gardens—Eucalyptus—Suicide and murders—Schools—American politics—The labouring class—Shoddy—Refinement—Literature—The Press—Advertisements—Side-walks—Street-cars—Occupations—A critic 166

CHAPTER XII.

SAN FRANCISCO TO MOUNT SHASTA.

The Bay—Education of turkeys—The sparrow—Larks—Golden grain—Stubble—Bad farming—Fruit—Marysville—Bank robbery—A humming-bird fight—Staging—Companions—Highwaymen—Scenery—No grumbling—'You bet'—Making oneself popular—Grizzlies—Spiritualism—Castle Rocks—Soda Springs . . 187

CHAPTER XIII.

MOUNT SHASTA.

Game—Foliage—Barrenness—Night—Morning—Clouds—The Crater—Boiling Springs—View—Sunset—Red snow—Sisson's—Play of colour—Packing—The trail—Our first deer—American deer—Destruction of game out of season 204

CHAPTER XIV.

CAMPING OUT.

A frying-pan—Castle Lake—Famine—Fishing—Dinner—A song—Fresh quarters—Deer-hunting—Ambush—Mountain-sides—Bears—Wild flowers—Home—Camp life—A duel—Woodpeckers—Maternal love 214

CHAPTER XV.

FROM YREKA TO THE LAVA BEDS.

Eaten by a bear—Forest fires—A desert—Sage-hens—Mountain-sheep—Modocs—Indians—Belief—Cost of Indians—a liberal Government—Indian Agents—Present policy—Reservations—Issuing rations to Indians—Santanta and Big Tree—Red Cloud—War Department. 226

CHAPTER XVI.

THE MODOCS.

Treachery—Treaties—War—Murders—Modoc success—Peace Commission—Captain Jack—An interview—Warning—Murder of the Peace Commissioners—Marvellous escape—Lower Klamath Lake—The camp—The Lava Beds—Panic—Savage squaws—Warm Spring Indians—Surrender—Execution—Pelicans—Graves—After dark 230

CHAPTER XVII.

FORT KLAMATH TO THE MYSTIC LAKE.

A custom—Fort Klamath—The Agency—Dead Indian country—The Lake of the Woods—An Indian workshop—A cañon—Snow-fields—The crater's rim—A snow-camp—An alarm—O-po-co-ninne—Mystic Lake—A canoe—The medicine-man—The island—Law of death—Midnight—Internal fires—Surmises . . . 253

CHAPTER XVIII.

FROM JACKSONVILLE TO THE COLUMBIA RIVER.

Oregon forests—The Umpqua Cañon—A poultry fancier—A female hermit—Willamette Valley—Eugene City—The Three Sisters—The Mackenzie River—Oregon City—Falls of the Willamette—Portland—The Columbia River—Scenery—The Multenomah Falls—Castle Rock—Cape Horn—The Cascades—A portage—Coffin Rock—Dalles—A Sahara—Catching salmon—Great Salmon Falls—Fish-eagles—A crane story 267

CHAPTER XIX.

KALAMA TO VICTORIA.

A tedious journey—A terrible threat—An epithet—Olympia—Puget Sound—Snokomish City—An Indian cemetery—Flat-heads—Use of Indians—American diplomacy—Washington Territory—Salmon not taking a fly—San Juan—Victoria—Dull times—Terminus—A view—Climate—Roads—Esquimalt Harbour—Sport—Indians—A red admiral—Superstition—Hospitality . . 282

CHAPTER XX.

UP THE FRASER.

New Westminster—Stumps—Halcyon days—Fishing—A panther—Ferns—Sal-lal—Burrard Inlet—Steam saw-mills—Up the Fraser—Anonymous gifts—Providence—Wood-cutters—Hope—A silver-mine—Rapids—Yale—Hudson's Bay Company—Christianised Indians—Missionaries—A waggon road—A trail—Fatal accident—Hell's Gate—Suspension-bridge—Scenery to Boston Bar—Indian larders—Salmon—Fishing establishments—Boundary line—Haro Straits—The Driard House—British Columbia . . 296

CHAPTER XXI.

RETURN TO NANAIMO.

Miners—Difficulties and dangers—Good and bad luck—Gulf of Georgia—Calculating birds—Nanaimo—Duck-shooting—An Indian guide—The beaver-dam—Fishing—A river—Stars—Merit—An entertainment—The coast 314

CHAPTER XXII.

BRITISH COLUMBIA.

Game in British Columbia—Grouse—Mud Bay—A day's shooting—Raccoons—No woodcocks—Summer ducks—Bears—Indians of British Columbia—Carving—Canoes—Chinook—Indian houses—Burials—Door-posts—Smuggling—Civilised and Christianised Indians—The 'Prince Alfred'—The coast—Grumbling settlers—A Bohemian—Sunset—The Golden Gate 325

CHAPTER XXIII.

SAN FRANCISCO TO THE GEYSERS.

The race for the blue riband—'Coasting'—Games in America—To the Geysers—Calistoga—The Petrified Forest—Foss—The Summit—Speed—The Geyser Hotel—The Devil's Cañon—The Witches' Cauldron—The Pulpit—Indian legend—Indian cuns—The Indian bath—Quicksilver mines—Quails—Return 337

CHAPTER XXIV.

CONCLUDING REMARKS.

Healdsburg—Porters—Jewellery—An art—Rainy season—Catarrh—San Diego—The abalona-hunter—Shooting—Hotel mania—Americans abroad—The West 354

LIST OF ILLUSTRATIONS.

Niagara Falls—Whirlpool Rapids . .	*frontispiece*	
Niagara Falls—Entrance to Cave of the Wind .	*to face p.*	23
Witch Rocks, Utah	,,	47
Devil's Slide—Front View . .	,,	71
Big Tree—Mother of the Forest	,,	103
Father of the Forest	,,	112
General View of the Valley from Prospect Point	,,	120
Sea Birds—Cormorants, &c.	,,	169
South Farallone Island	,,	186
Mount Shasta	,,	204
View on the Columbia River	,,	273
Vulcan's Steam Works	,,	346

Erratum.

Page 47, line 10, *for* Yauhton *read* Yancton.

WESTERN WANDERINGS.

CHAPTER I.

ACROSS THE ATLANTIC.

The poetry of motion—A growl—Rough weather—Fellow-passengers—A new-fashioned honeymoon—Emigrants—Life on the ocean-wave—An arrival—The pilot-boat—The harbour.

At the present day the voyage to New York is of as little importance and, generally, as devoid of interest as the trip between Dover and Calais. In fact, I think the latter, being shorter, has the more interest and variety of the two. Theoretically, hanging over the side of the gallant ship—a ship is always gallant till she comes to grief—and watching the blue waves as they dance in the sunlight, or shimmer with a phosphoric gleam under the pale moonbeams, is all very nice and poetic; but, practically, the stricken one seldom realises the poetry of his position, and his thoughts, if he has any, are apt to be very prosaic.

Will it ever be discovered that the safety of a ship is not incompatible with space, ventilation, and cleanliness, and the general comfort of its passengers?

People often say, 'Oh, it's no use grumbling; we are on board ship, and must put up with it.' Now, I cannot help thinking that a great many improvements, both on board ship and on land, are due to a little good-natured grumbling. But whilst I have been indulging in a quiet growl over the confined arrangements of my cabin—yclept 'state-room'—the ship has weighed anchor, and we are already some distance from the shore. In the morning a bright April sun was shining, a favourable breeze blowing, and there was every prospect of a speedy end to our troubles. But on returning to the deck to enjoy the sea-air and the conversation of my fellow passengers, how changed the scene!

The brightness of the morning has vanished, and a thick mist, evidently fresh from Scotland, shuts us out from the land. The waves are beginning to heave in an unpleasant manner, and it requires a pair of sea-legs—which at present I am not possessed of—to pace the deck with a gait which has any pretensions to grace. Rain, too, begins to fall. No sign is there here of a human being, save myself, and some two or three of the crew, ominously wrapped in huge tarpaulins. Not caring to occupy the deck 'alone in my glory,' I make the dreariness of the scene an excuse for a descent, more rapid than elegant, to the regions below.

The next day broke more propitiously. Acquaintances were formed, and even friendships, destined to last nine or ten days—that is, if nothing untoward should happen in the interval. We had amongst us no professional celebrities on their way to fortune, and had, therefore, to content ourselves with the companionship of beings of commoner clay. These consisted of some four or five merchants; two or three invalids; an old Californian, who told me he had never had a day's illness in his life, but who was as yellow as a guinea—a fact which set me speculating whether the inhabitants of that land gradually change into gold-dust; several children; a thin Methodist preacher, who was going out to improve the Pintes; and a very smart military gentleman, from Illinois. I never exactly ascertained the rank of this gallant son of Mars. Sometimes I heard him addressed as Captain, sometimes as General, but he was familiarly known as 'the Colonel.' He informed us that he was returning from Nice, where he had been passing his honeymoon. As the bride had not yet made her appearance, some one remarked that he was afraid she was suffering a great deal from sea-sickness; to which 'the Colonel' replied that she had been spared that misery, as he had left her at Chicago. I wonder whether this mode of enjoying a honeymoon is common with Americans?

For the first few days I fancied we had none but saloon passengers on board, but I was afterwards informed that we carried over eight hundred emigrants. The capacity they exhibited for living down below was something really wonderful. I hardly ever saw a dozen of them on deck; and how they managed to reach New York alive will ever remain a mystery to me.

Our amusements were not of a very varied description. There was only one complete set of chessmen, and to obtain this it was necessary to get up before daybreak, so great was the rush for it; and the amount of misery thereby entailed was hardly compensated by the most brilliant check-mate. Then there was an old jangling piano in the saloon, and upon this one lady, as 'the Colonel' said, 'played considerable;' and two elderly spinsters, who said they delighted in music, once favoured us with a duet, beginning with the appropriate words, 'Oh! ye voices gone.'

Whist and euchre whiled away a few hours for most of us, but the latter game absorbed ' the Colonel's ' every spare moment. He was indefatigable; morning, noon, and night he played. And to some purpose too, for I never entered the smoking-room without seeing there a victim to his rapacity.

The 'Heathen Chinee' was a joke to him, and the

only man I ever saw beat him was the Methodist preacher.

Life on board ship is very prosaic. At sea one day is far more like another than on land, and the smallest incidents assume there vast importance. Speaking with another ship is an event to be remembered, and the sight of a shoal of porpoises causes as much excitement as a pack of hounds running their fox through a country town on a market-day. Time, however, passed away pleasantly enough, in spite of sea tea, cracked piano, and narrow berths. As regards the berths, I am sure that walking the plank can be nothing to sleeping in one of them, and that their invention can only be due to the fertile brain of an ancient Inquisitor or that of a modern shipbuilder.

Our only event of any importance was the arrival one stormy night of a fresh passenger. Nobody could understand how it was possible for him to have come on board in such weather, and nobody remembered our stopping. Some of the ladies thought we might, perhaps, have picked up a shipwrecked mariner, but anxiety and conjecture were soon set at rest by the information that 'both mother and child were doing well.' There was much discussion as to the nationality of the infant, and I do not know that the question was eventually satisfactorily settled.

On the eleventh day a pilot-boat hove in sight,

and was the signal for numerous wagers amongst the betting-men; the number of the boat, and whether the pilot would first place his right or left foot on deck, causing as much interest as the running of a Derby favourite. I believe if anyone had remarked that the pilot would not stand on his head when he came on board, some one would have been willing to bet that he would.

One of the signs that we were approaching our destination was a change in the kind of beverage in request on board. No longer did you hear pale ale or claret called for, but mixed drinks—'cock-tails,' 'juleps,' 'smashes' &c.—were the order of the day; and the quantity and variety of these concoctions consumed by my Yankee fellow-passengers might have astonished me, had I not always heard that 'the bar' was a great and favourite Institution with the Americans.

We had a glorious day for entering the harbour, and the view was superb. Hills covered with trees, and dotted with picturesquely pretty white houses; forts, celebrated in history, Staten Island, Brooklyn, and the great city stretching away in the distance on its low level island, formed a picture as striking as it was novel; whilst the river, with its numerous monster ferry-boats, and crafts of all shapes and sizes, gave the traveller a very fair idea of the busy active life he might expect to witness in the city itself.

CHAPTER II.

NEW YORK TO NIAGARA.

Civil service—A free country—Street-cars—Hotels—Cookery—Sight-seeing—Billiards—Central Park—Flowers—A naval engagement—The Hudson—A 'Pullman' car—The old lady and her luggage—Susquehanna—An express train—Buffalo City.

ABOUT two hundred years ago the site of the City of New York was bought from the Indians for the sum of twenty dollars, or its equivalent; at the present day that is the amount exacted by the Custom-house myrmidons from every four or five individuals who have the privilege of landing there. The 'feeing system' is certainly the only well-organised arrangement in the Custom-house department. For, unless you would have your portmanteaus opened and their contents scattered over the floor, and are satisfied also to undergo a great deal of annoyance and badgering, called 'civil service,' it is absolutely necessary to slip five dollars into the expectant grasp of one of the rapacious officers. Nothing less will satisfy these harpies; but from the moment their wants are appeased your way is clear, and though your boxes may be filled with silks, laces, and other excisable articles, what is that to them? A friend of mine, who had weakly offered a five-franc piece, thinking to save himself the trouble of opening his luggage, was coolly informed by the inspecting officer that if he had no other money about him he would be happy to wait on him at his hotel the next morning. This piece of condescension my friend did not avail himself of, and consequently, though he had nothing subject to duty, he was soon surrounded by the contents of his portmanteau and hat-box.

The drive to our hotel was another five dollars. In England it would have been half-a-crown; but then we were not in England, as the driver very cleverly explained to us. But we quickly perceived we were in a free country; that cabby was evidently free to charge what he liked, and we, as we liked, free to accept his services or not. The excessively high rate of fares for carriages in New York entirely precludes the general use of them. But there are plenty of street-cars; and the amusing scenes constantly to be witnessed in them, and the necessity for a steady look-out that your pockets are not picked, are as stimulating for the mental powers as the jolts, jerks and struggles to obtain a seat are for the bodily ones.

New York is undoubtedly great in three things— hotels, oysters, and mixed drinks. In the first I was disappointed, with the second delighted, and astonished by the third. The hotels, magnificent externally, and sufficiently well-appointed, yet want a home-like air; and the continual crowd and bustle you find on entering some of the larger ones gives you the impression of being yet in the street. They have a terrible habit in American hotels of serving at meals all the dishes at once, so that by the time one is finished the rest are perfectly cold. Covers, apparently, are unknown luxuries, and the same may be said of a sufficient supply of clean plates, knives and forks, &c.

Mr. Henry Watterson, in a letter to the 'Louisville Courier Journal,' makes the following complimentary remarks on the English: 'The English are a gross, material people. They live on the coarsest food.' Now, anyone who has travelled in America must have noticed that at most of the hotels in large cities, and at all of them in small towns, coarse food and extremely bad cooking are invariably found. The *menu* makes a grand display, but will not stand analysing; and after a short sojourn in America you might easily, before arriving at any hotel in any town, write out the bill of fare that will be found there.

Of course there are exceptions. At the Brevoort House, in New York, as good food and as good cooking will be found as can be wished for; but the charge for these unusual luxuries is most exorbitant.

The hotel is conducted on the European plan, which for English travellers will be found far preferable to the American one. As for the wines, they are generally good, especially in New York; but the prices—I suppose on account of the heavy duties—are so enormous that milk, tea, and water entirely take the place of sherry, claret, and other light wines. It is the same with beer—a bottle of Bass costing four or five times its original price.

Finding fault is a very ungracious task; but hotels may be regarded as belonging to the travelling public. Besides, I have seen so many letters from Americans in England to the different New York papers, constantly abusing 'English cookery,' that it is only fair that the subject of 'American cookery' should be touched upon by an Englishman.

To the oyster-lover America ought to be a paradise. And to the great variety of those bivalves is added a still greater variety in the manner of preparing them for the table. The clams are not quite so good, and, as with olives, an acquired taste is necessary to appreciate them. When I first ate them I thought them like indiarubber boiled in brine.

Everybody has heard of Broadway, as he has heard of the Rue Rivoli and of Regent Street. Length is its principal feature; for the rest, it is ill-paved, badly lighted at night, and has very few shops, or stores, worth looking at. On the whole, Broadway is remarkable for little except the crowds that frequent it and their eager haste—each man, seemingly, being bent on making amends, as they say here, for having come into the world half-an-hour too late. The inventor of boots with wheels, which enable the wearer to go as fast as on a bicycle, ought to make his fortune very rapidly in New York. The hare will never be beaten by the tortoise in America.

Several of the New York churches are very beautiful, and some of the great marble buildings stand as monuments of what can be effected by the persevering industry of those who began life as penniless boys.

As London has its East end and West end, so New York has its Bowery and Broadway. But instead of the innumerable squares and streets of the West end of London, the West end of New York is confined to Fifth Avenue and a few of the adjacent streets; and just as Paris is the paradise which every good American hopes for when he dies, so, a house in Fifth Avenue is what he most covets in this life.

The theatres are mostly fine handsome buildings. They are well-managed, and you find there no disagreeable people on the look-out for a fee for showing you to your seat or for handing a programme, as in our London playhouses. The acting, generally, is indifferent, one 'bright particular star' being the magnet to attract an audience.

New York must be a very musical city, judging from the immense number of piano stores. I should say they are about as numerous, in proportion to the population, as the drinking-bars—which are calculated at one to every hundred and twenty persons. Yet the charge for hiring a piano is more than double what it is in Europe. However, as a shilling in England, or a franc in France, goes as far as a dollar (four shillings) in America, I suppose this is not a charge to complain of.

We went one day to see a 'great billiard tournament' between some of the champions of America; and in spite of the wonderful play of Garnier and Dion, the champions, we found the American game much more tedious for spectators than the English one. Cannons are apt to become monotonous after the first hundred, even when the stakes are silver cups and diamond cues.

In the large billiard halls it is very amusing to watch the different players, and it is not difficult to estimate a man's character by his play.

One player prefers 'following strokes;' quietly and delicately coaxing the hard balls to do what he wants without their being aware of it. Another, is always twisting and 'putting on side' and scoring just where you do not expect it ; whilst another, by sheer straightforward play, drives the balls about with far-seeing combinations. Then there is the cunning man, who gets the balls in a corner and keeps on scoring till the helpless opponent longs to hit him over the head with the butt-end of his cue.

But let us get into the fresh air; and the Central Park will be the very place to drive away the effects of the hot billiard-room.

This park, the pride of New York, is very picturesque ; it has a great variety of surface and ornamentation. But a short time ago it was a barren, bleak, unwholesome stretch of land, a place of deposit for rubbish and old bricks, with here and there a marshy spot and a few stagnant pools. Now, it is most admirably laid out, planted with trees and shrubs, and diversified by hills, rocks, slopes, plains, and lakes ; arranged, too, by the hand of a master, and with a most thorough effect of natural scenery. All sorts of means for elevating the surface and breaking the monotony of outline have been used. Doubtless, in future ages learned men will dig deep into some of the vast mounds and wonder how volcanic action could raise and collect in these spots such a wonderful assemblage of old Indian curiosities, in the shape of tin cans, oyster-shells, shoes, cast-off crinolines, and broken china.

The prohibition to walk on the grass seems rather

strange in a People's Park; but perhaps during the hot dry summers the grass would be so soon worn away that the rule is necessary. At all events, the place is a source of immense enjoyment and benefit to everyone.

In New York one misses very much the flowers and 'hanging gardens' which make London houses so gay. It is a pity that houses whose interiors are so lavishly adorned with works of art should not display on their exteriors a few of the works of nature.

Whilst passing a few days at Rockaway, on Long Island, we witnessed a very curious naval engagement. There was a great noise one morning in front of the hotel, and on going out to ascertain what was the matter we saw a number of large porpoises in hot pursuit of what are called 'drum-fish.' Such a noise! such splashing! the porpoises striking with their tails, and actually driving several of their enemies on shore. More than twenty dead fish were taken out of the shallow water. They must have weighed on an average twenty or thirty pounds each. One old porpoise nearly stranded himself in his laudable endeavours to outdo his friends in this onslaught; and he grunted terribly, and seemed quite put out when the battle was over.

We had reserved the Hudson river for a *bonne-bouche*, and very fortunately so, as we were thereby enabled to carry away with us more pleasing impressions of New York than we otherwise should have done. The banks of very few rivers display more beautiful and romantic scenery than do those of the magnificent stream which flows beneath the Palisades.

From Hoboken to beyond West Point (the Staff College of America) objects of great interest, historical and legendary, present themselves at every turn; whilst the natural beauty of the scenes, viewed from the deck of most capitally-appointed steamers, combine to make this trip one of the most charming imaginable. In these river steamboats food for the body is not lost sight of in the intellectual treat, and in my recollections of the first glimpse of Poughkeepsie there still lingers a reminiscence of the most delicious terrapene stew I ever tasted. To attempt any description of the beautiful river after one rapid journey up and down it would be absurd. It would require weeks to inspect but a part of its beauties, and even then I could not do it anything like justice.

Returning to New York, we said good-bye to the many kind friends we had met in that hospitable city; paid a last visit to busy Broadway and wealthy Wall Street—the latter destined so soon to witness a terrible financial crisis—gave ourselves a farewell dinner at Delmonico's, and finally left the most Hibernian city to be met with out of Ireland, and proceeded on our way to Niagara. We took the Erie Road, as it seemed by the map to pass through a more picturesque country than the other routes, and on a dull damp morning ensconced ourselves in a 'Pullman Silver Palace Drawing-room and Hotel Car.' Such a high-sounding title was enough to take one's breath away. It reminded me of a palace scene in the 'Arabian Nights.' The reality, however, was simply a long railway carriage, with chairs like music-stools with arms; some nets, of a size quite incapable of holding anything, and a brilliant array of spittoons. Nor must I forget the filter of water, with one glass or tin cup chained to it, out of which everybody, from the pea-nut boy and porters, was supposed to drink. What would life be to an American without his filter of iced-water!

For the privilege of entering these luxurious structures an extra three dollars per day (if I remember aright) had to be paid. And as the common first-class carriages in America are most uncomfortable, and the second-class quite unfit for anybody to travel in, the consequence is the 'Pullmans' are the receptacles for all sorts and conditions of men, and are often crowded in a manner conducive to anything rather than good-temper. In speaking of the cheapness of American railway travelling in comparison with that of other nations, this extra charge for the absolutely necessary convenience of a Pullman car is generally overlooked.

A first journey across a strange land is always

entertaining, even if the scenery should present but few attractions; but on our route, though the day was a wet one, we saw much that was interesting—quaint wooden villages, mountains covered with forest-trees, and rich valleys with their numerous farm-houses, giving evidence of a wealthy country and a thriving population. At Port Jervis, a most voluble old lady entered the car, bringing with her an extraordinary assortment of luggage. She had two bandboxes, a dog, a flower-pot, an umbrella, a jug of milk, a luncheon-basket, a parcel of figs, and a boy of fifteen, whose age she gave at the ticket-office as nine. I heard her tell her nearest neighbour of that fact, and she chuckled over it as if she had performed a most virtuous action. Her face, though, fell very considerably when the conductor, after inspecting the youth, informed her that unless she at once paid his proper fare they must go with him to the superintendent. That boy's life must have been a misery to him for daring to be over half-fare age; for when the pair got out at Buffalo the old lady gave him such a swingeing box on the ear that it resounded through the station. Certainly, the boy had given the wretched poodle a kick when he thought the old lady was not looking, but that alone could not account for the terrific force of the blow she inflicted.

Leaving on our right the Catskill Mountains, where

c

poor Rip Van Winkle slept his sleep of twenty years, the road runs along the Delaware River, and we presently enter the Valley of the Susquehanna—a splendid agricultural country, with neat farm-houses, broad fields, and rolling uplands. A picture of rare beauty, indeed, is this valley, with its river winding far down below us and reaching away through the undulating hills to the misty blue mountains in the distance. Our 'express' train was really a most obliging one; it stopped at all the small stations in the most thoughtful manner, not to let them feel of less importance than the bigger ones, I suppose, as we rarely ever took up or set down a passenger. We crawled over the Starucca Viaduct at a pace which gave us ample time to inspect one of the greatest engineering achievements of the route, and as darkness set in we found ourselves entering the city of Buffalo.

First impressions are the most lasting; therefore, Buffalo ought to be seen for the first time from the lake. It is a beautiful city, and worth more attention than is usually bestowed on it—we, in fact, had been advised not to stop there. A long breakwater protects it in front from the treacherous lake, whose waters sometimes rise suddenly and without the slightest apparent cause, and storms of the most appalling character then ensue. A whole navy might ride in the wide and spacious harbour formed by the breakwater.

Fleets of grain-laden vessels cover the lake, whilst on the shores the huge elevators and extensive storehouses are evidence of the source of wealth of this busy town.

The Buffalo people are apparently very fond of trees; two and sometimes three rows of elms and other trees line either side of many of the streets; and as they are constantly adding row to row, some parts of the city appear as if built in a forest. The view from the fort presents a charming panorama, extending over many miles of land and water. We passed a very pleasant day at Buffalo; then, taking the cars, we arrived in a couple of hours at Niagara.

CHAPTER III.

NIAGARA TO CHICAGO.

The Cataract House—Proffers of assistance—A soliloquy—The Falls—Tolls—A want of caution—Curiosities—An elevator—Birds—Over the Falls—A 'sleeping-car'—Tobacco-chewing—Snoring—Lake Michigan.

As it was late when we arrived at the 'Cataract House,' where we had engaged rooms, we deferred taking our first view of the Great Falls until the following morning. The bedrooms at the above-named hotel are about the size of an ordinary ship's cabin, their numerousness probably making up for their diminutiveness; at all events, in the eyes of the proprietor.

After an early 'current bath' of the most intensely cold water I ever bathed in, we made our way to the chief of the natural 'wonders of the world.' Guides and touts of all descriptions pressed their services upon us; urged us to take carriages, though the distance was only a few hundred yards, and generally proffered assistance, which, having no need of, we resolutely declined. Then, conscious of having brought on ourselves the utter contempt of the crowd of would-be showmen, yet remaining firm in our determination not to be 'done,' we were all the more prepared to enjoy the magnificent spectacle awaiting us.

Most of us, probably, have mentally pictured to ourselves the famous Falls of Niagara; almost as soon, perhaps, as we were able to read or first heard with shuddering interest the numerous tales that are told of boats swept with their human freight down the rushing rapids, never again to be seen. Having always had a great love for bold natural scenery, the pleasure experienced from it being intensified when water forms its prominent feature, it had ever seemed to me that the Niagara Falls must be the culminating point of grandeur in nature. I had looked forward so much to the day when I should first behold them; but now, when almost in their presence, I hesitated to look at them—so fearful, so almost convinced did I feel that in them, as in most other things, the reality would fall short of the ideal.

With this impression on my mind I walked rapidly over the small bridges to a point on Goat Island whence a good general view of the Falls was to be obtained. Reaching this, I raised my eyes to take in the whole scene at once, and, with an unpleasant foreboding that my overwrought expectations were about to be disappointed, I looked, and—the stupendous grandeur of the scene that met my gaze far surpassed all I had imagined.

Niagara has been regarded with various feelings and from various mental points of view. Men of business have thought it has a good site for building; John Bull has pronounced it ' a very nice waterfall, and a bigger stream than the Thames.' Sentimental girls have gazed into its misty splendours with superstitious awe, and fancied they saw their fates there. The Yankee calls Niagara ' *some,*' in the way of water-power.' The Red Indian prays to it, ' Oh, Father of mighty waters, grant a blessing on your child.' But with whatever feeling the traveller from the East may view the Falls of Niagara, his eyes can have looked on no grander picture; and far as he may wander towards the setting sun, he cannot hope to see another so splendid.

All this time we have been looking at the great Horse-shoe Fall, over which the enormous mass of water pours with tremendous force. Till it reaches half-way down, the water seems to hang like a green curtain as it rolls over the cliff; then, gradually breaking, the mighty mass spreads out in foam and falls into the gulf below. It is not its rapidity but its slowness which is so awe-inspiring:

> 'Wie das Gestern,
> Ohne Hast
> Aber, ohne Rast.'

NIAGARA FALLS.—Entrance to Cave of the Wind

But no words can describe the grandeur of such a scene.

We were told that the Horse-shoe Fall is gradually assuming a triangular form, the force of the water wearing away the rocky bed and forming a narrow chasm, so that in time the water will have the appearance of falling from two opposite walls. Strangely enough, the water never encroaches on the land on either side. The old tower which for so long stood sentry over this fall was becoming dangerous to ascend, and was blown up the day we were there.

We retraced our steps a short distance towards the American Fall, which is smaller than the Horse-shoe or Canadian Fall, but equally impressive. Descending a few steep steps, we suddenly found ourselves on the brink of the precipice over which the water was pouring and disappearing into a great blue cavern, 150 feet below. This Fall had a greater charm for me than the Horse-shoe Fall, perhaps because we were so much closer to it and were able to look straight down into its misty depths. This also is changing its form, and gradually taking a horse-shoe curve. The little islands in the rapids above, splendidly wooded and covered with all sorts of wild flowers, add greatly to the beauty of the scene. We walked round Goat Island and visited the Three Sisters; small islands connected by rustic bridges to one another and to the main island, and extending out into the middle of the rapids. Here, the river rushes down a steep descent, and the foaming and tossing waters are angry and disturbed like the waves of the sea after a fierce storm. The extraordinary fascination ascribed to Niagara is no myth, and its attractive power no mere fancy of the poet.

The minor drawbacks to visiting Niagara are the great number of tolls and the numerous touts. Regarding the former, if they would only charge so much on arrival, instead of giving you the trouble of putting your hand in your pocket every time you look at the Falls, it would be pleasanter; as for the latter, not one of them ought to be allowed near the place. If there is one thing more wanted than another, it is a pleasant drive or ride without a toll-gate at every mile, and this could be easily made along the shore of the Niagara river towards La Salle. The Goat Island toll is right enough, as keeping up the bridges and other expenses are incurred; but all other tolls are wrong, being wholly unnecessary.

On the second day we drove over the magnificent suspension-bridge to the Canadian side, whence we had a fine full view of both Falls. The garrulous driver was very careful to point out the exact spot where Blondin crossed on the tight-rope. It was a long way below the Falls, and therefore no more danger incurred than in walking on a rope stretched across the fountains of the Crystal Palace—perhaps not even so much. This and another spot, from which somebody once jumped into the river, were evidently of much deeper interest to the mind of our Jehu than the glorious Falls themselves. We were inveigled into a house in front of the Horse-shoe Fall by the assurance of the proprietor that the view from the top was magnificent, and that no charge was made; but the view did not seem to us finer from above than from below. Incautiously entering another room, we discovered a shop full of photographs, Indian fans, &c. (made in Birmingham, probably), and offered for sale by some fascinating young ladies, who could not allow us to leave without a *souvenir* of Niagara.

We were afterwards induced to change our clothes for waterproof ones, and to descend with a guide beneath, or rather behind the Fall. I am not sure that this part of the programme repaid us for getting very hot and wet; but the proprietor when he had pocketed our dollars seemed to think it all right—so we had to look comfortable and happy. A slight shade passed over his countenance when he found he could not induce us to be photographed 'in connection with the Falls,' as he expressed it. But that soon passed off, as he saw a carriage-load of gay tourists approaching, 'got up,' apparently, with the intention of having their likenesses taken, not only 'in connection with the Falls,' but in any other aspiring position that the artist might suggest. On our return to the American side we were asked if we had any articles to declare; but as we had no specimens of Niagara spar, fresh from Derbyshire, and no curious Indian-Parisian bead-work or embroidery, and the few photographs were considered too insignificant for duty, we were allowed to pass free.

The rapids, below the Falls, and the whirlpool, still lower down, well deserve a visit, although the romance of the former is rather diminished by an elevator which takes visitors up and down the cliff. The view on reaching the water's edge is exceedingly fine—the rushing torrent eddying down, and the wild waste of whirling water being a sight second only to the Falls themselves.

We saw a great many beautiful birds, both in the surrounding woods and on the islands. There were two or three sorts of orioles, blue-birds, cardinal grosbeaks, and numbers of the American robins; birds as ubiquitous as our sparrows, and about the size of a large blackbird. Unfortunately, they are considered good eating, and therefore, as they are very tame, become an easy prey to every little wretch who carries a gun.

Many stories are told of victims hurried down the rapids; now clinging to a rock against which the strong current has carried them, and now swept on again by its resistless force, until, with a last shriek, they disappear for ever in the cruel waters of the mighty Fall. These stories are all too true; since our visit two boats and their occupants have in this way been lost. When will thoughtless mortals learn that the treacherous current draws slowly but surely on till they are beyond earthly aid? Not, I suppose, until the great St. Lawrence is dried up, and the hanging cliffs of the giant Falls can be ascended from their base.

But we must be speeding onwards; and so with a farewell look at Niagara, as we cross the great suspension-bridge on our way to Chicago, we leave behind us one of the grandest of Nature's handiworks.

We make our journey to Chicago in a 'Silver Palace Drawing-room and Sleeping-car;' and as there is not much outside to claim our attention, we may as well occupy ourselves with an examination of this renowned invention of the New World. The only visible articles of furniture are sofa-seats, placed *vis-à-vis*, and the inevitable spittoons. The latter nasty articles intrude themselves everywhere. It is all very well for Americans to say, 'You do not find them in the abundance often stated;' all I can say is, you do find them wherever you go, and, what is worse, see a constant use of them. It is said they owe their origin to the devil, and the story runs·thus: 'When the Christian navigators first discovered America the devil was greatly annoyed, and was afraid (without reason, I think) of losing his hold on the people there. However, he whispered in confidence to some of his Indian friends and acquaintance that he had found out a way of being revenged on the new-comers. He would teach them, he said, to chew tobacco, and that the filthy habit should cling to them for ever, and make them a bye-word among the nations.' He certainly has kept his word.

As our 'sleeping-car' afforded no signs of sleeping accommodation, I waited with curiosity for bedtime. It came at last, and the chamber-maid, in the shape of a black-man, entered, and asked me to move, as he was going to make the beds. He then gave a pull upon the sofa-cushions on each side, and the bottom ones came together in the original space between the seats, whilst the back ones took the places of these; a sufficiently good sort of arrangement on which to make up a bed. A handle above was then pulled, and what had looked like part of the ceiling of the car came down to within about three feet of the lower bed. This formed the attic. From out of this concealed bedstead came a couple of mattresses, one of which was placed on the lower bed, the other remaining for the occupant of the story above. Sheets, blankets, and pillows were then produced from the same recess, and a walnut partition was disclosed, which divided these berths from those next door. A heavy curtain fell down in front of the beds, separating them from the rest of the carriage, and the chambers were ready for their guests. All these arrangements were very good in themselves, but there was no possible way of making use of them with the smallest degree of comfort. If there had only been a few hooks for hanging hats, coats, and other garments upon, and a place to put boots in, it would have been something to be thankful for. For, usually, boots were to be found in the morning at different ends of the car, or else on the wrong person's feet.

The space between what may be called the upper and lower deck does not allow of the occupant of the bed sitting up; the double windows are kept shut, that he may not be smothered in dust and ashes, and the night is passed in the most luxurious misery.

The man who slept in the berth next to mine snored frightfully, in fact, night was made hideous by the unmusical sounds issuing from all parts of the car; but no snoring came up to my neighbour's, and I was not astonished at this on looking at him in the morning. Evidently, he was a German Jew, and his nose, acoustically considered, seemed well adapted for the involuntary transmission of vast volumes of sound. An ingenious Yankee has patented a cure for snoring which all snorers ought to purchase previous to night-travelling. It consists, I believe, of an indiarubber tube, of which one end is fastened to the nose and the other enters the tympanum of the ear; so that the snorer is so terrified by his own noise that he instantly awakes, and a few nights of this agony suffice to cure him of any further propensity to snore. The horrors of that first night in a 'Pullman' car are indelibly impressed on my mind. The atmosphere ran a close heat with that of the 'Black Hole of Calcutta.' On my asking the porter why he had kept a fire burning all night, he said he had to sit up, and it would never do for him to catch cold.

If going to bed is misery, getting up in the morning is simply agony. If you are late, you have to wait some hours before you can get a turn at the one wash-hand basin. If you are early, you have to stand outside on the steps in the dust and smoke, until the beds are once more metamorphosed into seats, there being no room or other place to retire to until that operation is performed.

Leaving Detroit, we passed through a country thickly wooded at intervals, and scattered here and there with towns and villages, some busy and active, others looking sleepy and lazy—the latter by far the more attractive of the two.

After some hours of steady travelling, we arrived at Chicago, which is situated on the great inland sea whose shores are skirted by the railway up to the fine avenue that graces the approach to the city.

CHAPTER IV.

CHICAGO TO OMAHA.

Trials—Enterprise—A moving story—Pig-sticking—New version of one of the labours of Hercules—Hotel life *versus* home life—To the Mississippi—Reserve—Iowa—Farmers' granges—A bad track—Council Bluffs—Baths—The Missouri.

CHICAGO, within little more than the last two years, has been most sorely tried. The first disaster was the great fire, which burnt down about two-thirds of the city; in the following year business was almost suspended because of the raging epizootic; and, more recently, an almost unparalleled financial collapse has occurred, bringing with it distress and ruin. Phœnix-like, she rose from the ashes of the conflagration in an incredibly short space of time, and with handsomer buildings and more magnificent warehouses even than before. The vitality of Chicago is remarkable, and we may form in this city a correct idea of the wealth and prosperity of a great nation.

The statement may sound extraordinary, but it is nevertheless a fact, that there was built and completed in the burnt district of Chicago a brick, stone, or iron warehouse every hour of each working day during the space of seven months of 1872. So rapid a growth of a city is unprecedented in the history of any nation in the world, and equally unprecedented are the energy and pluck to which it was due, as evinced by a people who had just witnessed such an enormous destruction of their property by fire.

Nothing seems too bold or difficult for Chicago enterprise. A year or two ago it was thought that the business quarter of the city lay too low, and could not be properly drained; thereupon, the whole quarter was raised bodily about eight feet higher.

Everything must keep moving in Chicago. The houses are continually shifting their position, and a moving building is no longer an uncommon sight. We were greatly amused one day by suddenly coming upon a good-sized three-storied house, standing dejectedly in the middle of a street, as if it did not know where to settle down. The next day, and for two or three following ones, we were continually meeting this same house, and always at different places. The fading ivy which clung to it gave it so mournful an expression that I quite pitied it. It was evidently a little weak in the upper story, poor thing; but whether it eventually took it into its head to prance off to New York, or whether it was accommodated with an acre or two in the grounds of the State Lunatic Asylum, I never satisfactorily discovered.

There are numerous tunnels under the river, and they are of great importance in facilitating intercourse between the different parts of the city; for the river divides Chicago into three sections, and these are connected by drawbridges, which are great obstacles to traffic, as they are always open when carriages or pedestrians wish to cross, and closed when vessels want to pass through.

The enormous new Pacific hotel seems as if it had been intended to accommodate all the people who visited the Vienna Exhibition, only had been built in the wrong place. I do not see how such a caravansary can be made to answer in a town where there are already several very fine large hotels. I hear that, amongst other improvements, the 'Pacific' has a new kind of stairs, which are warranted not to creak when the gentlemen of the resident families return home late. I cannot answer for the fact; but if such stairs are there, they will doubtless prove an attraction.

Hog-killing is now recognised in America as one of the fine arts, and together with pork-packing may be seen to great advantage in Chicago. We were highly edified and amused by a visit to one of the large hog-killing establishments. The houses are spacious substantial buildings, two stories high; the pigs are driven up an inclined gangway to the second story and into the 'feeding pens' in lots of about a hundred at a time. About twenty of them are then driven into the 'clutch-pen,' where each hog is seized by the hind leg with a pair of tongs; a pulley then hoists him up head downwards, and puts him on wheels ready to be moved forward. After a train of about half-a-dozen pigs has been made up, the sliding-door is opened and the victims find themselves in the presence of the executioner, who cuts their throats and presently slides them down the incline into the scalding-vat. Then follows scraping, cleaning, washing, and drying; in fact, a sort of Turkish bath, only perhaps not so pleasant for the pigs. Afterwards, the cutting up and trimming takes place. The dexterity with which the men work is astonishing; a couple of blows severs the head from the body, and with a like number the hams and shoulders are separated. Each part is hurled to its own particular spot, and the air is positively alive with trimmings flying to their destination. Every place is neat and cleanly in the extreme; and after passing though such refining influences it is not surprising that such 'pretty pork' should be extracted from such ugly pigs. While visiting this poetic establishment, where all idea of such gross things as hogs was done away with, I was reminded of the boy who was once asked what pig was called when prepared for the table. He was rather puzzled at first, but a thought suddenly struck him, and he replied, 'Grunt mutton;' a very happy name for it, I think.

Shortly after our arrival at Chicago we went for a long drive by the lake-shore to Evanston, and past a succession of country houses and villas, with gardens and hothouses, quite in the English style. Very seldom are the beautiful lawns and the carefully-kept gardens so universal in England seen in America—the price of labour being too great to admit of its being applied to the uncommercial realm of flowers. The boldest project of the citizens of Chicago, and one which met with complete success, was changing the course of the Chicago river and making it flow south instead of north. The sluggish waters of that Stygian stream crept slowly under bridges, across which you had to run to escape the sickening odours that pursued you. Here and there, near where the waters were thickest and most polluted, placards might be read declaring in hideous irony that boys who bathed there would be taken up. If such an event had happened, the boys would certainly have been mistaken for the '*genti fangose*' in Dante's Seventh Circle of Hell. Nothing lived in these poisonous waters except bull-frogs, whose croaking must have made life a perpetual romance to the dwellers along the banks.

All this had to be altered. And as the sewage-laden stream flowed north into the lake, why not cut down the level inland to make it flow south, and thus bring the pure lake water in a fresh and abundant stream past their very doors? This scheme was carried out to perfection, and the Herculean task of cleansing the Augean stables by the rivers Alpheus and Peneus was equalled at Chicago by the engineering skill of Mr. Chesebrough.

Attracted by some flaming advertisements telling how an operatic company was about to give 'positively its last performance,' we visited the theatre, and, out of regard to the actors, I will only say that the 'Huguenots' were more vilely murdered that night than they could have been on the fatal eve of St. Bartholomew.

At Chicago, as well as in every other city in America, you cannot help being struck by the absence of anything like home, and the prevalence of hotel life. You are told that families can live so much cheaper at hotels, on account of the great difficulty in obtaining servants; but I cannot help thinking that the trouble of house-keeping has a great deal to do with the prosperity of hotels. Besides, only certain localities and only a certain grade of building and style of furniture are considered 'respectable.' 'Respectable' life in America is very expensive. The rent for a respectable house is enormous; for everything—business, living, hospitality

—must be done on a large scale. There really are no suitable dwellings for a family of moderate means. Low-priced hotels are not fashionable, and low-priced houses are either unfit to live in, or are not in 'genteel' localities. In New York there are only two classes, the rich and the poor. The middle class go out of the city to find their homes, and the words 'To Let' stare from the windows of a multitude of houses that nobody can afford to hire. Perhaps—yet I greatly doubt it—the late great commercial disaster may have the effect of overthrowing existing prices, and establishing another and better system of living. The effects of hotel life on the lives and manners of young people are but too evident. I have no wish to preach a sermon on the subject, even were I capable; all I would say is, home is not a name, a form, or a routine; it is a spirit, a presence, a principle, and I do not think these are to be found in hotels.

To gain information by travelling it is of importance to study a map of the country through which one is about to pass; so that the locations of rivers, mountains, towns, &c. may be observed and remembered. On this occasion, our map was spread out before us as we ascended to the top of a lofty grain-elevator, to enjoy a bird's-eye view of the surrounding country. But the panorama did not come up to our expectations; whether it was owing to the flatness of the prairies, the sharp wind from the lake, or the dust from the streets, with which the air was filled, I do not know; but, at all events, we returned to our hotel sadder if not wiser than when we started, and all the more ready to resume our Western journey on the following day. We chose the 'Burlington and Quincy' road, in preference to the other two routes to Omaha, and again had the pleasure of looking forward to another long night in a sleeping-car.

The road lies through a rich, flat, cultivated prairie worthy of its name, the 'Garden State.' The further we go the more thinly scattered become the white wooden houses; and gradually the finished neatness of a suburban district melts into the larger and freer forms of cultivation. The prairie land is the place for steam-ploughs, reaping, mowing, and threshing machines; for with them one family can do the work of a dozen men.

Until the Mississippi is reached you are hardly ever out of sight of farms or woods and plantations. And even by the railway-side tracts of prairie can still be seen— prairie in all its wildness—that looks friendless, desolate, and doomed. The long grasses sway heavily in the wind, and now and then a string of wild ducks rises from a weird-looking reedy lake close beside us, or a covey of prairie-chickens springs from the waving grass and flies away like a covey of the partridges of

Old England. We pass great flat farms of great square flat fields, with but little fencing between them; plantations of tall leafy Indian corn, as yet unripened by the hot summer sun. Here, are orchards laid down in regular rows, there, a line of poplars; but no fine spreading tree is anywhere to be seen. The vastness of the immense unconfined plain is oppressive, stretching onward for miles and miles with a silvery mist in the distance, which might be the sea; but still it stretches onward and onward—repaying with wealth and comfort thousands of toilers, gathered to it out of poverty and dependence in other lands.

There is great amusement, and a little instruction as well, to be derived from the people one meets in these long railway journeys. Like a parrot in a strange cage, they will not talk much the first day, but wait a day or two. Then if you will listen you may learn the personal and family history of most of your fellow-passengers. By the way, it has appeared to me that Americans at home are much more reserved than when abroad. In Europe, nearly every American you meet is 'hail-fellow-well-met,' and ready to discuss his private affairs with you on the very slightest encouragement. In their own country, they seem to have lost, in some measure, their colloquial propensities, not only amongst strangers but amongst themselves. In their public dining-rooms, you rarely hear the steady hum of conversation you mostly do in Europe. But this may be because the servants make so much noise that all other sounds are drowned by it.

But to return to our 'car.' Take, for example, two 'feminines' who have had the same section assigned to them, and watch how the reserve of the first day gradually wears away on the second, and by the eve of the third how completely the ice has melted. The family records have been faithfully aired, and a friendship has been formed which ends when they finally scatter and separate with a gushing 'Now do write to me,' from one, and a sacred promise not to fail doing so, from another. As a rule, the loving remembrance lasts about half-an-hour; and I do not believe the consequent forgetfulness ever caused the death of either from a broken heart.

We are now approaching Burlington, and having crossed the Mississippi, we find ourselves in that pretty, well-built town, where we are to stay for a couple of days, to recover from the effects of 'Pullman' and to see what we can of the great river.

After leaving the Mississippi we gradually ascend until we reach the high plateau which divides that river from the Missouri. There is no doubt about its being a 'rolling prairie,' as the undulations of the ground recall the round swell and deep dips and hollows of the roll of the sea. In Iowa the 'Farmers'

Granges' are most numerous. They number over two thousand in that State alone. A 'Grange' is a sort of co-operative society, and its grand object is not only the general improvement in husbandry but the increase of the general happiness, wealth, and prosperity of the country. First organised less than seven years ago, the number of 'Granges' at present amounts to over six thousand, distributed throughout the land, with a membership of probably over four hundred thousand persons. To resist railroad monopolies was their first determination; and now they have set themselves to resist monopolies of all kinds; avoiding politics, because they hold—and rightly, I believe—that the trade of politics in America is the source of all infamous impositions.

Their business embraces everything that can be advantageous to the members. They have a systematic arrangement for obtaining and disseminating information regarding crops, the aspect of demand and supply, and facilities for procuring help and labour at home, and from abroad. They have a ready means for the exchange of live stock, seeds, plants, &c., and a well-guarded system for testing the merits of new implements and other inventions. The 'Farmers' movement' may be also of great value when looked at from its social side. Anyone who has visited the agricultural districts in America must have remarked the loneliness and isolation of farm-life. This isolation is too often accompanied by an intellectual poverty, and a too great devotion to money-making and money-saving.

A pleasant feature, therefore, of the movement is the prominence given to social intercourse amongst the members; and the formation of 'Granges' would be almost impossible without a certain ratio of lady members.

The farmers take their wives and daughters to the 'Grange meetings,' and thus gradually discover that the tastes of their children are as well worth cultivating as their acres. A good library, an organ or piano, a microscope, botanical collections, &c., are amongst the items with which each Grange is furnished, and all sorts of means are employed for drawing out the hardworking, taciturn farmer, and inspiring him with a fellow-feeling for the neighbourhood. He is taught that to breed pigs and plant potatoes are not the only objects of life, but that books, flowers, and pictures have as real a value as threshing and mowing machines.

Ladies become 'patrons of husbandry' in more senses than one, and soon take a greater interest in agriculture than they perhaps otherwise would do; and there is little doubt that the establishment of 'Granges' will have a most beneficial effect not only on individuals but on the community at large.

But while we have been talking our car has been bumping about in a most extraordinary manner. On looking back at the long lines of rails over which we have just passed they seem so unevenly laid, so rugged with ups and downs, that it is a wonder how we kept on the metals at all. One of the passengers has meekly remarked to the conductor that the roads seem rather rough. 'Wal, yes,' he answers, 'guess they air; trains do jump about some, but it's enough for us if they keep anywhere between the two fences.' However, we have managed to keep not only between the fences but actually on the track, and are gradually approaching the town of 'Council Bluffs,' which stands on the east side of the Missouri, right opposite the more prosperous Omaha.

Council Bluffs is built at the foot of some steep banks which probably have at some time been the boundary of the river; but now, the Missouri, being a wayward, wandering stream, constantly changing its channel, has moved off to see what the Omaha side is like, and has left Council Bluffs high and dry about three miles east. A duller town, or rather village, than Council Bluffs I never saw; certainly it was very hot, and everyone may have been asleep when we arrived, but they could not have remained sleeping all day; yet hardly a soul was stirring, and at last we thought we must have found our way to 'Drowsietown,' so well described by the author of 'White Rose and Red,' where there was

> Nothing coming, nothing going,
> Locusts grating, one cock crowing;
> Few things moving up and down,
> All things drowsy—Drowsietown!

It was a relief to hear that this village and Omaha were at fierce war with one another about railroad matters, but I am ignorant as to where the energy for conducting such a conflict was to come from.

Black water is a specialty at Council Bluffs, and bathing in it is like bathing in ink. This reminds me that travellers in America will do well to provide themselves with indiarubber baths. Fortunately, I had taken that precaution, and found it of immense service. At the hotel at Council Bluffs they had never heard of such a thing as a bath, and were horrified when I produced mine and asked them to fill it. They said it would spoil the carpet. However, they filled it; but in the morning in emptying it they did not take it up in the right place, and the pressure of water on one side caused it to collapse, and in a moment the whole room was flooded. You should have seen the landlord's face when he heard of the disaster. Baths are prohibited in that establishment henceforth and for ever. In the large cities, if you are fortunate enough to get a bedroom with a bath-room attached, you are charged a dollar (four shillings) extra, per night; but that is better than having to wander about the hotel in your dressing-gown and slippers in quest of a bath that costs you only half-a-dollar. In moderate-sized towns the only baths to be found are in the barbers' shops. Hip or sponge baths are unknown; the reason for dispensing with them being, as I was told, that it would not do to give servants too much trouble. Perhaps the day will come when baths, large and small, will be considered as necessary an adjunct to every hotel in America, as they are in every other civilised country.

We very soon had had enough of Council Bluffs. We crossed the dull, muddy river, with its low, flat banks, on a fine iron bridge sixty feet above high water mark. The 'Transfer Company' put 'through' passengers to much unnecessary inconvenience here, and when they do arrive at Omaha they have more trouble still, with their luggage and changing of cars. Railway company disputes are the cause of all this inconvenience, which will probably not be remedied until more routes are opened to California and the Far West.

My travelling companion, much to my regret, left me here, as he had to proceed straight through to San Francisco, in order to catch the mail-steamer—for his destination was China.

WITCH ROCKS.—Echo Cañon, Utah.

CHAPTER V.

OMAHA TO SALT LAKE CITY.

Up the Missouri—Snakes!—Nebraska—Indians—Prairie—Buffalo—Eating-stations—Prairie-dogs—Denver—The Red Rocks—Indian races—Agates—Indian battle—Sheep mountain—A storm—Echo cañon—The Devil's Slide—Salt Lake City.

OMAHA is about as interesting as Council Bluffs Its hotel is large enough to contain all the inhabitants of the town; but it was closed, and the business done by the two or three wretched little inns seemed to be very small indeed. I was glad, therefore, to get on board a small steamer for a cruise up the Missouri as far as Yauhton. The hotel was built, I believe, by the well-known Mr. Train, and I should think he was hardly satisfied with his speculation. The wharfage at Omaha is of a very peculiar kind; steamers and other vessels simply run against the mud, and stick there. Indeed, mud-banks are the principal features of the place.

The steamer in which I embarked was a large flat boat, open at the sides like a raft, and with its furnaces in full view; above, resting on posts, was the cabin, extending nearly the whole length of the hull. Above that again was a smaller cabin, which was surmounted by the pilot-house, and the whole was crowned by the high smoke-stacks, which are necessary to secure a draught for the high-pressure engines.

It was like a card-house which children build up as high as possible without toppling over. Very often on these boats there is a band to enliven the voyage; on this occasion, however, the only music on board was one banjo and no 'bones.'

The navigation is very difficult, on account of the innumerable sand-bars and endless number of roots of trees, which, when washed away from the bank, float into the stream and stick in the mud, with their stems rising just above the surface of the water. They always lie with their sharp ends pointing down stream, and are consequently very dangerous to steamers when ascending it. The river was so shallow that I sometimes doubted whether we should be able to proceed at all; in fact, navigation for any distance is practicable only for a very few months in the year. A story is told of an old toper, who, when travelling on this river, was asked why he drank nothing but whisky, to which he replied 'that he felt absolutely compelled to do so, as every drop of water was required to float the boat.'

We passed a small village called Florence, whose only resemblance to its Italian namesake was that a river flowed past it. With all their inventions,

Americans cannot invent names, and not only are Old World names given to towns and villages in the New one, but there are sometimes duplicates of them in the same State.

Slowly we steamed up through the mud and sand. Hardly was the monotony of the boundless grass plains on either side broken by a bluff, and scarcely did a breath of air temper the fierce rays of the hot sun till late in the day; then, suddenly, the high-lying stretches of rye-grass were struck into long silvery waves by the evening breeze, and across the western sky a glare of pale gold, gradually opening out into a bewildering haze which extended far away to the horizon, gave to the surrounding country the appearance of a wild golden desert. 'Quite a scenery,' as a fellow-passenger ably remarked.

There is a very curious rock, called Rattlesnake Peak, a few miles up the Big Sioux river, near Sioux City. Steep ledges lead up to the top of the bluff, and hundreds of snakes of all sizes and descriptions may be seen basking on the limestone, dashing in and out of the crevices of the rock, and hanging from the boughs of the stunted oaks, like the ringlets on the head of Medusa. In fact, a more uncomfortable place for spending an hour on a hot summer's day cannot well be imagined.

After leaving Sioux City, where I had expected to

see a number of the red-skin warriors, and perhaps one of their encampments, but where there were only a few hideous specimens of demi-semi-civilised savages, I was told to keep my eye 'peeled' for buffaloes. As I supposed that meant I was to be on the look-out for them, I gazed steadily into the distance for hours without seeing anything resembling a buffalo. But just before we arrived at Yancton, the cry was raised from one of the upper stories that a large herd was in sight, and being driven towards the river by a party of Indians on a hunting expedition. Expectation was now raised to boiling point, and presently, over a low bank, there came snorting and foaming, with their tails over their backs, and, as those who had glasses said, looking terribly enraged, a large number of tame cows, hurrying to the river to bathe and drink! From that time buffaloes hunted by wild Indians had no charms for me; and after spending a short time at Yancton I returned to Omaha, to continue my journey Westward.

I was glad to get away without having my luggage entirely knocked to pieces, as Omaha is celebrated for its 'baggage-smashers.' There were several boxes lying about, whose owners could only recognise them by their contents. Many a handsome box must have left Chicago as a 'Saratoga' and arrived at San Francisco mere lumber.

At present there is but one route from Omaha to

the Far West—that of the Union-Pacific. For a few miles the traveller passes along high bluffs, and thence to the open prairie, in the fertile land of Nebraska. Groves of trees are scattered here and there, and tracts of cultivated land frequently intervene; but these soon disappear, and he is hurrying over that wide barren tract so lately known as the 'Great American Desert,' and which spreads out in one vast unbroken waste from the Missouri to the Rocky Mountains. The soil is rich and easily cultivated; but a serious check to agriculture is the scarcity of water. Hardly any rain used to fall on this immense region, but it is now much more abundant. Some people say that the railroad is the cause of this, on account of the displacement of the atmosphere by the rushing train. Probably the planting of trees and shrubs has more to do with it.

The great influence of forests on the climate, the moisture, and the fertility of a country is well known. The destruction of the forests of the Vosges and Cevennes has sensibly deteriorated the fertility of Alsace and the rich valley of the Rhone. Since the Alps and Appenines have been deprived of their forests the shores of the Mediterranean have lost much of their original verdure and fertility. The tremendous ravages of the settler's axe, and the still more destructive one of the lumber-men, in America, bid fair to introduce an era of climatic deterioration that must in time reduce its fair and salubrious aspect to the condition of a Sahara. The French have carried their system of tree-culture to Algeria, and have already added several rainy days to July and August. Perhaps in America the French system is impossible, but the work of preservation and careful husbanding can proceed from the people. One generation will plant for another, and the sapling of to-day will be a monarch of the forest fifty or a hundred years hence. Along the line of railway, plantations of 'locust' trees have been formed, not only as an ornamental improvement but to provide material for ties, &c.

Near the Platte river and other smaller streams that intersect the prairie, agriculture can be pushed most advantageously. The grass which grows over the whole is excellent fodder for cattle. Grazing, of course, is impossible without water; but more numerous and more widely-spread experiments, of how far this want can be supplied by sinking wells in places far from streams, are required, to solve this question, so constantly debated on the plains.

The extraordinary effects produced by the system of irrigation used by the Mormons and the farmers round Denver and elsewhere, will spread the influence of streams much further than the adjacent lands, and show that it is not merely close to rivers that cultivation can be successful. Western men are sanguine that as irrigation and culture gain ground and the old hard crust of soil is broken up, the climate will change and become more moist and rainy. Some of the new settlements seem thriving, but I know not from what source their support is derived; as *lager-bier* saloons, whisky-shops, and what they call hotels, are often the only houses to be seen in the village. And this is what is termed the 'march of intellect' across the continent!

Groups of 'noble savages' are now to be met with at most of the stations; but those who expect to see in them the heroes, or their descendants, of Fennimore Cooper's novels, will be woefully disappointed. The traditional Indian is a romance, and his 'wild turkey' appearance is pretty in a picture, though not in the reality—at all events, not near a railway station. The 'squaws' have certainly settled a point much discussed lately, relating to extravagance in dress; and a work entitled 'How to Dress on Nothing a Year like a Pawnee, by a Pawnee,' might be a success, but would hardly be approved of by Worth or Madame Elise. There is a quaint Indian proverb which says: 'The smiles of a pretty woman are the tears of the purse;' but where either the pretty woman or the purse is to come from is matter of conjecture. What the Indian woman would do with a purse if she had one I cannot tell.

The '*braves*' carry bows and arrows, with which they try to knock down any small pieces of coin that a sporting white man may feel inclined to put up as a target. They insert the coin in a small piece of stick which they fasten in the ground; then retiring about twenty paces, they begin shooting. As far as my observation went, they generally succeeded in knocking the coin down about once in twenty shots, and then only by firing short and the arrow accidentally ricochetting against the stick—the bow being held parallel with the ground.

The women will inform you that they are good squaws, and sometimes produce a dirty scrap of paper on which is written a certificate of good character and the information that they can wash well. From their appearance you cannot help thinking that they perhaps could wash well, but unfortunately never do.

After reading and handing back this interesting document a demand for ten cents will be made, and if not at once complied with you will be looked upon as a 'mean white,' and one who has obtained valuable information under false pretences.

The 'Pawnees' congregate at most of the railway stations, and are very fond of a short trip by train. They are allowed to ride free on any car on to which they can jump when the train is in motion; the consequence is, the tribe is being rapidly reduced. It has been proposed to introduce the same system at other places, wherever there are Indians.

All through Nebraska we pass broad valleys, which afford immense fields for grazing; rich farming lands, and deserted houses and cabins, once the resting-places of gangs of roughs and desperadoes, who followed in the track of the railroad as it pushed its way towards the West; whilst,

> 'Spreading between the streams are the wondrous, beautiful prairies,
> Billowy bays of grass ever rolling in shadow and sunshine;
> Bright with luxuriant clusters of roses and purple amorphas.
> Over them wander the buffalo herds and the elk and the roebuck;
> Over them wander the wolves, and herds of riderless horses;'

And for all we knew there might have been an 'Evangeline' in some of those small unshaded houses we passed; cheering with her bright presence the terrible loneliness of pioneer life in the wide prairie, and watching, with a mother's love, children destined to become types of the every-day, active, vivacious Western citizen—of the class of men who people the prairies, fell forests, reclaim swamps, and tunnel the mountains.

Now and then, a few antelopes may be seen in the early morning, gazing curiously at the passing train, and after a minute inspection bounding gracefully away. Sometimes, one braver than the rest will not move at all, but with a little stamp of its foot will express its indignation at our trespassing on land owned by its grandfathers and great grandfathers from time immemorial.

Along the Platte valley may be traced the old emigrant-road; and sometimes a lonely grave with a rude head-board will be seen, marking the resting-place of some poor traveller, struck down by sickness or by the arrows of the savage Indians.

After leaving Grand Island we are constantly passing scenes of Indian massacres; and near O'Fallon station we see the bluffs on the opposite side of the river, where was a celebrated lurking-place of the redskins, the abrupt cañons and gulches affording them excellent hiding-places whence to swoop down on the unfortunate emigrant trains, when a general slaughter ensued.

On the south side of the Platte, at Fort Kearney, buffaloes used to be so numerous that orders were issued forbidding soldiers to shoot them on the parade-ground. We did not see any until we passed a station called Brady Island. There, a fine herd was feeding along the banks of the river, well in the open, and far removed from any chance of a surprise. It was a relief to see the long-looked for animals at last; for only those who have felt it can understand what a dreadful thing it is to want to see a buffalo, and not to be able to do so.

It was near this spot that, on one occasion, an old

lady, alone and unattended, except by an umbrella, was obliged to cross some miles of prairie to visit a sick friend; hearing a snorting behind her, she looked round, and found herself face to face with a huge buffalo. With great presence of mind, she instantly opened wide her umbrella which so exasperated him that he turned round and rushed off! Since then, old ladies crossing the prairie always carry umbrellas.

The eating-stations, all along the route, call for great improvement; some of them are moderately good, but, as a rule, the food is ill-cooked and worse served. Morning, noon, and night, the same cry greets you at every meal: 'Mutton-chop, beefsteak, ham and eggs, sir?' No change of any sort, from the time you leave New York until you arrive at San Francisco.

Everybody has heard, and too many have partaken, of the dry chops, the gutta-percha steaks, the bean-coffee, and the currant-leaf tea to be found at railway eating-places. Then there are desperate skirmishes with the waiter, who persists in bringing tea when you want coffee, and who tells you 'it's all the same, sir;' the struggles with your *vis-à-vis* for the bread or sugar; and, if you happen to be late, the hateful cry of 'All aboard' ringing in your ears, and obliging you to rush off, leaving the proprietor counting his money and arranging the victuals for the next batch.

It is wonderful how expert the people who keep

these places become in collecting their money. Needless to say, the ubiquitous pie is to be found in all its glory at these places. The number of victims to intemperance in pie-eating must be enormous in America. I believe pumpkin-pie is the least injurious of all pies, as it contains only half the poison of the double-crusted mince-pie. A 'light hand for pastry' would be useless in making these pies; a hand that can manufacture a pie, every inch of which means nightmare for a week, is the one most in request here.

On approaching Potter we meet with the suburban residences of the prairie-dogs, and presently a large city of them appears. These little animals are not dogs, but rabbits that make a curious barking noise. Their dwellings consist of a mound with a hole in the top. When anyone approaches they scamper off to these houses, and having arrived there, sit on their hams, or stand up on their hind feet and bark.

The plains about here are arid, and produce little except the prickly cactus, thistles, and white poppies; but we soon again enter a great grazing country, with low hills covered with the nutritious 'bunch' grass, and evidently better watered than any we have yet passed. Before long, we catch a first glimpse of the Rocky Mountains, and after a few more miles arrive at Cheyenne, whence I branch off to Denver.

This journey of about six hours through the Colorado

plains was dreary enough, and with little but the dog-cities to enliven the prospect. After Greeley, the country becomes more interesting, and there are fine stretches of grassy plain and upland. Water-courses are easily traced, and there are actually trees of good size and in tolerable abundance. Denver is certainly blessed in its climate, as well as in its site. The view is magnificent from the outskirts of the town. The Rocky Mountains rise abruptly from the plains, about fourteen miles off, range piled above range, and the long white sky-line in sharp contrast with the brilliantly blue sky.

The plains are covered with flowers of various kinds, gold and red being the predominating colours. There are quantities of our common garden flowers, such as marigolds, sunflowers, yuccas, and numerous others. The most beautiful of them was a large white flower, growing in numberless blooms on branches to a height of about two feet. The blossoms open only at night, and close soon after sunrise.

One of the pleasantest excursions to be made from Denver is to the famous Red Rocks and the Platte cañon. We (a very agreeable American gentleman and his wife; the host of the hotel, who acted as guide, and myself) started very early one morning, and soon found ourselves crossing a great prairie farming country, on our way to the cañon. Those who have seen the never-ending sweep of the Great Plains can understand the feeling of—well—call it self-sufficiency, that Western men have been accused of displaying. The sight of, and the possession of these boundless seas of wealth give a sense of power and freedom hardly to be estimated by the inhabitants of the city. The prairie is indeed a silent land, but it is full of charm, and never wearisome. We passed a small cabin, once the home of Jim Beckwith, a celebrated Indian scout. In his youth he fell in with the Crow Indians, who adopted him and made him a chief. Tired at last with the monotonous country life of scalping and bear-hunting, he left the Crows and roved over California and Mexico. He then paid his old friends a visit, to their great joy, and they determined he should not leave them again; so they made a great feast, and in his favourite dish they put poison. His ashes are still preserved in the dismal recesses of the Rookery.

Mrs. F. remained at a small farm-house, where we intended passing the night, while we explored the cañon as far we were able. After two or three hours of hard scrambling, we at length reached some cool shadows on the bank of the stream which flowed at the foot of the rocky precipices that formed the walls of the cañon. A beautiful vale stretched away, bordered with trees, forming a long arched lane, and carpeted with bracken and briar-roses. Squirrels were nut-gathering; the garrulous and important jay flitted about; the woodpeckers hammered away on the dead boughs, and for a moment I fancied myself in the quiet glade of a far-off English woodland. Ah! in spite of the surroundings of mighty cliffs and the solemn grandeur of great natural wonders, there is, after all, no scenery like English scenery, no resting-places like our old English homes!

After several hours of exploration and the expenditure of a great amount of shoe-leather (an extravagance to be avoided in these parts) we returned to a capital supper and a good night's rest at the farm.

Next morning we wended our way towards the Red Rocks, where we soon arrived, after crossing the Platte. These rocks, which give the territory its name, are of red sandstone, and extremely grand and picturesque. They lie at the foot of the mountains for miles and miles. Some of them are in the shape of towers and turrets, others have graceful spires and pinnacles, while numbers of them, several hundred feet high, are perched on one another like the family of a Cyclopean acrobat balancing on the top of a pole which is sustained by the uplifted chin of their steady-going old parent.

On our return to Denver we saw some Indian races, which were not in the least suggestive of Ascot or Goodwood. The Utes performed wild acts of generosity which would hardly have been countenanced by civilised jockeys ; although instances have been known, I believe, of similar performances on their part, though from very different motives. If, for instance, a Ute thought he was coming in too far ahead of the other ponies, he would pull up and wait for his competitors, a proceeding which in several cases would have lost him the race, had not etiquette forbade the winning of it by the distanced red-men.

The Utes are, if possible, uglier and more repulsive-looking than the Pawnees, and have as much expression in their countenances as a turnip.

After a day at Greeley, where nothing goes on except irrigation and irritation (the latter on account of the mosquitoes), I returned to Cheyenne, and went out for a day's agate-hunting. Colorado is rich in precious stones, and around Cheyenne beautiful moss agates are frequently found. I only succeeded, after several hours' search, in obtaining a few indifferent specimens, and therefore turned my attention to prairie-dogs.

I got an old Indian to dig out a few of their holes, as I wanted to see whether it was true that their habitations always contained owls and rattlesnakes.

I found the former—pretty little blinking ground-owls—but no signs of the latter. I fancy owls are too wise to make bedfellows of rattlesnakes. I had a couple of the 'dogs' cooked for supper, and found them excellent—quite as good as rabbits. They live on roots and grasses, and are invariably very plump and tender— much better, in fact, than the tasteless and tough antelope and buffalo steaks which they feed you on in these places.

It seems—and I ought to have mentioned it before—that a very exciting scene had taken place in the Republican Valley, not far from Omaha, a few days before we arrived there. The Pawnees had prepared for a buffalo-hunt. Their enemies, the Sioux, being aware of this, stripped their ponies and distributed them round an adjoining hill, to lead the Pawnees to believe them to be buffaloes. As soon as the Pawnee '*braves*' left their camp the Sioux immediately attacked it, and succeeded in killing about fifty squaws before the warriors returned. When they did return they fought bravely for about ten hours; but they were at last obliged to retreat, and fled across the river, having lost over a hundred men. The Sioux loss amounted to about thirty. The soldiers from Fort M'Pherson arrived after the fight, and drove the Sioux back to their 'reservation.'

The Pawnees were at Elm Creek Station when we arrived, and I never saw more miserable-looking objects.

They brightened up a little at the sight of some food, and a few dollars which were collected for them. Somebody having offered to buy from one of them a knife which had a very cut-throat appearance, they all began to offer for sale whatever they had about them—and that was not much.

One of them offered me a most disgusting-looking scalp, with the remark, 'One much heap hair, one dollar,' and seemed surprised that I did not at once close with the offer. Finally, he disposed of the horrid object to a veteran relic-hunter for the sum of fifty cents, and I should think the proprietor would have been glad to have paid double that amount, a short time after, to any one who would have taken it away. On the occasion of the fight, the Sioux were commanded by 'Young Spotted Tail'—'Old Spotted Tail' having preferred remaining at home. The Pawnees were under Sky-Chief, who, with a very natural determination, under the circumstances, has sworn to avenge his losses. But as the Sioux know how to take very good care of themselves, and invariably get the better of the Pawnees, and as the latter are not particularly fond of fighting unless they are in overpowering numbers, I think revenge for the buffalo trick and the subsequent slaughter is likely to be handed down, as a pleasure to come, to future generations.

After leaving Cheyenne we ascend a very steep grade, through Granite Cañon, with wild rugged mountains of granite piled up on either side, and with an occasional opening, through which we see the lofty mountain-tops away to the south, and Pike's Peak—

plainly visible three hundred miles away. At Sherman we are at the most elevated railroad station in the world, and enthusiastic tourists are much given to telegraphing that information to distant friends. Here a lady, with what some one expressed as a rush of lace to the head, entered the car; she had evidently been astonishing the natives of Sherman with the latest fashions, and was proceeding on her philanthropical expedition still further West.

At Laramie I made a long tedious excursion, in company with two officers of the U.S. army, to Crystal Lake, about forty-five miles distant. The road was dreadfully rough for the unfortunate ponies, besides being very steep; but the view from the summit of Sheep mountain was superb. On the way, we passed a lonely little cabin, whose sole occupant was a poor melancholy-looking white woman. She asked us in to rest ourselves, and refreshed us with some most deliciously cold water. Her husband, she told us, had gone to the town, as she called Laramie, and she seemed quite frightened at being left there all alone. Amidst bursts of tears, she said they had lately lost their only child, a little girl of about five years old. It was really painful to see anyone so nervous and so utterly broken down. She insisted on our going in to look at a small neat white-curtained inner-room, where her little daughter had lived and died. Everything was left as if she still expected her, and the poor creature would listen every now and then, as if she heard the footfall of her child—yes,

> 'There was a little white rose of a bed,
> But its fragrance had passed away.'

We pleased her with a promise to pay another short visit when we returned, which promise we kept, and found her and her husband packing up their household goods, as they were going to settle in the town.

The dense forest through which we passed has abundance of game, in the shape of bears, panthers, and wild sheep; but we saw none of them, though we now and then came across the track of deer. When we arrived at the top of the mountain and emerged from the deep gloom of the forest into the sunlight, we looked down on banks of fleecy cloud floating far below us, whilst around and above rose innumerable peaks whose snow-clad heights were lost to view in the hazy distance. The black masses of rock visible through the glistening misty vapour, and the gleaming clouds of a passing thunder-storm, seemed the realisation of Shelley's fancifully descriptive lines :—

> 'The billowy clouds
> Edged with intolerable radiancy,
> Towering like rocks of jet,
> Crowned with a diamond wreath.'

Away down the mountain was a wide open green

space, and in its centre lay the beautiful lake, clear as crystal, and reflecting every object on its banks. It looked like a huge basin of quicksilver with the sun shining on it. It was difficult to believe that it was water, so still and mirror-like was its surface. The contrast between the lovely view of the lake and the distant grandeur of the mountain-peaks was particularly striking, and more impressive than anything I had then seen, or indeed afterwards saw, in the Rocky Mountains.

On our way back the following day, we found some hideous horned toads, and they were about the only specimens of animal life that we saw.

After leaving Laramie and entering the district of alkali and sage-brush, I must say I began to get rather tired of the monotony of the view. It is all very interesting, as long as you are on the prairie, on the perpetual look-out for antelopes, and are constantly seeing (in your mind's eye) buffalo herds pursued by wild Indians, with the white waggons of emigrants corralled to receive the attack of the scalping gentlemen; but when nothing but sage-brush greets the eyes, except small particles of alkali, which makes them smart terribly, the scene is apt to become rather tiresome.

We were relieved at last from absolute monotony by a tremendous storm; but I think the remedy was worse than the disease, for we were thereby detained for fifteen hours on a siding. It was evening when the storm began, and the guard was afraid to go on in the dark, lest the rails should have been washed away, or a bridge have been broken down anywhere.

Towards sunset the clouds in the west had assumed a most threatening aspect, and every form of storm-like beauty was then combined in the sky. To the south-east, the most lovely blue was bordered with vast mountains of fleecy white clouds; right in front of us, and rapidly extending overhead, was an enormous mass of black clouds tipped with fiery red, whilst away towards the north was an expanse of grey-coloured mist, from which torrents of rain were pouring and fast approaching us. The air was suddenly charged on all sides with electricity, and from the huge dense black mass burst forth an overwhelming rush of water, while the lightning afforded as magnificent a show of fireworks as can be imagined—the whole west sometimes appearing as a ball of flame, from which the crags and peaks of the mountains stood out distinctly and grandly. The storm continued far into the night, the crashing, echoing, and re-echoing of the heavy peals of thunder entirely preventing sleep. There was an old lady in the car who was quite unmoved by the raging of the storm, but was so dreadfully afraid of being scalped that she kept continually running to the door and looking out, in the expectation of beholding the approach of her red-skin horrors. I was the more surprised at this fear on her part, because, 'raising her hair' would only have been performing an operation which she went through of her own accord every evening. Before retiring, she combed out the disordered wig, and hung it up in the most conspicuous place over her berth, ready to be put on the first thing in the morning; and this she did with an air of the most complete nonchalance, and a coolness only to be acquired by a long course of travelling in a Pullman's car.

It was very fortunate, as it turned out, that our engineer did stop the train; for when we proceeded on our journey next day we found the track being repaired in two or three places, and in one spot we had a further delay of some hours, while at least a ton of rock was removed from the line.

At Evanston I was told I should find everything 'real nice;' and certainly it was the best dining-station along the line. The table was neatly arranged, the napkins and tablecloth were white and clean, and the cooking far better than usual. Fortunately, there was no military post near, and so it was impossible to obtain the condemned articles of the commissary for the passengers' consumption.

From Evanston our way ran through Echo Cañon, and we soon plunged amongst its red rocky bluffs, peculiarly bold in form, and of great beauty and variety of colour. Grand indeed are the pictures presented in these strange ravines, and the effect is increased by the unexpected manner in which the traveller comes upon them. The shapes, too, taken by these rocks, like those in Colorado, are wonderful. Sometimes you see a cathedral, with spires and windows; then a castle, with battlements and turrets; domes and pillars are everywhere. The Witch rocks are also peculiarly striking and weird.

Presently, we pass the spot where the Mormons erected their fortifications; and on a precipitous rock, a thousand feet above us, are the huge stones that were piled up one upon another ready to be hurled down on their foes. The huge boulders were never used, and now stand as a monument of folly and superstition. A little farther on rises 'Pulpit Rock,' from which Brigham Young preached his first sermon, on that side of the Rocky mountains, to his strange, devoted people. Vast circles of rocks rise story upon story, and lofty precipices frown down upon us as we pass, whilst right across the smooth broad brow of a towering cliff may be read in letters several feet in height, 'A thing of beauty and a joy for ever'—'Try our rising sun stove-polish!' After such a sudden fall from the sublime to the ridiculous half the poetry and romance of the scenery vanishes for ever

DEVIL'S SLIDE.—Front view.

On we go through Weber Cañon, picturesque certainly, but not to be compared to Echo, and we come then to the 'Devil's Slide.' What a gymnast the old gentleman must have been, if he really accomplished a quarter of the feats we put down to him! in fact, a great part of his existence must have been spent in jumping through rocks, like a clown through a paper hoop, and sliding down hills and mountains like a naughty boy down a bannister. In the case in question, he was probably well whipped when he went home, as, from the rugged state of the rocks, his pantaloons must have been in a most unenviable condition by the time he reached the foot of the mountain.

The river Weber frets and rages along its course just beneath us, and presently we pass a solitary pine tree on our left. A board on it states that the distance from Omaha is 1,000 miles. Here another storm passed us, taking the usual north-easterly direction; we therefore only came in for a very small part of it. Just where the river rushes between two great walls of rock the road crosses the stream, and we enter the valley of Salt Lake. Passing through a cultivated country, with well-tilled farms on either side, we soon arrive at Ogden, where I was very glad to leave the the main road, and after a few hours of slow travelling reached Salt Lake City, the capital of Utah, and the 'desert home of the Mormons.'

CHAPTER VI.

SALT LAKE CITY TO VIRGINIA CITY.

Early days—The Tabernacle—A vision—Mormons—Ann Eliza—Brigham Young—Mormon shops—American Fork Cañon—Salt Lake—A pageant—The theatre—Mormonism—The great American desert—Euchre—Tricks that are vain—Nevada—Train-robbers—Americanisms—Reno.

WHAT a wonderful change there is in the Salt Lake valley of the present day compared with its aspect before the arrival of the Mormons! After encountering almost superhuman difficulties, after leaving scores of their companions dead on the long terrible road they had journeyed over, they arrived in 1847 in this valley; and finding that the parched sandy desert and the high mountain-peaks were insuperable barriers against their foes, they determined to make it their home, and to live there according to their own peculiar ideas. Persecution had strengthened their faith; they believed implicitly in the divinity of their martyred prophet, Joseph Smith, and considered themselves the 'Chosen People.' With the greatest religious enthusiasm —a little augmented, perhaps, by personal requirements —they built houses, planted trees, and irrigated and cultivated the land. The circumstances in which they were placed furnished an incentive to exertion. There was no way of escape for them out of the valley, and they could only exist by toiling to the fullest extent of their powers. The success they have achieved is evident in the garden-like appearance of the beautiful valley.

On the morning after my arrival I set off to visit the town. The first thing that struck me was the number of trees bordering the streets, along the sides of which runs a clear stream of water from the mountains.

The houses are not particularly tasteful, but the great amount of foliage surrounding them gives them a secluded home-like air.

Orchards of peach, apricot, cherry, and apple trees abound everywhere, and the soil is evidently extremely fertile, where it is irrigated.

The great object of interest is the Tabernacle, whose huge oval roof gives the building the exact appearance of a roc's egg. On entering its precincts I met a gentleman, who, seeing that I was a stranger, kindly offered to show me over the building. He proved to be one of the Apostles, and a very entertaining and agreeable one too. The Tabernacle is about two hundred and fifty feet long, and a hundred and fifty feet wide, and will hold fifteen thousand people. The enormous roof is self-sustaining, and springs from a number of stone columns. The large organ, built by a member of the flock, is the most conspicuous object in the interior. In front of the organ is the pulpit from which Brigham preaches. Next below is one for the councillors, then one for the bishops, and finally one for the deacons. The seats are all of plain pine, and the absence of paint gives the building a very cold and formal appearance.

Adjacent to the Tabernacle is the Temple, or rather what will be the Temple, as at present the foundation is but little above the level of the ground. From the plan which my friend (if I may so call an Apostle) showed me, it will be a most magnificent building, if ever finished; but there is not, I imagine, the very slightest probability of it, as it was begun near twenty years ago, and funds are now at a very low ebb, in fact, so low that there was not a single workman then at work on the edifice. The plan, they say, was given to Brigham Young in a vision; if so, it must have been by the united spirits of Sir Christopher Wren and Brunelleschi.

The Apostle introduced me to his house, but I saw nothing of his wives, of whom he had three, as I was later informed. From the quiet home-like look about the place, there seemed to be more peace in it than I should have thought probable from the presence there of such disturbing elements. I believe, however, before a Mormon takes his second or third wife the consent of the first is usually obtained.

I noticed a peculiar air of depression, and even sadness, amongst the Mormon women—a patient suffering look, which seemed the natural consequence of adopting a creed many of whose doctrines must be repugnant to the chaste impulses of woman's nature, however sincere her faith may be in its strange delusions. The Mormon men looked particularly jolly and free from care, and certainly appeared to leave the burden of the ' cross,' about which they talk a good deal, to be borne by their wives.

My kind guide was unable to obtain for me an introduction to President Young himself, but showed me what he could of his dwelling-houses, chief of which are the Lion House and the Bee-hive House, so called from the carved figures over them, emblematic of strength and industry. They are surrounded by a high wall, which gives a dignified and secluded air to otherwise unimportant-looking buildings.

From the account of Mrs. Young, *née* Ann Eliza Webb—the seventeenth, and, I believe, the last wife of the President—his family life does not run very smoothly. She (the seventeenth) had lately left the house he had provided for her, and had taken apartments in one of the hotels. Amongst other grievances, she showed that Brigham, like Socrates, had his Xantippe. This

Xantippe was allowed *carte blanche* at the Lion co-operative store, and arrayed herself in silk attire, while the more meek and humble, but not less deserving, Ann Eliza could only dress herself in homespun. She further objected, and with good reason, to the extremely frugal means of subsistence allowed by her husband. A lawsuit ensued, in which she endeavoured to obtain an annual allowance suitable to her position. How it was settled I do not know, but the case was a difficult one. The law did not recognise her as a wife. To do so would be to put a premium on polygamy; and if she was not a wife she could not legally be allowed alimony. However, should the revelations made by this seventeenth wife find their way to Europe, they may act as a warning to young women against being deluded by Mormon doctrines, and in that case Ann Eliza will have done something for her sex.

Within the precincts of the Lion house and the Bee house are the 'tithing-houses.' Thither, the Mormon farmers and gardeners bring yearly a tenth part of their produce. Merchants, miners, mechanics, &c. bring a tenth part of their income.

On Sunday I attended service in the Tabernacle, and there saw the President in his accustomed place of honour. I was in hopes he was going to preach, but in this was disappointed. He is a tall, quiet-looking man, with a calm firm face; but I could see nothing to which to attribute the extraordinary influence he has obtained over the minds of his followers. He looked like a man to whom physical exertions for the benefit of the state were of greater consideration and importance than spiritual ones; and yet he calls himself a Prophet, and declares he has received revelations from God himself.

The service was very simple; prayer, music, and singing by the choir, with a sermon, followed by a discourse, and a blessing from the Prophet constituted the entire ceremony; after which the congregation of about two thousand souls departed to their homes.

The Mormon shops are known by a sign placed over their doors, on which is written 'Holiness to the Lord. Zion's Co-operate Mercantile Institution.' The true followers are expected to trade there; but I have strong suspicions that even Mormons like trading where they can obtain the cheapest and best goods, and that the Gentile stores are as much patronised as the others.

The scenery of Utah is magnificent. A long excursion I made to the American Fork Cañon, about thirty miles distant from the city, was full of picturesque surprises. The old mill, in the Cañon, presented as charming a picture as could well be found. The ride to it was over hanging hills, whose tops were fringed with trees and at whose base flowed a winding stream, and through a narrow gorge filled with all sorts of wild flowers. After rounding a high barren rock, the old mill suddenly appeared, perched up amongst the trees, and surrounded by the foaming white water that was rushing down the ravine. The country around is very rich in minerals; the Emma mine, said to be the richest in Utah, is situated in Little Cottonwood Cañon, adjacent to the picturesque scene of the mill.

The Mormon city lies east of the south end of the great Salt Lake, and some miles from it. There is no doubt about the saltness or the buoyancy of its waters, for while bathing I found it difficult, indeed almost impossible, to stand on the bottom. In spite of all efforts to maintain my ground, my heels would fly out of the water. Eggs and potatoes will float in it like corks, and any but a swimmer would fare badly if he trusted himself to the tender mercies of its briny depths, as his head would go down and his feet fly up. Bathers in the salt lake are said to come forth from its waters white and sparkling. For my own part, I must confess that I was not more dazzled by my appearance after coming out than before going in, although the salt coating I received necessitated a plunge into a fresh-water stream before dressing. The Mormons say it is good for the health to leave the salt on the body, and dress without drying the skin.

There are numerous islands on the lake. One of them, called Antelope Island, is about fifteen miles long; it swarms with deer, but shooting is not allowed. One day, whilst enjoying the view over the lake from Ensign Park, above the city, I saw a gorgeous procession advancing, glittering with silver and all 'the pomp and circumstance of war.' I hastened down to the streets, and met people hurrying along from every direction to view the pageant. I thought that it was, probably, some municipal display, and that I was about to witness some curious demonstration of the Saints. Slowly the procession wound its way through the shadow and sunshine, glistening like some gigantic monster with scales of gold and silver. Ladies in historical costumes swept by on their cream-white palfreys; knights in armour, and mounted on magnificent chargers, trooped past. A magnificent chariot, with pink and white plumes, and drawn by eight camels, with their African attendants, rolled proudly on; and by the time a cage of lions and other wild animals had passed me I began to realise the fact that the 'New York and New Orleans Great American Circus and Menagerie' had arrived, and that a performance would take place in the 'Mammoth Tent' that evening. Indians in full dress—that is, hideously painted with streaks of red and yellow ochre—followed the procession in great numbers, and for once looked astonished. They evidently thought the gaudy pageant the most imposing spectacle they could possibly witness. Part of the evening's entertainment was the exhibition of a fat woman; I forget what she weighed, but she created immense amusement by singing, the then popular song, 'Put me in my little bed.' Even the red-skins saw the joke, or the laughter of the audience proved infectious—for they gave vent to their delight in many guttural 'Ugh! ughs!'

At the theatre one has a good opportunity of observing the Mormon ladies. The President is often present, with several of his wives and endless sons and daughters. The Apostles are also in force, attended by their wives; whilst the rest of the house is composed of the lesser Saints, some with only a modest couple of wives, and some with but one wife. Yet everywhere may be seen the same sad dead-alive look amongst the women that I had before remarked. Whether they would have allowed that they were unhappy, or whether they even knew that they were, I cannot tell—they looked so, and that was enough.

Discussion on the subject of polygamy in Salt Lake City is useless. But we Gentiles have one argument against it which cannot be gainsayed. Looking at the question from a purely social and domestic point of view, is not woman man's equal, if not his superior?

Most undoubtedly she is. But to the Mormon she is not even his equal—she is simply his slave.

Mormonism has also its ludicrous aspect. A man may not wish to have more than one wife, but if Brigham chooses he can order him to marry some poor forlorn creature, and should he not like her, all he can do is either to turn her out to grass—that is, send her to his farm, if he is fortunate enough to possess one—or pension her off, as best he can. How odd, too, it must be for the wives to talk of 'our husband,' or 'our piano,' and they all seem to have a joint-stock even in 'our baby!' I was told that one particular trait in the Mormon women's character is a total absence of the love of scandal. The story of the woman who used her tongue to slander other women is a favourite one in their schools. This woman confessed her sin to the priest and desired a penance. He gave her a thistle-top and told her to go in various directions and scatter the seeds, one by one. She obeyed, then returned to her confessor and told him she had done so. He then bade her go back and gather the scattered seeds. She answered that it would be impossible. Still more difficult, he replied, would it be to gather up and destroy the ill effects of the evil reports she had circulated about others. As to Brigham Young, it must be admitted that, considering the elements he has had to deal with—men from the poorest and most ignorant classes—considering also the enormous toil and labour caused by the hard conditions of early emigration, his formation of the colony is an unparalleled achievement. He has ruled and guided his people with wonderful skill and tact. And though schisms and divisions are now common amongst them, and the Mormons, as a religious sect, are fast losing their footing; yet, in spite of his mysterious doctrines and the many faults attributed to him, he will leave a name behind him as a benefactor of the poor and the founder of a new commonwealth. I was quite sorry to have to say good-bye to the quaint Mormon capital, but did so, bearing away with me a bag of its most delicious peaches, by way of consolation; then, returning to Ogden, I resumed my journey.

After skirting the north side of the Great Salt Lake we entered upon that vast plateau which is the true Great American Desert. And it is worthy of its name. For more than seventy miles nothing is to be seen except dull sage-brush and white dust, and in the distance dry, brown, bare mountains. The showers of alkali-dust make the journey most painful for the eyes; but, as there is nothing to be seen, you have no loss if you keep them closed. Lizards are the only living things found on this desert tract; and as there is no rainfall it must always remain a desert, and a very bitter one too. With ordinary rainfall, the water, percolating through the soil, would carry off the alkali into the lakes and rivers, and an agricultural future might possibly be expected.

The Palisades are grand and picturesque; and the Humboldt Valley, through which we ran, has many pleasant features, not the least of them being that at the eating-stations we were waited upon by quiet Celestials instead of uncouth, rough-mannered white men.

At one of the small stations we were startled by the entrance into our car of a very finely-dressed individual. His appearance was quite dazzling. His coat was of velvet, and his hat—a tall white one—had a deep crape band, whilst on his immaculate shirt-front reposed what was apparently the wreck of a large tumbler.

At the next station a big jolly-looking man, in appearance a well-to-do farmer, entered and sat down by the last comer, whom he did not recognise as a friend, but with whom he soon entered into a little light conversation about the crops, mining, &c. Presently a game of cards was proposed, just to while away the time, and the two played for about half-an-hour, when the farmer said he was tired of playing. Our friend in the black velvet with a bland smile then asked his *vis-à-vis* if he would like to take a hand. Now, the individual to whom this question, was addressed was a young man from the country, who had entered the train the day before, and was going to see the city—San Francisco—for the first time. His father bade him good-bye at the station, and his last words to him, in our hearing, were 'Beware of card-sharpers, swindlers, and all such cattle,' as he expressed it. The young man imagined himself too shrewd to be taken in by anybody; in fact, it was this shrewdness, I fancy, which made him prefer slow death in the city to slow life in the country. He had played euchre before at the store up in his village; so he answered, 'Wal, I guess I will take a small spell at the keerds.'

As he crossed over and sat down at the board prepared for the occasion by the kind gentleman in velvet, it was just possible to detect the suspicion of a wink between Velvety and his late opponent, the farmer. Just to make the game interesting, they each put up twenty-five cents. Our country friend could never have had better luck. Pool after pool he wins; becomes astonished at the facility with which money can be made, and gives it as his opinion that playing euchre is better than hoeing corn. Presently the velvet gentleman says, quite carelessly, that he has a good poker hand. Our rural friend is surprised to find that he too has a good poker hand. A little bet of five dollars is made, and Rurality wins again. The farmer here makes the remark, 'You always was a fool, Bill.' This, to say the least of it, was a strange remark from a man who, from his previous manner, had never before met the gentleman he thus addressed. However, the game was resumed, and after a few more deals the countryman got four kings. Here was a chance of making a small fortune; such an opportunity might never occur again. Strange to say, the gentleman in black velvet thought that he also had a good hand. Rurality bet fifty dollars and gasped, Black Velvet went fifty more and smiled. Rurality then bet a hundred, which was quickly covered, and the pool further increased by yet another hundred. Rather tremblingly our rural friend threw down his cards, saying, 'Four kings—what have you got?'.

'Four aces,' replied our bland friend, showing his cards with one hand and raking in the money with the other. The country youth swore and raved, but all to no purpose, and the two gentlemen smiled as sweetly as ever. At the next station they were just about to get out for 'lunch,' as they said, when the conductor, who had recognised them, and two gentlemen, who had watched their proceedings, seized them and marched them off to the office of the station officials, where they were made to disgorge their ill-gotten gains—much to the delight of our country friend, who then said he thought ' hoeing corn was after all better than " poker." '

Thieves and gamblers are to be met with all along the line, and notices in all the cars bid you beware of such people. They dog the steps of persons leaving a town, and by means of the telegraph and other agencies known only to the initiated, their accomplices are advised of any 'game' that may be passing.

One of their contrivances is called the 'green-back reflector,' and consists of a one dollar green-back note, having a stiff piece of paper pasted on it. A small piece of wood is pinned to the paper, having on its face a small glass mirror. When the game commences this is laid on the table, and dollars are placed upon it, so as to conceal the mirror. The cards are dealt directly over this reflector; and thus, knowing his opponent's hand, the gambler has easy work in fleecing his victim.

All through Nevada the scenery is most forbidding: nothing but vast tracts of sand, and sage-brush, and glittering alkali. Occasionally near the stations there may be a small patch of cultivated land, but that will be all. The only incident likely to occur is the stopping of the train by a band of the 'Train-robbers;' but as this only happens on an average two or three times a year, it is difficult to suit your journey so as to hit off the exact time.

A few months ago a train with cars containing some Chinese of high rank was stopped and ransacked. The moon-faced Celestials must have been pleased with their first adventure in a strange land! I believe they simply remarked on the occasion, 'Hi-yah! too muchee gun; no can fightee all that bobbery!' and wished themselves back in Pekin.

We are now in the region of 'square meals,' whatever they may be, and slang terms are more prevalent than they were in the East. I had often been told that Americanisms were only to be found in novels. My experience differs entirely from that assumed fact. Slang is heard only amongst the lower classes (if the Great Republic will admit of there being classes), but Americanisms are heard everywhere. America originally forgot to furnish herself with an independent language, but she is working hard to supply the deficiency, and in time there will be an American language, concise and significant. One cannot help being struck by the number of words and even sentences that are repeated on all possible occasions. Such a poverty of expression becomes at last quite annoying. 'Hurry up' are words that can never be forgotten by a traveller in America; and I do not believe it is possible to converse for five minutes without hearing a dozen times the remark, 'You don't say so.' In the West that terrible word 'say' (not 'I say') is prefixed to every sentence; and the epithet 'elegant' is bestowed on the most inappropriate objects. Fancy an 'elegant day,' and yet you hear that expression continually! Our 'awfuls' and 'awfully jolly' are bad enough, but they are not reiterated with the provoking frequency with which domestic Americanisms assail the ears.

You meet 'real (pronounced 'reel') nice' people wherever you go, and are constantly asked if you have had a 'real fine time.' It may be said they are not the 'best' people who use those expressions—I beg to differ—and besides, in travelling you must judge from the people you meet. I have lately seen papers denying the existence of Americanisms at all, and virtually agreeing with a lady who once said to another in my hearing, 'Oh! I knew you were English by your accent;' so I like to add my testimony in a humble way and show what my experience of the American language has been.

You certainly do not hear so much slang, in the ordinary acceptation of the word, as in England; but what is slang, after all, but an effort to be concise? And, for my part, I prefer an ocasional slang term to the constant use of hackneyed Americanisms.

Thank God we are approaching Reno; and although it is two o'clock in the morning I am very glad to leave the train and make my way to Virginia City and the mining districts of the Sierras.

CHAPTER VII.

VIRGINIA CITY TO STOCKTON.

Politicians—A silver mine—Sutro tunnel—A commercial crisis—Geysers—Lake Tahoe—Shakespeare—Donner Lake—The old traveller—Two American forces—Cape Horn—Alabaster cave—Sacramento—Mosquitoes—The pedlar-boy—The poor man's carriage—Gold currency—Wages.

OF all the desolate, grim scenery to be found in America that around Virginia City takes the lead. The great brown hills are scarred and seamed and bare. No wonder the town itself obtained the distinction of being the 'cussedest' in the land; but even that proud epithet no longer distinguishes it, and the title has been assumed by newer and less frequented villages.

The hotel at which I was staying was crowded with people who called themselves politicians, but who might have been more appropriately designated agitators—men who seemed angry because they could not get into Congress, that they might become people of some importance.

What they were doing in Virginia City I cannot imagine, as it seemed to me a very inappropriate place in which to air their sentiments. They all appeared to think, and I believe the belief is widely spread in America, that the Republic of the United States was founded after mature deliberation upon the comparative merits of the various forms of government. People who believe this will not understand that it was American society that produced their form of government, and that the founders of the Republic merely provided the machines for administering that form, and simply took existing materials and built up with them such a political fabric as society demanded.

The Republic of the present day is very different from the old Republic; and this change has been brought about, not by lectures from political agitators on forms of government, but by changes in the national manners and the material conditions of the country. One of the politicians asked me how we would like a republic in England, and seemed quite astonished when I answered that very few would like it at all; but that, if such a calamity ever should happen, the red-hot republicans would probably like it least of all, as we had too many great and well educated men—men of position and good feeling—who would come forward, as they do now, to see that the country was properly governed. And what would become of the noisy agitators then? In spite of our differences of opinion he seemed very sociable; and as he knew the superintendent of one of the mines, he kindly offered to accompany me on a visit to it.

We descended into the silvery deeps by means of a 'cage,' a sort of elevator, and a great improvement on the 'bucket,' by which you are taken down in some of the mines. We went down several hundred feet, and walked about the tunnels and saw all the different processes of mining, and had a very enjoyable and instructive expedition.

The number of mills around Virginia City which work on the silver ore from the great Comstock Lode is about eighty, and this lode is the richest in the country. It extends in a broad belt along the mountain-side, and under Virginia and Gold Hill Cities, which are thoroughly undermined. The whole mountain is a series of tunnels, shafts, and caverns, from which the ore has been taken.

Enormous as is the amount of silver taken out of these mines, yet the net profit is ridiculously small; so true is the saying that 'it takes a mine to work a mine.' A tunnel is now being driven into Mount Davidson, on whose slope Virginia City is built, to intersect the Comstock Lode at the depth of 2,000 feet.

Mr. Sutro is the projector of the tunnel, and it has been named after him. There are different opinions regarding this gigantic enterprise, but one thing is certain, it will either ruin its promoters or make each of them a Crœsus. The distance to be pierced is over four miles. The drive to this tunnel through Six-Mile Cañon is very interesting, but not picturesque. There are numbers of sluices, reservoirs, and crushing-mills to be seen, besides other buildings and appurtenances of a mining district. I went into the tunnel for a long way, where the blasting of the hard granite was going on, and I must say I cannot believe that the work will ever be accomplished unless Government takes it in hand.

The rise of Nevada was very sudden. When the 'Washoe' range was first prospected and pronounced to be a mass of silver, the 'rush' to Mount Davidson was unprecedented, even in that era of 'rushes.' Cities were laid out, and every available piece of flat ground was sold for town lots, and the maddest speculations were entered upon. But of all the so-called 'cities' that were then founded, about two, and those on the very smallest scale, ever were built; and of all the companies formed to work the claims but a very small proportion ever paid a dividend.

The only sign discoverable at Virginia City of the great commercial crisis at New York was that one morning, when I asked for some butter at breakfast, I was informed that there was none, as butter lately had been very 'panicky;' a circumstance so unusual that I thought it worth while making a note of.

From Virginia City I went to Carson, where there are some famous hot-springs, said to be a certain cure for rheumatism. All the springs have wonderful legends and stories attached to them. Hot-springs are numerous in Nevada, and are utilised in various ways, some families dispensing altogether with patent stoves and doing all their cooking by means of a domestic geyser.

From Carson a capital road, but a very steep one, took me to Glenbrook House, a pleasant little inn, situated on Lake Tahoe. Mark Twain, in one of his amusing books—'Innocents Abroad,' I think—says that this lake is superior to the Italian lakes. I suppose he means its situation is higher, as, although very beautiful, it wants the variety of scene and the lovely islands and villas which give such wondrous views to those delightful lakes.

Entirely surrounded by mountains covered with sad forests of gigantic pines, Lake Tahoe would present rather a sombre aspect if it were not for its marvellously clear and sparkling water, in which you may 'try and drown many worms,' as the poacher said when caught fishing in preserved waters. Perhaps I was more disappointed with the lake than I should otherwise have been from having been told there was capital shooting amongst the surrounding hills, but finding, after many long trudges and many conversations with wood-cutters, &c. on the subject, that there was no game at all worth speaking of, as all birds and animals had been driven away by the advance of civilisation. There is a singular natural curiosity on the face of a high rock in full view of the lake. It is a profile of Shakespeare, and not at all a bad likeness. It has been formed by depressions in the stone like a gigantic natural intaglio.

A little steamer carried me to Tahoe City, on the opposite side of the lake, crossing the line on its way, as the division between Nevada and California runs north and south through the lake. The lake is about twenty miles long and ten broad, and there are many points of interest around it. Caves, hot-springs, and beautiful little bays and inlets abound, and the valley of Lake Creek is one of the most fertile in the Sierras, and is dotted over with farms and milk ranches. The shores of Lake Tahoe have been chosen for the site of the Lick Observatory, the princely gift of Mr. Lick to the State. Another point of interest will soon, therefore, be added to the charming scenery.

From Tahoe City, a drive of about twelve miles along the river-bank and across green meadows brought me to Truckee station, whence, after visiting Donner

Lake, which is a miniature Tahoe, I proceeded on my journey.

Tunnels and snow-sheds now begin to appear, and continually shut out from view the finest scenery along the road. Just before reaching **Summit** Station we caught a glorious view of Donner Lake, which lay three miles **below** us, and which is infinitely more picturesque when seen from a distant height than it looks when standing at its **edge. When we** saw it, the morning sun had just spread a glittering sheen over the lake, leaving some corners hidden in deep shadow, which presented the strangest contrasts of sombre purple hues. The soft yellow tints of early morning enveloped the north side, whilst the eastern slopes were **shaded by a dark purple haze,** wonderfully contrasting **with** the brightness of the sun and the lake. From our distant point of view, it looked deserving of its name—'The Gem of the Sierras.'

How easy it is to distinguish the **old traveller from** the new **at the ' meal stations! ' As the train draws up** he is already on the platform outside the carriage, and before the train stops is dashing wildly towards the saloon, and straight **to a seat,** ordering coffee as he goes, and taking up the right thing at once. He is aware **of** the exact time allowed, **and at its** expiration, he is **out** on the platform picking his teeth and talking of ' real estate ' before the young traveller has got his first cup of tea. At these stations, too, the knife-swallowers may be seen in great numbers, giving entertainments 'quite gratuitous.' Sometimes, if there is a wearisome delay before the train starts, some fiery republican will give vent to his feelings through that animating power known as 'stump oratory,' giving decision to his arguments by the handling of that other great American force—the revolver. He is aware that he would not be listened to unless he is known to be capable of knocking anybody down who interrupts him; and so he likes it to be generally understood that he is quite able to take care of himself. One of these individuals was holding forth at Summit Station when we were there, and really gave a most amusing and intelligent discourse.

Summit Station is over 7,000 feet above the level of the sea, and in the next 70 miles after leaving the grade descends 6,000 feet. The railroad passage over these mountains is the greatest engineering feat on the whole line. The track is carried along the edge of precipices stretching downward for 2,000 and 3,000 feet, and in some parts men had to be swung from the upper rocks in baskets in order to excavate the mountain-side.

It is fortunate that the envious snow-sheds do not shut out the view on rounding Cape Horn. The scene there is magnificent. The train is close to the brink of the precipice, at the bottom of which the river, 2,500 feet below us, looks like a winding silver thread, whilst far above, on our right hand, rise towering masses of rock, forming a colossal wall of unbroken granite.

At Auburn, we left the train for a visit to 'Alabaster Cave,' and reached it after a drive of about ten miles through a country uncommonly dry and yellow-looking, but relieved by the rich dark foliage of the white oaks and the bushes of handsome 'buckeye,' the flower of which is something like our horse-chestnut.

Just before reaching the cave we passed a lime-kiln, where a large portion of the lime used in San Francisco is made.

After entering the cave and descending a few steps we found ourselves in a large room, in which was the inevitable register. In America you are always registering your name, and you cannot get a room at the hotels until that formality has been gone through. I once heard a passenger in a stage-coach say that he would have liked to have gone to the Vienna Exhibition, if only for the pleasure of seeing his name in the registers of the large hotels.

But to return to the cave. After traversing another passage we came to the 'Dungeon of Enchantment;' a large broad chamber, about a hundred feet in length and sixty in breath, and varying from four to twenty

H

feet in height. Here, irregular rows of bright stalactites hang down, in every variety of shape, and every tint from snow-white to salmon-pink—in brilliant relief to the dark arches above, and the black and brown ridges on either side. Some of the groups of stalactites are most beautiful, and vary in size from fine needle-like pendants to miniature pine trees, growing head downwards, and thus adapting themselves to circumstances with an amiability hardly to be expected from such hard-looking creatures. Presently we come to 'Lot's Wife;' and if the stalagmite at all resembles her, the poor petrified lady must have been a dwarf, and of a very peculiar shape, as its altitude is only about four feet and its circumference three.

Passing on, over what is apparently an ice-covered floor, we look down into an immense abyss whose sides are covered with icicles and transparent moss. Entering another chamber, with formations in the roof like streams of water turned to ice, we pass a beautiful bell-shaped bower, and emerge into the most magnificent chamber of all, called 'the Holy of Holies.' This room is completely draped with the most wonderful alabaster sterites, of a light creamy pink. Brilliant stone icicles, coral, moss, and what look like fleeces of fine wool covered with petrified dew, adorn the walls. On one side stands a most magnificent pulpit, dome-shaped at the top, and covered with undulating folds, arranged with wonderful grace and seemingly carved out of alabaster. When brilliantly illuminated with coloured lights the scene is grand and most imposing. Our Aladdin's cave seems then a stern reality, until Abanazar, in the shape of the custodian, knocks loudly at the entrance and intimates that our time is up and that another party of sight-seers wishes to inspect the wonderful grotto.

As it seldom rains in California from March to November, you may imagine the parched dried-up appearance of the country by about August. It is difficult to understand where cattle and sheep find sufficient food to keep them alive. Very little verdure is to be seen until we approach the Sacramento river, which we cross before reaching the State capital, and which, from the colour of its water, looks as if it were liquid mud. The Capitol building is the grand feature of Sacramento, and is a very conspicuous landmark. In appearance, it somewhat resembles the magnificent structure at Washington, but on a very diminutive scale, and might in fact be taken for a junior member of the same house. The city may be very remarkable, but I was not particularly struck with it, and the intense heat drove me away sooner than I had intended. The mosquitoes, too, warned me that I was in the 'Mammoth' State, and from their size I began to think there was some truth in the story they tell of a band of these terrible insects having once attacked and killed a mule; and when they had eaten all the flesh several of the largest were seen sitting on the carcase picking their teeth with the ribs.

After leaving Sacramento, that terrible nuisance on the trains, the youth who sells books, fruit, &c. seemed to become more annoying than ever, I suppose because the weather was so hot. This dreadful bore on all American trains begins his persecutions and proceeds on his rounds as soon as the train starts. He first offers books, new and second-hand; if you say you do not want any, he at once throws two or three into your lap or down by your side, and begs you just to look at them. On his return from his journey through the cars, he sweeps them up again with an injured air, if you still do not want one. He then leaves you, but only to return in a few minutes with decayed pears, pea-nuts, apples, and peaches. When that round is completed you lie down perhaps in a corner for a doze, when suddenly his shrill voice yells in your ear, 'Figs, cigars, and chewing candy.' Indignantly you return to your seat, only to find he has made a stall of it by piling up his books and depositing his basket of pea-nuts in it. If you go to the smoking carriage for a quiet smoke, you encounter this young pedlar in all his glory, as the smoking-car is the stronghold where he keeps his supplies, in sundry large chests, and where he can enjoy passages of arms and wordy warfare with the breakmen and rowdies of all sorts, who generally occupy the second-class cars. I have often wondered how people who cannot afford the high fares of first-class and Pullman cars get through the long journey from New York to San Francisco, or *vice versâ*.

The second-class are the smoking-carriages; they are without carpets, the seats often without cushions, and not a place for a sick man or child to lie down, day or night, and no room for change of position. Crowded indiscriminately with whites, blacks, and Chinese, people of cultivated minds and habits have to herd with the vulgar and low mannered, and the journey altogether must be as near an approach to a seven days' purgatory as is possible.

The name of the 'Golden State' is very appropriate to California: everything is golden—the light, the landscape, and the soil. The currency is in gold also, which is anything but pleasant. Paper-money for travellers has many advantages over coin, in being more easily carried, and affording fewer opportunities for robbery. Besides, with gold the loss is very great.

In the East, for an English note say of twenty pounds, you will receive nearly one hundred and twenty dollars in green-backs; in California, you will not receive for it one hundred dollars in gold. And yet prices are just the same. It is very well to say you receive more value for your money, but you do not in fact; at all events, travellers do not. You pay the same number of dollars per day at the hotels in the West as in the East, and a dollar is a dollar in both places, no more and no less. Retail traders, and hotel and bar keepers are the people who chiefly gain by it—and their gains must be enormous.

It has appeared to me that throughout America the high rate of wages is merely nominal. As wages rise so do prices. The price of clothing in America is so high that persons accustomed to European prices would hardly believe what the cost of a coat or a pair of boots is. Yet if the Irish bog-trotter hears that he can get two dollars a day for his work in America, off he rushes to receive his high wages, without the slightest consideration of the still far higher price he will have to pay for his daily necessaries. No wonder the duty on imported articles of clothing is so enormous in America, for if it were not, I think everything would be obtained from Europe. As it is, smuggling has obtained quite a prominent place amongst the arts practised in the East.

But here we are at Stockton, which is my starting-point for the Big Trees of Calaveras and the celebrated Yosemite Valley.

BIG TREE.—Mother of the Forest.

CHAPTER VIII.

STOCKTON TO THE YOSEMITE VALLEY.

Stockton—Dust — Gophers — Quails—Staging—Tarantulas—Hydraulic mining—Mammoth trees—A curious flower—A theory—Table Mountain—Deserted villages—Chinese camp—Wine—The Siamese twins—Manzanita—The summit.

I SHALL always look back on my visit to Stockton—the City of Windmills—with a pleasant remembrance of its beautiful gardens. All sweet-scented flowers seemed to grow there, and with a greater luxuriance than I had seen anywhere else.

Some of the gardens were a little unkempt and overluxuriant, like gardens to which the hired man comes once a week only, or tends in the intervals of knife-cleaning and boot-blacking; but the houses were covered with roses, myrtles, and honeysuckles, which climbed to the very roofs, and every window was set in a frame of heliotrope and jessamine. The borders were all filled with Old World flowers, and numbers of our hot-house plants grew there as trees and bushes.

Stockton is neither a pretty nor a well-situated town, as it is on the borders of the tule-lands which are formed by the overflow of the San Joaquin and Sacramento rivers. Numbers of little channels, with long wooden bridges over them, run in all directions, at least, they run when there is any water in them, which is seldom. The outskirts of the town seem to be entirely under water, as the main channel winds all round them. There is, however, one beautiful view, that of Mount Diablo; miles away, but standing out boldly across the flat country, and the spectacle at sunset is worth a visit to Stockton to see.

I had the good fortune to meet there two American gentlemen—one of whom was an ex-colonel of the United States army—who kindly asked me to join them in their expedition to the Big Trees and the Valley. I gladly accepted their invitation, and most delightful and agreeable companions I found them. The Colonel was just as enthusiastic and as determined to see everything that was to be seen as he could have been when twenty years younger, and he had a fund of quiet humour, which entertained us as much as his knowledge of botany and other subjects instructed us.

A branch line of the railway took us to Milton, a small station about thirty miles from Stockton, and thenceforth our journey was by stage-coach. If you are so unfortunate as to be unable to obtain a box seat, staging in this part of the world is simply agony. From the moment you get on the coach till the time you get off, you are in one perpetual cloud of thick yellow dust. Dust-coats, veils, &c. are useless, although you must wear them. Every halting-place has its supply of basins of water, and innumerable brushes to assist you in getting rid of some of the dust. But in less than two minutes after you start again, eyes, hair, mouth, ears, and clothes are once more filled with the penetrating sand, and you become irritable to a degree if you think about it and try to keep clean. It is better, therefore, to bear it stoically, and to become as begrimed and dirty as you possibly can at your earliest convenience. Our thirty miles' journey to Murphy's, where we were to remain for the night, was through a country, yellow of course, parched, and without much variety of scenery, but alive with squirrels and gophers. These pests to the farmers increase every year, and do almost as much damage to the crops as a flight of locusts. For every one that a farmer may destroy on his land, ten survive to avenge his death. Individual efforts to exterminate them have hitherto been ineffectual, and to get rid of them entirely, some general system will be necessary, which must be carried out fully and thoroughly, so as to leave no corner in which the enemy, once routed, can take refuge and recuperate. A gopher is like a small mole, and is even more destructive than a squirrel.

We saw many of the beautiful Californian quails,

dusting themselves in the road, and looking so 'game' with their erect feathery top-knots. These, and the black-and-white woodpeckers and small doves, are the principal birds found in these regions, and they make up by their numbers for the scarcity of other varieties. The only animals we saw were jackass-rabbits—thin gaunt-looking animals, with enormous ears, from which, I suppose, they derive their name.

Stage-driving in California is widely different from staging in other parts of the world. The drivers, as a rule, are quaint, clever, companiable men, and splendid whips. At first, the break-neck speed at which they always drive down-hill is rather appalling, but you soon get accustomed to it. To find yourself whirling down a very steep hill, along a narrow road, round sharp corners with a steep precipice on one side, and as fast as four and sometimes six horses can go, is so novel a sensation, so exciting, and so opposed to the usual steady down-hill sort of pace, that you cannot help cheering on the horses, in spite of a very probable upset on the brow of an almost perpendicular rock several hundred feet in height. The horses, too, seem to enjoy it, and I must say I attribute the absence of accidents as much to their knowingness and sure-footedness as to the certainly brilliant attainments of the 'knights of the whip.' Generally, each driver has some specialty of his own—for instance, one is well up in botany; another knows something of natural history; and I remember one who knew the height of every mountain we saw, the length of every bridge we crossed, and the number of inhabitants in each village we passed through. His successor afterwards informed me, that he was of so statistical a turn that he had counted the hairs on his children's heads and pasted the number in their hats; but I am inclined to think that must have been an exaggeration.

Murphy's Camp is a quiet little mining town. Perhaps we found it quiet because we happened not to be there on a Saturday night, which is anything but a quiet night at most mining towns. It is then that the 'poor but honest miner' spends his week's earnings in liquor, and the village whisky-shops and bars are the scenes of one long round of general dissipation. Murphy's is a great place for tarantulas' nests; indeed, the chief business of the little village consists in the sale of these curiosities. The nest is composed of a house of clay, rough outside but polished in the interior, and having a little clay door swinging on a perfect hinge. If you look at this door carefully on the inside you will see two very small holes, and into these the tarantula, when at home, and an intruder wishes to open the door, sticks two of his hind legs, holding on at the same time to the other end of his room with his fore legs; by which means he makes it impossible to gain access to him. Sometimes you are asked to buy a nest with the huge spider inside, but that is an advantage I should advise no one to avail himself of.

Mining is carried on to the very back door of the hotel, and by this time, I have no doubt, underneath it. We had there a good opportunity of seeing hydraulic mining, which is, I think, the most interesting kind of mining. For this sort of work, the water is brought down from a river or stream, in narrow ditches dug around the sides of the hills. In some places, where water is scarce, ditches have been made extending for more than seventy miles. From these ditches the water is conducted through a long narrow trough of wood, called a 'flume,' stretching out over the 'claim' or tract which is to be worked. A hose, with nozzle, is attached to it, from which the water flows in a continual stream, and is directed by the miners against the hill-side. By this action the soft dirt is washed away from the gravel, and, forming one liquid mass, is carried through a 'tail-race' into long 'flumes.' Within these 'flumes' are placed 'riffles'—little steps, as it were, attached to the bottom of the 'flume'—for arresting the gold, which, on account of its own weight, sinks to the bottom, and thus is caught. When these 'riffles' are supposed to be full the water is turned off and the dirt is taken out.

The next process is using the 'long-tom,' which is

a box of sheet-iron with a duplicate perforated bottom, extending diagonally over a little more than half the box. Under it, in pockets, is placed the quicksilver; the 'long-tom' is then attached to a sluice-way and the water turned through it—the dirt being taken from the 'riffles' and shovelled upon this perforated plate, when the particles of gold fall through and unite their atoms with the quicksilver. The amalgam is then removed, placed in a retort and heated, when the quicksilver being sublimed passes away in vapour, leaving the gold. The economy of human labour effected by the hydraulic method of mining is very great; but it is immensely expensive where long ditches and flumes have to be built; and besides, with every precaution, much of the gold is carried away. The whole tract of the mining-land at Murphy's, as at most other places where the hydraulic method is used, was doubtless once the channel of a large mountain stream, which piled up the great beds within which are found the fine particles of gold, worn away from the great quartz mountains by the action of the water. It is extraordinary what this constant flow of water has done in so short a time. The soil has been wasted clean away from the underlying rock, which presents a most jagged and strange appearance; the denuded rocks standing up in enormous fangs and reefs, resembling the gnarled and twisted stumps of old oak trees.

The drive from Murphy's to the Big Trees, a distance of sixteen miles, was all up-hill, consequently very tedious, and the dust was worse than on the preceding day. The road winds up a narrow gorge by the side of a picturesque stream, and groves of oaks and pines give a pleasant shade from the hot rays of the sun.

The grounds of the hotel are entered by a road between two splendid specimens of the Sequoias, or Big Trees, and are called 'The Sentinels.' The Mammoth Tree Grove of Calaveras is situated nearly 4,500 feet above the sea-level, and consists of about one hundred of the Big Trees, a species now known as the 'Sequoia gigantea.' The valley and ridges are heavily timbered with spruce, fir, sugar pine, and cedar trees—the latter much resembling the Sequoias.

We first paid our respects to the 'Mammoth Tree Stump,' on which a pavilion has been built, and where church-service was performed on the Sunday we were there. This tree was cut down several years ago, and it took twenty-three days to accomplish the sacrilegious act. The solid wood of this stump, which is perfectly smooth, and sound, and stands about six feet from the ground, measures thirty-one feet across. Just imagine the stump of a tree over ten yards in diameter!

Botanists say that each concentric circle is the growth of one year; and as nearly three thousand of these circles can be counted in this stump, there is little doubt that the age of the Big Trees in this grove is nearly three thousand years. 'This,' says the 'Gardener's Calendar,' 'may very well be true, if the tree does not grow above two inches in diameter in twenty years, which we believe to be the fact.'

In my humble opinion the growth of these trees is at least four inches in diameter in twenty years, and I base it upon the appearance of the bark, which gives the idea of extremely rapid growth; also from the fact that several of the plates inscribed with the names of these trees, and which had been firmly nailed on the trunks, have, after a comparatively short period, been burst open and dislodged by the growth of the bark.

A short walk brought us into the heart of the grove; and there, like stately guardians of their smaller brethren—such as enormous sugar pines and lordly cedars—towered high above them these majestic monuments of the solemn silent ages. Nearly the whole of the trees have been injured by the desolating fires which have swept over the forests at different periods, and most of them have been deformed by the wind-storms which at certain seasons traverse these hills and valleys with irresistible fury. The 'Mother of the Forest' presents a very melancholy appearance, as she was flayed alive some years ago. The bark on an average was about twelve inches thick, though in some places it was over two feet. It was stripped off to a height of about 120 feet, and sent to England, where, at the great fire at the Crystal Palace, it was burnt. Of course the poor 'Mother' died when she lost her skin, but that did not matter to those who profited by the sale of it.

The 'Father of the Forest' lies prostrate, and is half-buried in the soil. This tree measures 112 feet in circumference at the roots. It is 200 feet to the first branch. The whole of it is hollow, and you can walk through it erect. It is estimated that when standing the tree could not have been less than 440 feet in height. At 300 feet from the roots it was broken off by striking against another large tree in its fall, and at that height it is twenty feet in diameter. Near its base is a spring of clear cold water. Ladders are placed against some of the fine old prostrate trees, by which means you can mount the trunk and walk along by a good path to the top branches—a grand trunk road, in fact. One fallen tree you can ride through on horseback for a considerable distance.

The height and circumference of a few of the largest of these wonderful trees, as far as I have been able to ascertain them, are as follows:—

Name	Height	Circum.
Mother of the Forest	325 feet	95 feet
Father of the Forest (estimated)	440 ,,	115 ,,
Empire State	330 ,,	90 ,,

FATHER OF THE FOREST.
115 Feet circumference.—Near view, Mammoth Grove, Calveras County.

P. 112.

Name	Height	Circum.
The Mammoth Tree	310 feet	102 feet
Pride of the Forest	280 ,,	65 ,,
The Two Sentinels	315 ,,	70 & 66 ,,
Uncle Tom's Cabin	310 ,,	95 ,,
The Burnt Tree	340 ,,	100 ,,

We rode out one day to the South Grove, which has only lately been made accessible by tract. It is the largest and finest grove of Sequoias yet discovered in California, and contains about fourteen hundred Big Trees, some of which are much larger than any we had before seen. Sixteen horsemen may congregate in one of them, and through the prostrate trunk of another a large stage-coach crowded with passengers might be driven for a distance of 200 feet. If ever you wish to feel yourself a pigmy, go and stand at the feet of these giants, or lie on your back and look up at their vast lofty canopies.

The 'Sequoia gigantea' belongs to the same family as the Red Wood, of which magnificent specimens are constantly seen in California. The wood is red like the cedar; much harder than that of the Sequoia, and the shape of the tree is more symmetrical. Indeed, but few of the big trees are symmetrical in their outlines; they have battled too long with the storms of centuries to preserve a graceful appearance. The enormous weight which each tree carries makes it more difficult for it to bear the force of the gales, as it overtops other forest trees and receives no shelter. Its leaf is very like that of the cedar. The cone is small and insignificant, and the wood is wonderfully light, almost like cork. The bark is also very light, porous, and reddish in colour.

In the **North Grove** we found some very curious plants, called by the natives ' snow-plants,' from their springing up in great profusion when snow is on the ground. There was no snow when we were there, but we found several of these plants. The flower is blood-red; it is of a flesh-like substance, and in growth much resembles a hyacinth. Its stems are clustered, from five to ten inches high, with long erect scales.

We gathered several specimens, but could not preserve the wonderful red colour. The flower when plucked turned black. That, however, did not prevent the Colonel from carrying away several large bottles in which he had placed the flowers for preservation. But these, together with a quantity of the enormous cones from the sugar pines, and several blocks of petrified wood and pieces of bark from the Big Trees, formed an amount of extra luggage that was so strongly objected to by our Jehu, that most of it, on our return from the grove, was perforce left at Murphy's, where most likely it was afterwards disposed of to stray travellers at exorbitant prices.

Our drive back to Murphy's was much pleasanter than the ascent had been; and as we each had our own theory about the Big Trees, the discussion was very animated. I was looked upon as a heathen, because my idea was that each tree had been originally two or three trees growing near to each other, the stems of which, as they grew, had gradually approached until they touched; the quick-growing spongy bark then uniting, and thus in time forming one tree. The concentric circles to be seen in the trunks of the cut-down trees had in some degree confirmed me in my idea. Besides, the trees are hardly ever single, but are divided, at different heights from the ground, into two and often three distinct stems, which look as if they yet might unite entirely.

My hypothesis was well laughed at, but I intend to hold to it until I hear of more likely conditions for the production of these forest monsters. The isolation of the Sequoia is almost as remarkable as its size. A belt of them runs along the slopes of the Sierras, and near Visalia there is a group of them, but there are very few other places where they are known.

In China I once saw a tree called the 'Glyptostrobus,' and in Japan one of the same kind called the 'Gingko;' both were of the Red Wood species, and were looked upon there as of extraordinary size. But they were not to be compared to the Big Trees of California; and though they were classed as specimens of the 'Sequoia gigantea' they had not much more right to that distinction than a mushroom has—at least, not when put into competition with the trees of the Mammoth Grove of Calaveras.

From Murphy's our road ran for the most part through old mining districts, abandoned now, but suggestive of all the struggles, sorrows, and passions to which flesh is heir. I do not know which looked the more desolate, the worked-out diggings or the closed and ruined houses of the mining villages.

We crossed the 'Stanislaus,' and there saw one of the most interesting features of scenery on the journey. This was 'Table Mountain,' a long level ridge of solidified lava.

Ages ago a vast stream of lava must have poured down from the mountains beyond the Big Trees of Calaveras, and after flowing some forty miles, hardening in its course, at last stopped altogether. It must have run between mountains and have followed probably the channel of some river. The mountains which formed walls for this enormous stream of lava being of slate, have gradually wasted away, and now nothing remains but this flat smooth mountain of hard basaltic lava, upon which thousands of centuries have hardly made a furrow. The surrounding country has been nearly washed away, and all round, as well as beneath Table Mountain, the miners have been very busy. In some cases, the profits have been very large, but, as usual, more, on the whole, has been put into the mountain than has been taken out of it.

Passing through Sonora—a quiet shady little village—we traversed the melancholy deserted mining district. Here and there might be seen a persevering Chinaman, pensively shaking his rocker, and gleaning what he could from what had already been sifted over and over again. Soon after, we arrived at Chinese Camp, where we purposed remaining the night. Camp seemed the proper name for these almost abandoned mining towns. Destined to exist only so long as the hunt for gold proved profitable, when fortune turned, tents were pitched in fresh places, and these in their turn were deserted, leaving only long streets of empty drinking saloons and gambling hells as relics of the past. When I think of the hotel at Chinese Camp it brings vividly to my remembrance a terribly hot night, a certain spring-bed with all the springs broken, and the worst food met with during the whole of the journey. I can only hope that the incapable landlord, who was a Pole, and consequently a Count, has ere this closed his hotel and returned to his native land.

We started very early next morning, so as to be some miles on our way before the dust, which had been partly laid by heavy rain that had fallen in the night, should again rise in clouds on the roads.

We passed a large vineyard, which the driver told us was the most famous one in those parts. The vineyard may have been, but I hope it did not produce the most famous wine; for we tasted of the vintage, and, to say the best of it, found it but indifferent. The owner, however, thought it excellent.

We crossed the Tuolumne river, rushing along in a tremendous hurry, and again found ourselves in a ravaged and disfigured district. We dined at a little village bearing the suggestive name of Garotte; and after toiling up steep hills, from which there were magnificent views, we arrived at a small *ranch* called Hardin's, where we remained for the night. On the following day we drove through the Tuolumne grove of Big Trees, consisting of about thirty Sequoias, two of which grow from the same root, and unite a few feet above the base. They are called 'The Siamese Twins.' Together, they are about one hundred and fifteen feet in circumference at the ground, consequently about thirty-eight feet in diameter. According to my theory, these two trees will gradually unite and in a century or two become one tree, that is, if they remain undisturbed; but I believe the intention is to widen and heighten the present unconnected parts, so that the carriage-drive may pass through the Twins.

Our road lay through what are in the spring, grassy meadows interspersed among the mountain districts;

but we saw no signs of vegetation, flocks of sheep having eaten up all the grass and as much as they could of the shrubs. At the dividing ridge of the Tuolumne and Merced rivers, there are beautiful views of the snow-clad peaks of the Sierras; and timber-covered gorges and ridges stretch away to the distant horizon. We are here 7,000 feet above the level of the ocean.

Everywhere are seen the red flesh-like arms and limbs of the Manzanita—a wood which takes a most brilliant polish—enormous sugar pines, oaks of different kinds, and the chaparral, forming a thorny, impervious shrubbery, which at certain seasons has a very unpleasant smell. Singular groups of granite rocks are now passed, many of them most quaint and picturesque in form, and therefore, probably, named after objects which they least resemble.

At this point, the fresh track of a large bear caused us some excitement. But Bruin was too shy to show himself; and by the time we had recovered from our disappointment at not seeing him we had arrived at the summit, where we mounted our ponies to descend into the Yosemite Valley.

CHAPTER IX.

THE YOSEMITE VALLEY.

The descent—A patient steed—The valley—The hotel—A philosopher—Riding astride—The Yosemite Falls—Mirror Lake—A legend—Bridal Veil Fall—Glacier Point and Sentinel Dome—The Nevada and Vernal Falls—A rapid—The Cosmopolitan—Improvements—Impressions—Digger Indians—Departure.

THE descent of the mountain is very gradual as far as Prospect Point; a rocky promontory from which the Merced river is seen, winding its way under steep cliffs and through rocky cañons as it rushes, cold and sparkling, from its snowy home among the Sierras. Nearly opposite to us, and beyond a thread-like waterfall of about 800 feet, is 'Inspiration Point.' This Point is passed when entering the Valley by the Mariposa route. We were to visit it later, as the view from it, looking up through the cañon and into the Valley, was said to be inexpressibly grand.

Here the descent really begins, and certainly one or two places are 'real steep.' But the animals knew every inch of the trail, and were as sure-footed as goats. Mine happened to be a mule, which our guide informed me was a strong patient animal. I had very little

GENERAL VIEW OF THE VALLEY FROM PROSPECT POINT   P. 120.

opportunity to test the former quality, as the latter was so marked that after the first half-hour nothing would induce the brute to move, and I at last reluctantly dismounted and left the obtuse animal patiently standing and looking over a precipice, several hundred feet deep, at the view below. I never heard of the arrival of that mule at the hotel; but I suppose it did eventually succeed in reaching it, or I should on leaving have seen in my bill, amongst other items, 'To one mule lost,' so much.

The pack-mule did not make his appearance till some time after we had arrived, and might just as well have picked up his patient brother and brought him on with him.

After about an hour and a half, slowly but surely descending, we arrived at Mecca—*i.e.* we found ourselves at the end of our pilgrimage and in the Yosemite Valley. We followed the trail along the right bank of the Merced, a broad rushing river, which gladdens one's heart to hear and to look at, and out of which some wretched-looking Digger Indians were then taking trout. After a ride (or rather walk in my case) of about a mile, we found, at a spot where the trail widens into a road, a carriage waiting, which was to take us to Hutchings's Hotel.

I must here attempt to give a general idea of the Valley.

Its length is a little over six miles. Its breadth varies from half a mile to a mile and a half, and its sides rise up almost perpendicularly; sometimes quite so. Its area is nearly flat, and sunken about a mile below the general level of the mountain region around it.

Its principal features, and those which make it so different from other valleys, are the altitude and verticality of its walls, the absence of broken rock and *débris* at the base of the cliffs, the great height of the waterfalls, and the variety and beauty of the flowers that bloom there as in a vast garden.

On our way to the hotel we drove by many grand points of interest. The length of time it took to reach and pass some of the more prominent of the mountain-walls is a proof of their unrealised altitudes.

Large pines and shady oaks grew along the road, and perpendicular cliffs rose on either side, between 3,000 and 4,000 feet in height.

We slowly approached the naked granite wall called 'El Capitan,' whose white broad brow and bold form make it, as its name indicates, the Great Chief of the Valley. There is no slope to 'El Capitan,' its massive sides are destitute of vegetation, and its aspect is more majestic and grand than words can describe.

Opposite the 'Chief,' and across the Valley, is the beautiful waterfall named Pahono—Bridal Veil Fall—

which leaps a distance of 940 feet before it touches the rocks.

Then come in sight ' Pom-pom-pa-sus '—mountains playing leap-frog—and a glimpse is caught of the ' Yosemite Fall,' the huge ' North Dome,' ' Clouds Rest,' and other magnificent sights—all to be closely inspected later—and after twice crossing the river the hotel is reached.

The hotel and its surrounding cottages are decidedly light airy buildings. Too strong a gale might blow them away.

The partitions of the bedrooms are of cotton cloth, and the doors are sheets, consequently, conversations conducted under these circumstances have to be discreet.

Mr. Hutchings himself is a poet, author, and philosopher; presumably, therefore, extremely ill-suited for the post of hotel-keeper, an employment requiring more practical qualifications.

Crowds of tourists—you may call yourself a traveller, but on this expedition you will have to own yourself a tourist—all bent on different excursions, and all looking for the distracted proprietor, would turn the brain of the most matter-of-fact and most experienced host. But when Mr. Hutchings is up in the clouds, and dreaming of nature and her grandeur, he smilingly and thoughtfully assents to whatever you may have to say, and the next moment forgets all about you and your pleadings, and philosophically returns to the contemplation of the magnitude of his waterfalls. But Mr. Hutchings' good nature and desire to please, make ample amends for any little discomforts; and if you can only find him—that's the difficulty—when you want any help or information, and stick to him when found, you are sure to obtain all you wish.

On our first expedition in the Valley we took a guide with us, but soon found that there was no necessity for one, and that there is no difficulty in finding the way about alone. We hired our horses for the day, and were perfectly independent. Unless a great many visitors should happen to be in the Valley, horses are easily obtained, numbers of them being always kept tied up under the trees near the hotel, saddled and bridled, and only waiting to be mounted.

Strong-minded ladies here ride astride, and declare that it is easier and more comfortable than the orthodox mode; it certainly is not so graceful. A grim Amazon in a short skirt, thick boots, large hat, and green spectacles, riding astride a horse or a mule, is about as ludicrous—not to say ungainly—an exhibition as you could well contemplate. One of the best ways of enjoying the Yosemite is simply to ride up and down the Valley, under the trees and by the river-side, and to gaze in a state of pleasurable sensation on the new aspects which open freshly upon you, at least, every half-mile. The atmosphere is delicious; days bright and warm, nights cool and pleasant. Perhaps the sun is sometimes a little too hot; but there is nearly always a breeze blowing in from the Pacific.

The most important of the numerous waterfalls in the Valley is called the Yosemite—which means 'large grizzly bear'—and it is exactly opposite the hotel. The stream flows over a precipice into the Valley below— a depth of 2,634 feet. The Fall has almost the appearance of one grand shoot of water, but it has in reality three leaps. At the first leap of 1,600 feet it plunges into a vast rocky basin; gathering strength, it again takes a leap of 434 feet—finally, after another fall of 600 feet, plunging into the Valley. There is sufficient water to give a bright foaming sweep to the entire cataract. To my mind, the immense height of the Falls does not make up for their want of breadth, although the breadth of the Yosemite Fall, at the top, is nearly forty feet. Seen from a distance, however, this width dwindles down to apparently four or five feet. For grandeur I think it is not to be compared to Niagara, though many people consider it far superior. The rumble and roar of the Falls are heard at all times, and the sound has a peculiar double tone—a distinct monotonous boom, broken into at intervals by a loud thundering crash like the sea and the breaking of the surf on a rocky shore. Our first visit was to those falls, to get a closer inspection of their beauties.

Having crossed the bridge over the main stream, we presently arrived at a most picturesque ford. Oaks, maples, and cottonwood trees, overarched the broad shallow stream, and in the background the lower fall of the Yosemite was descending in a sheet of mist and spray, behind a dark middle distance of firs and pines. As we approached the Falls a change of temperature was perceptible, and a heavy shower of spray soon brought us to a stand-still. When seen from such close quarters they are certainly very grand. Overhanging mountains of solid granite hemmed us in, huge boulders of sharp, angular rocks lay scattered about, and ferns, flowers, and grasses grew in profusion all around. The great mass of falling water, apparently grown so wide now we were near it, seemed more like a snowy avalanche than a liquid stream; and we lingered there for some hours, gazing on this wonderful scene of wood and and water, and even then we were loth to leave. But our appetites finally prevailed, and we returned to the hotel for luncheon.

The rides in the fresh morning were very delightful. My favourite gallop was to Mirror Lake, the ride for a great part of the way being over fresh springy turf. The path takes you to the base of the great North

Dome, a mountain of bare granite, which towers up to a height of nearly 4,000 feet. Its sides are perpendicular for over 2,000 feet. Colossal arches have been formed in them, doubtless by the falling of sections of rock.

Crossing a plateau, then following a very rough rocky trail, you reach a small sheet of clear water with the most picturesque surroundings. On the north and west lie enormous rocks that have been detached from the mountains above; various kinds of trees and shrubs grow among them and overhang the margin of the lake. On the south-east stands the splendid 'South Dome,' about 4,600 feet above the Valley. Half of this immense mass has fallen, but its strange oval head and majestic appearance make it one of the greatest attractions of the Valley. The great beauty of the Mirror Lake consists in its marvellously clear reflection of the surrounding trees and mountains. The best time to go there is before the sun has appeared above the hills. The calm of the water is then usually undisturbed, and the reflection of the sun rising over the mountains has a very charming effect.

Around this spot was the traditional home of the guardian spirit, the valley of the angel Tis-sa-ack, after whom her devoted Indian worshippers have named the majestic mountain called the 'South Dome.'

I heard the following legend of Tis-sa-ack. It is

interwoven with the story of El Capitan, or Ta-tock-ak-na-lak.

'In the great long-ago the sun-children dwelt in Yo Semite. All was happiness. Ta-tock-ak-na-lak sat on high in his rocky home and cared for his well-loved people. Leaping over the plains, he herded the wild deer that his people might choose the fattest for their feasts. He drove the bears from their caverns, that the *braves* might hunt. He prayed to the Great Spirit for rain, that the seed in the valley might grow. The smoke of his pipe curled into the air, and through its blue haze the yellow sun shone warm and bright and ripened the crops, that the women might gather them in. When he laughed, the face of the river was rippled with smiles; when he sighed, the wind swept sadly through the singing pines; when he spoke, the sound was like the deep voice of the cataract. His form was straight like the arrow, and supple like the bow. His foot was swifter than the red deer, and his glance was strong and bright like the rising sun.

'One morning, as he roamed, a bright vision came before him, and then the soft colours of the West were in his lustrous eyes. A maiden sat upon the southern dome of granite that raises its bare head above the high peaks.

'She was not like the dark maidens of the tribe below, for golden hair rolled over her dazzling form, like golden waters over silver rocks; her feet shone like the snow-tufts on the wintry pines, and were arched like the spring of a bow.

'Two cloud-like wings fluttered on her dimpled shoulders, and her voice was like the sweet sad tone of the night-bird. "Ta-tock-ak-na-lak" she softly whispered; then, gliding up the steep dome, she vanished over its rounded top. Keen was the eye, quick was the ear, swift was the foot of the youth as he sped in pursuit; but the soft down of her wings was wafted into his eyes and he saw her no more.

'Every morning did the love-stricken Ta-tock-ak-na-lak wander over the mountains to meet the beautiful Tis-sa-ack. Each day he laid sweet acorns and wild flowers upon her dome. His ear caught her footstep, though it was light as the falling leaf, his eye gazed on her wondrous form and into her gentle eyes, but never did he speak before her, and never again did her sweet-toned voice fall upon his ear.

'So strong was his love for the fair maid that he forgot the crops of Yo Semite. Without rain they quickly drooped their heads and shrank. The wind whistled mournfully through the pines, the wild bee stowed no more honey in the hollow tree, for the flowers had lost their freshness and the green leaves turned brown.

'Ta-tock-ak-na-lak saw not this, for his eyes were dazzled by the shining wings of Tis-sa-ack. She looked with grief over the neglected valley, and kneeling on the **smooth** hard **rock,** besought the Great Spirit to bring again bright flowers, grasses, green trees, and waving corn.

'With an awful sound the dome **of** granite opened beneath her feet, and the mountain was riven asunder, whilst the melting snows from the Nevada gushed through the wonderful gorge. Quickly they formed a lake between the perpendicular walls of the cleft mountain **and sent a** sweet murmuring river through the valley. All was then changed. The moisture crept silently through the parched soil; the flowers sent up a **fragrant incense** of thanks; the corn raised its drooping **head, and** the sap with velvet footfall ran up into the trees, giving life and energy to all. But the maid, for whom the valley had suffered, and through whom it was again clothed with beauty, had disappeared. Yet, that all might hold her memory in their hearts, she left the quiet lake, the winding river, and the half-dome which still bears her name, "Tis-sa-ack," and **w**hich every evening catches the last rosy rays that are reflected from **the snowy** peaks.

'When Ta-tock-ak-na-lak knew that she was gone for ever he **left his rocky heights and** wandered away **in search of his lost love.** That the Yo Semites might **never** forget him, he carved with his hunting-knife the outlines of his majestic head upon the face of the rock that bears his name. There they still remain, and may be plainly distinguished, guarding the entrance to this much-loved valley.'

The excursion to the Bridal Veil Fall is a very favourite one with the ladies, and a very delightful ride it is. The trail leads first through groves of white azaleas, which grow to perfection near the river's banks. But after skirting Sentinel rock—a lofty solitary peak, on which the Indians used to light their **watch-fires**—it passes under the Cathedral rocks, **which look like** granite church-spires, their rugged sides rising abruptly from base to pinnacle.

Threading our way over rocks and through streams, we at length arrived at a spot where we were obliged to dismount. We then tied our animals to the trees, and proceeded on foot for the rest of the way—which, fortunately, was but a very short distance.

The 'Pohono,' or 'Bridal Veil' Fall, is exceedingly graceful and undulating. The glittering sheets of spray throw a misty drapery over the falling torrent, which is said to receive its waving motion from a strong wind that always blows on the lake which is the source of the stream.

Towards evening as the sun sinks in the west a glorious rainbow is formed in the glistening spray. The effect is magical, and most **lovely—only by** being seen can the faintest idea be formed of it. The Indians think the stream and its fall are bewitched; hence its musical name, Pohono, *i.e.* an evil spirit, whose breath is a blighting and fatal wind. On this account, too, when passing it, they hasten by as fast as they can.

Nothing would induce them to sleep near it; but that feeling may arise from their intense dislike to water in any form—at least such is my unpoetical belief.

We had not been many days in the Valley before we were anxious to ascend to some high peak and look down upon what we had hitherto been looking up to. We started, therefore, early one morning to make a long day's excursion to Glacier Point and Sentinel Dome.

A steep but well-made trail, winding amongst ferns and flowering shrubs and under the shadows of great rocks, brought us, after a nearly three hours' ride, to the summit of Glacier Point. The view from this Point is the most comprehensive of any, as it embraces the upper waterfalls, rocks, and cañons, and the magnificent views of the High Sierras.

Standing near the edge of the precipice, you look down into the Valley, which lies below at a depth of nearly 4,000 feet. Mirror Lake appears only as a little silver speck, and splendid trees, some of them 200 feet high, look like the trees in a child's toy farm-yard. The Merced winds along like a silken thread, and the high mountains seem so to narrow the Valley that from some points, you fancy you could almost jump over it. The North Dome, the magnificent Nevada Fall, the Cap of Liberty, the Vernal Fall, and the Yosemite Fall are all visible; but the Great South Dome stands out pre-eminent above them all, and eclipses the lesser wonders by its commanding appearance and the extraordinary formation of its untrodden summit.

Half-an-hour's ride brought us to Sentinel Dome, on which there is no vegetation, and from whose barren heights rise up all around, thousands of snow-clad peaks—shining like mountains of silver in the morning sun. The view of the valley itself is nearly the same as that from Glacier Point, but farther off—and to my mind not so impressive. The Coast Range can be distinctly seen, and the valleys of the Sacramento and the San Joaquin spread themselves out like a garden; while the great heights—Mount Lyell, Mount Dana, Mount Hoffman, Mount Star King, and others; averaging between 12,000 and 13,000 feet—give a strange Alp-like appearance to the vast snowy regions in this grand and beautiful panorama.

We found, on our way back to Glacier Point, several of the curious snow-plants; but we refrained from gathering them, remembering our experience at the

Big Trees. We also **saw a pretty** golden cavy, basking in the sun on the rocks. I dismounted and tried to intercept him in his retreat, but he was too quick for me, and I had the pleasure of seeing him disappear through a narrow fissure from which it was useless to attempt to turn him out.* This was the only wild animal we saw during our visit to Yosemite. There were also very few birds **in the Valley**. It would seem as if they, as well as Indians and wild animals, **were** afraid of it.

After another long gaze at the wondrous scene from the Point, and after watching for some time the splendid colouring of El Capitan and hosts of other precipices, some pearly grey, others reddish purple, their tints incessantly varying with the receding light, we retraced our steps, carrying with us the pleasant memory of a grand and never-to-be-forgotten picture, and arriving at our hotel with agonisingly stiff knees, caused by the great strain on them from the **extreme** steepness of the descent.

Of all the **delightful** excursions in the Valley none equal that **to the Vernal Fall**; and of all its glorious

---

* I do not know what the little animal was doing there, for the cavy is a native of South America—Brazil, I think. I was near enough to see its golden-brown hair. It sat up, too, as the cavies do; and when it ran off I noticed the absence of tail. There were acorns strewed about also. So altogether I think I could not have been mistaken about it, though these animals are not supposed to inhabit the Sierras.

scenes I prefer the view of the rapids between the Nevada and Vernal Falls to anything else.

The trail to these Falls winds up the Merced Cañon and past acres of azaleas—

> 'One boundless blush, one white empurpled shower
> Of mingled blossoms.'

Over sparkling streams, under high granite walls, through green woods, fragrant with all sorts of aromatic shrubs, and along the side of a swift brawling river, whose banks are covered with ferns and rare grasses, you are finally led to the Pi-wy-ack, or Vernal Fall. The former name means 'a shower of crystals,' and a more appropriate one could hardly have been chosen. It is a vast shower of sparkling diamonds. The height of the Fall is about 350 feet; I do not know to whom it owes its English name. I could see nothing 'vernal' about it; and the Indian name is more suitable and infinitely prettier. A vast body of water flows over the precipice, for the Merced is a broad, deep river, rising high up in the mountains. It makes a descent of over 2,000 feet in two miles, and forms in its course the Nevada and the Vernal Falls. At one side of the Fall, ladders have been raised, by which the perpendicular wall of rock can be ascended, and a short walk then brings you to the Nevada Fall. The spray through which you must pass to reach the Ladders soaks you to the skin almost immediately.

We therefore put off our ducking until we returned, and, remounting our animals, continued to ascend by a long steep trail.

The Nevada Fall is superb, and grander than any other of the Valley Falls, on account of its great volume of water. It differs in shape from the others, having a peculiar twist in the upper part of it; the whirling motion being caused by a projecting rock at the lip of the Fall. It descends perpendicularly for about three-quarters of its height—600 feet—then, striking the smooth surface of the rock, it spreads into a magnificent sheet of white spray, 200 feet in width. I enjoyed gazing on the wonderful cataract between the two Falls more than anything I had seen. The distance between them is some hundred yards, and the water rushes through a deep narrow gorge—over which a bridge has been built—with a rapidity and noise far greater than the rapids above Niagara. Nothing is to be seen but running foam, as white as snow, amidst which enormous logs are tossed about and hurried along like feathers; the angry waters in their irresistible force and power having a fascination even more spell-like than the Falls themselves. The Cap of Liberty, a great mass of perpendicular rock, stands boldly out on the north side of the Nevada Fall. It can be ascended on its western side; and we were told that the view from the top of the vertical precipice of the Nevada Fall is magnificent; but we did not make the ascent.

On our **return we sent** our horses round by the trail and made the descent of the Vernal Fall by the Ladders. Before descending we reached a natural **wall of** granite, breast-high, and looking exactly over the Fall. **It seemed** as if it had been made **on** purpose to prevent those people who always feel inclined to throw themselves over, when looking down an abyss, from doing so. **At** the **foot of the** Ladders there are beautiful little grottos, full of all kinds **of** ferns and mosses. They are kept green and fresh **by** the perpetual spray from the Fall. After leaving these hanging gardens we found ourselves enveloped in blinding mist, driven with such force as to resemble a storm of rain. Gasping and blinded, it was difficult to keep to the slippery and narrow path, and in **the few** minutes occupied in rounding the cliff we became **so** thoroughly wet through, that we had to hang ourselves out to dry on the rocks for **a long** half-hour before returning home.

For full half a mile below the Falls nothing can be **seen but** torrents of foaming water, and the scene is wild and picturesque in the extreme. One visit to these Falls is sure to lead to others, as there is more variety and charm to be found here than anywhere else in the Valley. **For my own part,** I recall Pi-wy-ack and

Nevada **with** greater satisfaction than **any** other part of **the Yosemite**.

I was pleased **to** see that a large flat **rock**, from which a fine view of the Vernal Fall can be obtained, was pointed out to us with some pride as Lady Franklin's rock; that brave lady having visited the Yosemite in her travels, and having often watched the descending waters from this her favourite standpoint.

And all this time I have **never mentioned the** greatest wonder of the Valley—'The Cosmopolitan Saloon,' kept by Mr. John Smith! This gentleman visited the Yosemite about four years ago, and foreseeing a brilliant future in store for it, resolved to anticipate its needs. Consequently, he built a spacious house close to Hutchings's Hotel, and fitted it up with capital hot and cold baths, billiard-tables, a reading and writing room, hair-cutting establishment, and a bar, where he concocts the most refreshing drinks imaginable. The undertaking was no light one, as furniture, **supplies, and** the materials for building, with the exception of the rough lumber, had all to be packed on mules and brought into the Valley over a mountain-trail of at least ten or twelve miles. But he conquered **all** difficulties, and now his bright 'Cosmopolitan' **is** the resort of all Yosemite pilgrims, who generally leave the Valley with a feeling that J. Smith has certainly done a **very** great deal to render **their** visit most thoroughly **enjoyable.**

I shall say no more about picturesque river-scenes, waterfalls, and cliff-views, for I have mentioned what seemed to us the principal sights. **Other** rides and **rambles** would be merely a wearisome repetition. But let me sum up, if **I can**, the general feeling **and** ideas of our party about the Yosemite Valley. Too much credit cannot be given to Mr. Hutchings for his skill, and the trouble he has taken, in providing capital trails along precipitous mountain-sides, or for his general superintendence and careful endeavour to make a visit to the Valley even as comfortable as it is. But surely it is time for the Government to take in hand the improvements so sadly needed, now that the Yosemite has been granted to the State of California as a national park. The Valley itself should be cared for like a garden; trees and shrubs tended, swamps drained, bridges built, drives made, **and grass sown** where it is **necessary.** Irrigation **would be simple,** and where now there is nothing but marsh, or tracts of **dust,** there would very soon **be flowers and** verdure. If a good roomy hotel were built, visitors would remain weeks instead of days, and what is at present **a mere** scrambling resort would soon become a favourite summer residence. The rights of tollgate-keepers should be bought up; for although their charges are by no means excessive, considering the enormous amount of labour that has been employed in making good paths up the mountain-sides, yet a public park ought to have no tolls, I should imagine.

I wonder whether others have felt the same vague sense of imprisonment and oppression that was general with us in the Valley. This feeling drove away some English friends of mine sooner than they had intended to leave. In their Sussex home, they must since have had many a laugh over their Valley sensations, and many a wild dream of domes, waterfalls, and precipices, mixed up with steady steeds, steep trails, and Smith's sherry cobblers. While in the Valley, a longing is felt to get to the top of the mountains again and into the world once more. There is a strange weird perception of indefinite vastness, as if the ghostly precipices and solemn Falls had no right to be there; as if it would occasion no surprise if the waters were to vanish, the rocks to grow higher, and the smooth plain to sink lower and lower till it reached the distant abode of the winged mortals of the 'Coming Race.'

There were various opinions as to whether the Valley is seen better from above or from the plain itself. For my part, I infinitely preferred looking up at the giant rocks; they seemed then so much grander, and it was so much easier to appreciate their immense perpendicular heights and their strange fantastic outlines. However, all were agreed as to the awful grandeur of the Yosemite, and the stupendousness of the wonders contained in its Valley. But, whilst some thought one visit sufficient for a life time, others would have been glad to return year after year and to linger long by the banks of the swift and sounding Merced.

As we rode out of the Valley we passed a small encampment of 'Digger' Indians. These Indians are the aborigines of California, and are perhaps the lowest tribe of the human race. They are probably a branch of the Aztecs. They have very dark skins, high cheek-bones, deep bushy eyebrows, and masses of long straight black hair growing low over their foreheads. The men are short and very small-limbed, the women a little taller in proportion, and all filthily dirty. They live on roasted acorns and manzanita seed, but their favourite dishes are crickets and roasted grasshoppers. They hardly ever hunt, seldom fish, and never cultivate the soil. They have no skill in carving ornaments or images, no war implements, no idols, and no religion. They have a tradition that they descended from animals, and they believe that their progenitor was a *coyote*, a sort of wolf, and that when the *coyote* died his body became filled with spirits in the shape of deer, foxes, and squirrels, most of which took wings and flew away. To prevent the depopulation of the earth by such a continual flight, the old *coyotes* determined that the bodies should in future be burned, a custom still kept up by the Diggers. From that time the bodies of the *coyotes* gradually assumed the form of man, first walking on all-fours, then acquiring a finger then a toe, and so on. Soon this creature got into the habit of sitting, and wore off his tail.

This, to this day, is a subject of great grief to the Digger, who considers a tail an ornament of considerable beauty, and often adorns himself with one on festive occasions. Thus, the Digger Indian, at all events, is not opposed to the Darwinian theory, and his appearance is certainly conducive to the belief of its correctness. These miserable-looking creatures did not seem out of place in the Valley, any more than their forefathers the wolves would have been. They chattered like apes, and waved us a friendly good-bye in a most cheerful manner. We soon lost sight of their little bough-huts and their beds of leaves, but for some time after we could hear the Diggers laughing and jabbering as we slowly pursued our upward trail. After a few hours' struggle on our spiritless horses and dejected mules, we again reached the summit, and our visit to the glorious Yosemite Valley was ended.

CHAPTER X.

TO SAN FRANCISCO.

Stage jokes—The Golden City—Site—Vegetation—Dust—Over-work—Lone Mountain—Seal Rocks—Mission Dolores—Bits—Bars—Free lunch—Julep—A character—Architecture—Chinese—High wages—Hoodlums—Chinese facetiæ—Visit to the bad Chinese quarter—Chinese superstitions and troubles.

We returned to Stockton by a place called Knight's Ferry, where there were the most magnificent oleanders I had ever seen. For miles away the masses of pink blossom could easily be distinguished, and several gardens were entirely filled with large bushes of both the pink and white sorts.

Our driver informed us that this was the town which was so healthy that when they wanted to 'dedicate' the cemetery a man had to be shot for the purpose. His anecdote, however, did not gain much applause, as we had been told the same story by two other drivers at other places. We therefore set it down as a standing 'stage joke.' We were ready to believe many of the stories we heard; but when the same terrible struggles with grizzly bears and robbers were repeated by successive drivers, each one being the hero of the same tale, we began to have doubts of the strict truth of some of the enthralling events. The stage-drivers doubtless are, as a rule, very intelligent, and may be relied on; but some of them have really such excessive regard for the truth that they use it with almost penurious frugality.

From Stockton to San Francisco, through the Sacramento and San Joaquin Valleys, and over the Coast Range, is an uninteresting journey. We were very glad when we reached Oakland, which is to San Francisco what Brooklyn is to New York. Here the train ran out into the bay, for a distance of more than two miles, on a substantial pier. We were then transferred to the ferry-boat, which took us three miles across the water to the City of San Francisco. The sudden change from heat to cold was rather severe. A perfect hurricane was blowing in through the Golden Gate. A gentleman informed us, with tears in his eyes—whether from sorrow or from the coldness of the wind I do not know—that it was always the same in the summer months. The wind in the bay, he said, was nothing to the breeze on shore, and that the consequent dust was the eyesore of 'the Golden City of the West.'

It was getting dark when we approached San Francisco. Lights twinkled from thousands of houses rising tier above tier to all sorts of heights and distances; and with the forest of masts in the foreground the city presented almost a fac-simile of the view of Genoa when entered from the bay. Fortunately, landing is not the same dreadful business as at the latter place, and we walked on shore from the huge ferry-boats as comfortably as we embarked from the railway-carriages. The hotel-runners, and touters in general were in far too great force to be pleasant; but as we had already chosen our hotel there was little difficulty about our luggage, and the coach speedily deposited us at our destination. San Francisco is all ups and downs, rather annoying for building purposes, perhaps, but giving a wonderfully picturesque appearance to the city. It is a much easier matter to distinguish the hills on which San Francisco is built than it is to make out the Seven Hills of Rome.

The difficulties of building the town must have been immense. No street could be made without cutting down a hill or filling up a ravine. Half the site was occupied by the shallow waters of the bay, and the other half was composed of sand-hills, destitute of even the scantiest vegetation. Now, the present ever-improving great city stands there a proof of what can be accomplished by perseverance and energy.

The extraordinary luxuriance of vegetation, wherever plenty of water is used, shows the power of the mild and equable climate. I believe that if a walking-stick were planted in a patch of sand, and irrigated well, in a week or so there would spring forth a crop of young canes. Every garden makes a splendid show of flowers, which bloom perennially. Verbenas and heliotropes become shrubs; scarlet geraniums form thick hedges, ten and fifteen feet high; passion-flowers and jessamines climb all over the houses; oleanders and arbutilons grow to a height, and blossom in profusion and beauty perfectly amazing. One of the most beautiful shrubs I ever saw, and which on enquiry I was told was the *Pittisforum nigrum*, a native of New Zealand, is to be seen in every garden, sometimes growing to a height of twenty to thirty feet. It bears a strong resemblance to the ebony-stemmed fern—I do not know the correct name—and has an extremely graceful appearance. Many houses have beautiful lawns, always kept green by a hydrant. From the hydrant a hose is led to a sprinkler, which stands on the lawn, and can be moved from place to place.

Artesian wells are everywhere; the windmill standing on the top of a tank from which water is distributed to the house and over the grounds. The garden-hose is kept playing morning, noon, and night, and the result is a most astonishing vegetation. There are no trees lining the streets; but in the few squares and in the *plaza* there are various kinds of choice evergreens, as well as cedars, loquats, pepper trees, acacias, and palms.

The great objection to San Francisco in the summer

months is the strong wind which blows from the Pacific, bringing with it clouds of dust from the sand-hills. It is wonderful that these acres of shifting sand are not r‑claimed. Shrubs and plants—such as the beach-plum and yellow lupin—would soon imprison the sand and form a complete barricade against drifts. The western side of the city is at present made desolate by these sands, and many people who would like to live in San Francisco during the summer months leave on account of the sand-storms. Thus this carpeting with verdure would add greatly to the wealth of the city, to say nothing of the increase of comfort. It is the wind which modifies the climate, which is said to be the most exhilarating in the world. It is never too hot or too cold for outdoor work or exercise. With a sun as hot as in Southern France, and with the cool Pacific breeze and an air crisp and dry, people work on without relaxation till, abruptly, the vital cord snaps. Men die here most suddenly, without any warning. The temptation to overwork is excessive. There are no useful avocations rendered necessary by a long spell of hot weather, as on the Eastern coast, and a man feels under a constant pressure of excitement. Doctors say there is nowhere so much insanity, in proportion to the population. In time, I suppose, people will learn to adapt their mode of living to the climate and its requirements.

Summer is considered the severest season; it is

undoubtedly the most unpleasant, on account of the wind and dust. It is the fashion for Californians, when away from their country, to say they wear light clothing in winter and warm wraps in summer. From my own short experience of the climate, I can only say that the winter is very cold, and warm clothing indispensable; fires, too, are often very necessary. In summer, in spite of the wind, light clothing is essential to comfort, although overcoats may be worn towards evening.

Our first drive was to the Cliff House, to see the wonderful 'sea-lions' and their play-house. We started pretty early, so as to return before ten o'clock, at which hour the wind generally rises. We drove through some fine streets, all having wooden side-walks, and many entirely paved with wood. The houses were gay with flowers, and from the white walls were wafted the delicious odours of the jessamine, honey-suckle, clematis, and myrtle. These gardens looked strangely in contrast with the bare sand-hills between which we continually hurried, and which render the space that separates the town and the ocean most bleak and drear-looking.

Our road lay between the cemeteries of Laurel Hill and Lone Mountain. Peaceful and beautiful spots they are; suitable resting-places, whether for the wealthy, whose names are engraved on the tall obelisks and marble monuments raised there to their memory, or for the poor man, whose lowly grave is marked only by the buds and blossoms of the lilies and fuchsias and scarlet geraniums, which loving hands have planted there and carefully tended.

After a drive along a broad, splendidly kept, and well-watered road—which was very lively with numbers of celebrated 'fast-trotters,' and is in fact the Rotten Row of San Francisco—we arrived at the Cliff House. It is built on a bluff overhanging the sea, and has a glorious outlook toward the Farallone Islands and the 'Golden Gate,' of which we had caught occasional glimpses on our journey. From the verandah of the hotel we saw the Seal Rocks, only a few hundred yards off, and covered with sea-lions, who filled the air with their strange dismal roaring. Of all California's 'natural wonders' these are, I think, the most curious. The huge, grotesque, ungainly creatures crawling up the steep rocks, taking magnificent headers into the sea, or lashing the rocks with their finny tails, and eternally bellowing 'Yoi-hoi,' with their deep-mouthed bay; the thousands of sea-birds—gulls, guillemots, pelicans, and cormorants—flying around or perched on the rocks amongst the seals, form a natural curiosity that has a wonderful fascination for spectators, and is all the more astonishing from its close proximity to a large city. Some of these sea-lions are of enormous size, and weigh, we are told, over ten or twelve hundred pounds. The extraordinary thing is, how they manage to climb to the top of almost perpendicular rocks; but they do, and without much apparent difficulty. A *siesta* on a pinnacle in the hot sun seems the height of enjoyment to them. The sea-birds appear to get on very amicably with them. Now and then when a pelican settles on the back of one, or approaches too near to his majesty, he will look the bird steadily in the face and then give a roar, which effectually disposes of the intruder; but, on the whole, they do not quarrel much.

The law, fortunately, affords the benefit of its protection to the Seal Rocks, and allows nobody to fire a gun in the neighbourhood. The creatures would otherwise soon be driven away. Already an outcry has been made about their consumption of fish, some people going so far as to declare that there will soon be no supply for the market. If there is a falling off at all, it might much more reasonably be accounted for by the immense and wanton destruction of fish going on at all times and seasons in the bay of San Francisco.

After breakfast we drove back by the old Mission Dolores, the road for some distance being over the firm sandy beach. Very few relics of the early Spanish occupation of the country are now to be found. The old-fashioned church called San Francisco, in honour of the patron saint, St. Francis, yet exists, but the attached monastic buildings are used as stores and saloons. The Franciscan fathers had considerable power over the Indians, who used to congregate at the Mission two or three times a year to enjoy a week's holiday, bringing with them their own cattle and provisions—thus making up a sort of tribal picnic. A few of the buildings that were set apart for the natives may still be seen; but most of the mission lands and houses have been destroyed, or taken possession of by strangers. The priests who taught and educated the people are all gone, and have left only a few Spanish MSS. and printed volumes behind them, which, with the old church, alone serve as remembrances of the devoted lives of the early missionaries.

Amongst the peculiar 'institutions' of California that of the 'bit' is most singular. A 'bit' is a small coin of the value of ten cents, or five pence. In general use, there is no coin of less value than a 'bit,' though, I believe, a five-cent-piece is now and then met with. A quarter-dollar is called two 'bits,' a half-dollar four 'bits,' and there is no copper currency. The system is absurd, and ought to be stopped at once. A quarter-dollar, or shilling, is, or rather ought to be, twenty five cents; but if you purchase anything the price of which is one 'bit,' and offer a quarter-dollar in payment, for change you will receive back only one ' bit,' the seller always getting the best of the exchange. If you buy anything for two ' bits,' and pay for it with two ten-cent-pieces instead of a quarter-dollar, you are looked upon as ' very mean,' and sometimes they are actually refused. The loss on every retail purchase is twenty-five per cent.; but the dealers, who of course buy in quantities, do not lose. The price of a cigar, a newspaper, a glass of beer, or having your boots cleaned, &c., is a ' bit,' or has a ' bit' imported into it for the sake of the exchange.

As at every other place in America, drinking-bars may be counted by the hundred at San Francisco. But there they are frequently fitted up in the most gorgeous style, and often very artistically. The wood of the beautiful California laurel is that most frequently used for the purpose. In some cases the entire room is fitted up with it, and the appurtenances of the bar are of pure silver. At all these places a ' free lunch ' is ready at certain hours; and often it is a most elaborate set-out. One can hardly understand how it can answer, and allow a man profitably to carry on the establishment; yet not only does it succeed, but immense fortunes are thus made. After lunch you are supposed to take a ' drink ' at the bar, for which you pay two ' bits,' and in some places only one. Supper is carried on in the same way. I never could comprehend how a man could have the audacity to eat the greater part of a roast leg of mutton, and a lobster, finishing off with bread-and-cheese and fruit; and then, after tossing off a huge julep, offer fivepence in payment, and walk away with a contented conscience. Yet I have seen that done, and doubtless the same sort of thing often occurs. By the way, juleps are not an American drink, as is generally supposed. I think they must have been prepared from Milton's receipt in the 'Masque of Comus,' where the son of Bacchus says :—

> "And first behold this cordial julep here,
> That flames and dances in his crystal bounds,
> With spirits of balm and fragrant syrups mixed;
> Not that nepenthes, which the wife of Thone
> In Egypt gave to Jove-born Helena,
> Is of such power to stir up joy as this,
> To life so friendly or so cool to thirst."

There is the name—julep—and even the ingredients—mint, sugar, spirits, and ice—are mentioned.

A great patron of 'free lunch,' and free everything else he can obtain, is a local celebrity known by the sobriquet of 'Emperor Norton.' The strange appearance of this individual invariably attracts attention, and he lives, I believe, by being the butt of the town. He scorns all attire, save military garments, and is always dressed in the cast-off uniform of some military or naval officer. Often he sports a mixture of the two—despising the costume of no rank, from a full private to that of a general. He carries with him on all occasions a huge carved stick. His appearance and method of getting promoted reminded me strongly of a well-known character who was once pointed out to me in Paris. 'General' Van—the man I allude to—was a Dutchman, and a lieutenant in the Dutch army. Anxious to rise in his profession, and believing his merits to be ignored, he took to promoting himself. He made Paris his residence, lived on his means, and always wore uniform. After being for some years a lieutenant he felt that he deserved promotion, and raised himself to the rank of captain—of course, making the necessary change in his uniform. Again, in due time he conferred on himself further advancement; he became major, and afterwards lieutenant-colonel. At the time of the Crimean war another rise in his profession naturally suggested itself, and a full colonelcy was the result. In 1860 he bestowed on himself the riband of a Dutch order; and in 1870, finding his health fail, he assumed the rank of general. In all probability, he would have received more honours and distinctions had not death shortly after brought his brilliant military career to a close. In the announcement of his death, which I saw in the papers, it was not stated whether he was buried with military honours, but I presume that he was not.

San Francisco, like other cities on the Pacific coast, is subject to occasional earthquakes, consequently new houses are now nearly all built of wood, and of no great height. Some builders undertake to build a house 'earthquake-proof'—rather a difficult matter, I should think. American architects build houses as if for the purpose of feeding a fire. It is well and right to build them of wood in a country subject to earthquakes, but there surely is no necessity for hollow partitions and combustible staircases. Stop the draft and you stop the fire. The Fire Department of San Francisco is extremely efficient, but the rate of insurance is nearly ten times higher than in Europe. The difference in combustibility, arising from the manner of placing the wood and its surroundings, is worth considering when building wooden houses.

There are great varieties of architecture in San Francisco, and all kinds of quaint conceits and whims of form and shape; but very often they are attractive and charming.

Perhaps there is a redundancy of ornamentation about some of the houses; but they invariably look so clean and airy—sometimes perched on cliffs, sometimes sliding down slopes or nestling in gardens, and girt with strange trees and beautiful flowers, and always wearing a pleasant and comfortable air. The houses, too, not only give an idea of the character of their occupants, but also of their personal appearance—perhaps I ought rather to say of the appearance of those who ought to occupy them. There is, for instance, the dwelling not much bigger than a good-sized baby-house, with two great staring windows, resembling the wide-open eyes of the infant who ought to be the proprietor. Then there is the tall, narrow, prim-looking building with a neat old-maidish appearance. Then comes the habitation with a decided matronly aspect; and finally the tottering, tumble-down old thing that a breath would topple over, and which has a beseeching air, as if asking for a strong gale to come and end its miseries. Houses, in fact, differing as much in style as characters and dispositions differ in individuals.

Throughout the whole of California the Chinese emigrant forms a striking feature amongst the population, but in San Francisco he seems to form the chief part of the stream of humanity that flows through its streets. The violent prejudice against the Celestials is so marked in this city that strangers naturally seek for the reasons for this antipathy.

Amongst the lowest classes—those who persecute John Chinaman most—the reason is evident enough, viz. because the Chinese are extremely industrious, and will work for less than half the wages of a white man. The better classes say that the Chinese impoverish the country, as they send all their savings home, and even import their own food and clothing; that they have no land, no real estate, nothing to give them an interest in the country; that they are heathen, and, worst of all, they are yellow.

It is generally admitted that John is sober, peaceable, hardworking, and patient. If he had not possessed a vast amount of meekness and patience he would long ago have been driven back to his own country. As a labourer, he is most industrious and steady; as a servant, clean, quiet, and attentive. As a business man and a good hand at a bargain, 'the heathen Chinee' is a match for even an American; and as a poker-player he has no equal—but, he wears a tail, and that counter balances his good qualities, and he is despised.

White labour can never compete with Chinese as long as clothing and necessaries remain at their present enormous prices, and as long as whisky, high wages, and universal suffrage, which are the real enemies of the people, occupy the prominent position they now do. There is no likelihood of there ever being a strike against high wages; but I believe a considerable reduction would do a great deal towards putting the Chinaman out of work. How are the common wages of eight, ten, or twelve shillings a day usually spent? Why, in the bar-rooms, at the theatres, and in the purchase of cigars. Ten shillings a day is poor wages for a thirsty free man. But making cigars is a favourite employment amongst the Chinese, and so the injured white man spends half his time and money in giving them employment.

There is in San Francisco an order of beings of the

type of 'roughs' and 'loafers,' but known there by the name of 'hoodlums;' these individuals are rapidly becoming a formidable element in the population, and often cause considerable annoyance and trouble to white people. But their chief delight is to attack and ill-treat a Chinaman, especially if a number of them can catch him alone. A Chinaman very seldom walks about the streets of San Francisco with his pig-tail hanging down his back, as he does in other countries—except in his own part of the town. If he did, he would stand a very good chance of having it cut off, and that would be the greatest misfortune that could happen to him; for he knows he could not then go to heaven, as there would be nothing to pull him up by.

Fortunately, the general sentiment of the people is just, and they agree that the Chinese who arrive here under the stipulations of the treaty with China ought to be protected from violence and persecution. At the same time they feel that their emigration has reached to such a pitch that the Govenment ought—by making some re-adjustment of the treaty—to restrain it for a time.

The Chinese are by no means the cowards they have been represented; and I have been gratified on three or four occasions by seeing a very complete thrashing administered to some great hulking hoodlum by an inoffensive-looking John Chinaman, whose patience had been exhausted by the attacks of his cowardly and astonished enemy. There are placards in some of the shop-windows stating that no Chinese labour is employed by the proprietors. One man—a bird-dealer—carried his hatred to the Chinese element so far as to inform the public that 'No Chinese birds are sold here.'

The Chinese are great in the laundry business, which they have almost entirely monopolised; and the only instance I ever saw of John's facetiousness was on the signboard over the door of one of their houses. On it was written in very large letters, 'Wa-Shing and Iron-Ing.' Underneath was the supposed resemblance of a flat-iron and a tub of soapsuds.

Whether the firm really bore that name or whether it was a Chinese joke, I am unable to say.

Of course there are the bad as well as the good Chinamen; and as one of the sights that should be seen in San Francisco is the 'bad Chinese quarter,' we went the rounds one evening, accompanied by a detective, who possessed the 'open sesame' of the various dens.

We were first introduced to a house with an open court in the centre, and containing small rooms fitted up with shelves one over another, like the berths in a ship. This was a favourite resort of the thieves who, previous to the passing of the 'Space Ordinance,' used to pack themselves away here like herrings in a barrel.

The Chinese are certainly great in the science of

stowage, and packing is their chief *forte*. The few we saw were quietly smoking opium; and though most of them had villanous countenances, they seemed not at all discomposed at the sight of the police-officer, but treated us with silent contempt until we were ready to depart, when they opened the doors with much alacrity. They bade us a sulky good-night, and then chattered away with supreme disgust at our unwelcome intrusion.

Hurrying on over a treacherous bridge of loose planks, we descended a flight of rickety steps leading to the mouth of a blind alley, which twisted about into the centre of a block of buildings that towered three and four stories high above us on one side, whilst on the other the houses were more like neglected hen-roosts than dwellings. The alley was dark, and strewed with rubbish from end to end, so that in case of a hunt after a criminal the chase might be impeded as much as possible.

After dodging about in a labyrinth for some time, and taking care to keep as near our guide as possible, we stopped in front of a small door, which the officer kicked open, and disclosed to view a most disgusting-looking apartment, without a window or ventilation of any sort. This box of a building measured about eight feet square, and was occupied by two receivers of stolen goods. Their repulsive appearance is indescribable. One of them gave a ghastly grin, and tried to appear guileless, and happy to see us, when, by the light of the candle he carried, he caught sight of the officer's face. The other remained on the couch—which was made of a lot of loose boards—and, in spite of the prods he received from our conductor, steadily refused to show his face. The floor was heaped up to the ceiling with miscellaneous articles of a most untempting aspect, and we speedily made a retreat from this loathsome den.

We visited other haunts of the heathen thieves—all answering to the same description, and all extremely filthy. Some of the narrow winding passages led us into the basements, where it would be very easy to lose one's way, even with the light of a candle, and where an unprotected stranger would fare but badly. But we met with no opposition; and having glanced at them, were glad to breathe fresh air again.

At the gambling-houses the usual game was going on. It is simply this:—The proprietor sits at the head of a long table, and before him is a large heap of 'cash' —a Chinese copper coin. A handful of these is taken up and placed in the middle of the table. Bets are then made on the number in the heap, whether it is odd or even. The coins are then slowly drawn away two at a time with an ivory stick, and the number left determines the winning of the bet. If one remains, odd wins, if none are left, even is the gainer.

M

Our last visit was to the home of a venerable heathen who had attained quite a celebrity amongst his people on account of his skill as a 'snapper up of unconsidered trifles.' His habitation was 'on the cold ground,' and only to be approached by steps dug out of the earth. It was more like a cave than anything else, for water trickled down the sides and oozed from the roof. The floor consisted of a couple of planks, floating about at will in a bed of slimy water, and the only articles of furniture to be seen were a filthy couch of boards and a wooden box.

From what we heard, the skill of the wretched being lay in contriving habitually to dispose of articles of value before he returned to his domicile; by which means he generally evaded the clutches of the police. He had no companions, and always lived alone; no one, it was said, cared for him, and I should imagine that he himself had not much regard for anyone.

The streets in the Chinese quarter of the city are very like those which are seen in every town in the Celestial Empire, and a stranger suddenly deposited in the middle of one of them might well imagine himself in China. There are the Joss-houses, in which they carry on many of the heathenish observances and the superstitious rites of their native land.

Here they have their hideous images of good and evil, before which fire is always kept burning, and small dishes filled with food for these idols to eat. The priest is always in his little office, writing prayers or muttering the words of a legend. The former are put into boxes, called 'praying-boxes,' which are placed before the idols, and are so constructed that they unroll the strips of paper on which the petitions are inscribed. This has all the efficacy of oral prayer, with the advantage that the petitioner, meanwhile, can be attending to his worldly business or pleasure, as the case may be.

In the little town of Amoy, which lies between Hongkong and Canton, there dwells an ingenious Chinaman whose praying-machine was attached to a water-wheel by the side of a running stream. He was thus free from all anxiety in regard to his devotions. The praying-wheel went round day and night, and its owner had the satisfaction of knowing that, whether asleep or awake, he was always praying. There is another favourite mode of praying. You bring your prayer, and having set fire to it in the flame of the lamp that burns before the image of your deity, you devoutly watch the smoke as it ascends into the air. Sticks of incense will do just as well, and are supposed to be very acceptable to the divinities. Thus your devotions need only be limited by the extent of the resources of your pocket.

The Chinese have another custom similar to 'prayer-burning,' that of sending home letters by the dead. No Chinaman allows his remains to be buried in a foreign land, if he can avoid it; and very often, when a man dies who is too poor to pay his own expenses, the necessary funds are provided by his friends. When a native of the 'Flowery Land' dies abroad, his spirit is supposed to return to his own country, and all his countrymen, far and near, entrust him with letters to their friends and relatives at home.

The missives are laid around his dead body until it is enclosed in its coffin, when they are solemnly burned, and the soul of the deceased is supposed to carry the messages to the shores of the Celestial Empire and there faithfully to deliver them. There is no return mail, for the ghosts of deceased Chinese do not visit alien shores; the failure to receive replies, therefore, does not diminish their faith in 'the dead man's post.'

When Chinese leave their homes for foreign lands bits of paper may often be seen on the deck of the ship; these are prayers for their safe return offered by the spectators of their departure. Scattering prayer-papers is a very favourite and certainly an innocent employment. In San Francisco the Chinese have also secret societies (notably the Hip Yo Sing), which exercise a very baneful influence, and before whose tribunals the poor wretches of their own nation who have incurred their displeasure are frequently mulcted of large sums of money. If they refuse to pay they stand in great danger of losing their lives. So, what with hoodlums, and secret associations, and a general feeling of insecurity, John Chinaman's existence is not altogether a safe or a happy one. But he adapts himself to circumstances, smokes opium and gambles; buys prayers, keeps his tail tight round his head, attends his theatre to witness interminable dramas, and generally makes enough money to enable him after a few years to return to his native land, there to pass the remainder of his life in the universal abuse of and utter contempt for 'the foreign devils.'

CHAPTER XI.

SAN FRANCISCO.

Peculiarities — Quacks — Farallone Islands — Woodward's Gardens—Eucalyptus—Suicide and murders—Schools—American politics—The labouring class—Shoddy—Refinement—Literature—The Press—Advertisements—Side-walks—Street-cars—Occupations—A critic.

MONTGOMERY and Kearney Streets, the two principal ones in San Francisco, afford a fund of amusement and instruction. At the intersection of California and Montgomery Streets crowds of eager-looking men are always assembled, who appear to do nothing but talk, and whose conversation is only of stocks, mines, real estate, and the condition of the money market. This spot is the San Francisco Stock Exchange, where 'bulls' and 'bears,' and other hopeful or despondent animals, of a species known only to brokers and business men, most do congregate.

There is a pleasant custom in San Francisco of fastening horses to a ring in the side-walk whilst their owners pursue their business inside the stores or saloons. As the animals object to be run into by passing vehicles, they move on to the pavement, and thus the passage intended for pedestrians becomes wholly occupied by horses.

The hardware dealer decorates the pavement before his door with old boxes and bundles of straw. Over these you stumble and climb only to find yourself opposite a second-hand shop, whose proprietor also has placed his entire stock of furniture outside his front door. There are chairs of all sizes and designs; tables, round and square; sofas that can be converted into beds at a moment's notice; old dishes, watering-pots, carpets and pieces of oil-cloth; in fact, everything appertaining to domestic use, lies carelessly scattered around. Presently you pass a laundry, or a carpenter's shop. As soon as you have been able to get round the large pile of wood, invariably heaped up before the door, and intended for at least a month's consumption, your toes are run over by a large barrel— that is, if you have escaped being knocked down by a street-car—for the wine-merchant, whose house you are passing, will probably be taking in his consignment of new vintages and, of course, through the front door.

Quack doctors, and vendors of all sorts of curious and valuable compounds, ply their trade in the street, with much energy and much cunning. I was often amused by one of these persons, who used to deliver a long lecture on geography, concluding with a description of the situation of some place lately visited by a pestilence, yellow fever, or cholera. He would then show how San Francisco might, and probably would be scourged in a like manner; in which case it would be as well to be provided beforehand with a small bottle of his elixir. Fortunately he had a few bottles left, which he would reluctantly dispose of at a very reduced rate.

Another individual would stand for hours giving a free course of instruction in mathematics. According to him, all arithmetic was in future to be done by 'dodges.' Half-an-hour's study, he said, of one of his books was worth all the schooling you could get in a year, and it would be downright insanity not to avail yourself of an opportunity like that, and for the ridiculous sum of one dollar. He called himself the 'Lightning Calculator.'

All these people are 'Professors,' a title which has become so common in America, that, when some wag on once entering a drinking-saloon called out in a loud cheery voice, 'Now, Professor, come and have a drink;' six men who were sitting in a row reading the newspapers; a shoe-black who had his stand just outside the door, and a corn-doctor who chanced to be passing, all smilingly stepped up to the bar.

Having accepted an invitation to visit the Farallone

SEA BIRDS.—Cormorants, &c.   P. 109.

Islands—a small rocky group lying about thirty miles west of San Francisco—we passed through the Golden Gate one lovely calm day, and in about four hours reached the islands. The Farallones are of importance, on account of the great quantity of sea-birds' eggs which are gathered there for the California market. As we approached the islands the air was literally black with birds, which at first seem disposed to prevent our landing. The scene on these islands completely eclipsed that on the Cliff House rocks. The sea-lions were there in thousands, and were of all sizes and ages, from the tawny grandfather to the few weeks' old baby. The old ones evidently did not like our intrusion. They moved away, showing their two long tusks, when we touched their children, and either disappeared in the water or sat at the edge ready to plunge in, should we approach too near.

The rocks were covered with myriads of birds—pigeons, tufted puffins, coots, cormorants, and gulls. But the most numerous were the murre, or guillemot, whose eggs are very large, for the size of the bird, and are extremely good to eat. They lay their eggs on the bare rock, both the male and the female taking their turn at incubation. The gulls are great enemies of the guillemots, and take every opportunity of stealing their eggs.

A pathway up the rock brought us to the lighthouse, which resembled all other buildings of that nature, and had everything about it beautifully bright and clean. On our way down to what is called the 'West End,' we passed through rows of foolish guillemots, standing strictly to attention, like white-breasted soldiers. After crossing a narrow inlet we obtained a most picturesque view of sharp rocks, caves, deep fissures, and, in the distance, an arch not less than fifty feet in height, and completely covered with birds. Through the window thus formed in the rock the birds flew in flocks, and the seals made use of it as a short cut to reach the other side.

The 'Big Rookery,' on the north-west of the island, is well-protected from winds, and is the favourite resort of innumerable birds. It is almost impossible for the imagination to realise how extraordinary is the multitude of sea-fowl that make these islands their home. It is almost as extraordinary that so few people ever take the trouble to pay a visit to the Farallones. But some persons I believe would not go a yard out of their way even to see an angel.

Sunday is a great holiday for the people of San Francisco; most of the shops are closed and all the theatres open. Half the population pic-nic in the adjacent country, and the other half swarm to 'Woodward's Gardens.'

These gardens belong to a public-spirited gentleman, sent by Providence to California to provide for the comfort and amusement of his fellow-citizens. The gardens contain in themselves a museum of stuffed birds and animals, a collection of curiosities, an art gallery, in which may be seen copies, gorgeously framed, of many celebrated pictures from the Roman galleries; conservatories, sea-lions, aviaries, an aquarium, a large skating-rink, swings of the boat order, in which you can make yourself ill in company with four or five other social beings equally bent on pleasure; and swings on which you may gain a proud pre-eminence alone. There are bars and poles, on which you can exercise your skill as a gymnast; and when tired of muscular employment, you may retire to a cushioned seat in a circular vessel which is propelled round the little pond without the trouble of oars or sails, and you may remain there with the pleasant illusion of being at sea, until an attack of vertigo drives you on shore again.

Afterwards, you may proceed to the Hippodrome, which is surrounded by cages containing wild animals; and, if you are fond of driving, there is a little four-in-hand goat-carriage, always ready; whilst for the equestrians, camels are constantly in attendance. The more ambitious may gratify their taste by trying to ride the accomplished jackass which is warranted to throw any-one who may attempt to mount him. Hoodlums are great at this exercise, and it would seem as if there were some natural affinity between them and the animal they try to ride.

'Feeding' the sea-lions is a great attraction. The monsters know the accustomed hour, and swim about as restlessly as lions and tigers pace their dens when the gratifying time approaches. Sea-lions and seals are more intelligent even than porpoises, and may easily be tamed. They would certainly be somewhat cumbersome for a person moving about much to carry, and as pets they might be in the way in a room; still, they are very docile and affectionate. At the Gardens there is one tremendously big fellow. He can catch in his mouth anything that comes near him, and would make an admirable point at cricket. He always gets great applause when, after climbing to the top of a rock and there exhibiting his skill, he plunges into the water, splashing it over the wistful spectators, whose interest in him is, after that feat, considerably damped.

Balloons, too, are continually 'going,' but seldom get up; fire or high winds invariably preventing the ascent. People who have visited the Gardens on five occasions, on purpose to see the ascent of a balloon, are apt to be disappointed if, on the sixth visit, the balloon still steadily refuses to be inflated. But those who have been disappointed of seeing the balloon capsize and the aeronaut come to grief, can enter the 'Great Pavilion' and witness performances on the trapeze, and acrobatic feats just as likely to end with broken necks or dislocated limbs.

The quaintest bird I have ever seen is the venerable pelican, which stalks about the gardens with an air of absolute proprietorship. Perhaps you are looking at the seals or the ducks, when suddenly you hear a deep croak and feel a slight tap. On looking down, there will be the old gentleman at your side, gazing up at you with his little twinkling black eyes, and with his enormous bill wide open; evidently asking for your pocket-handkerchief, or a newspaper, or anything with which to stuff his capacious pouch. I once saw him take off a child's hat and waddle on demurely as if nothing had happened. But his chief delight is to steal the fish intended for the dinner of the sea-lions; and unless a very sharp look-out is kept, he will not only pouch the greater part of the provisions but also walk off with the basket. Altogether, Woodward's is a very amusing place, and, for the present, supplies a great want in the city.

A very fine park is now being laid out beyond the limits of the town, but it will be some time before the trees and shrubberies have attained a sufficient height to be effective and picturesque; although wonders may be worked by the Eucalyptus, which has been extensively planted.

This tree—the Australian blue-gum tree—grows well in California, and with great rapidity. It has been known to grow fifteen feet in one year, and ought to be planted all over the plains and valleys. It would give verdure, shade, and rain to desert places, and would be a fortune to farmers who had a few acres of such beautiful forest. The timber, too, is good and valuable. The Eucalyptus also possesses extraordinary power of destroying the influence of miasma in marshy districts. When planted in swampy ground it will dry it up very soon. In Algeria I have seen several plantations of the Eucalyptus on farms once noted for their extreme unhealthiness, but on which, since the planting of this tree, no cases of fever have occurred. Near Constantine, too, where formerly there were several acres of marshy fever-haunted soil, a few plantations of these trees soon transformed the land into a dry salubrious park, from which fever has entirely disappeared. It is known that many strong-smelling flowers develop ozone in sufficient quantities to counteract the influence of a malarious situation; there is, therefore, all the more reason to give credit to the health-giving qualities of the Eucalyptus. Planted singly, the tree is not picturesque, but in numbers is very pleasing.

One evening in San Francisco I witnessed a sad occurrence. Whilst in the act of crossing a street I heard the report of a pistol, and a man on the opposite pavement fell down, having shot himself through the head. The poor fellow lived but a short time, and it was ascertained afterwards that he had lately married, and had since lost all his money by speculation. Suicides and homicides have obtained a terrible prominence in California.

Some statistics of the latter were lately given in a newspaper, to the effect that, while in Great Britain the average of murders was four to the million, and in the Papal States 113, in California the average was 250. Such an average seems almost incredible; and although deduced from statistics of 1871, yet, from the wholesale butcheries recorded in the papers nearly every day, I doubt whether the estimate is far out at the present time. Whether the number of homicides is to be accounted for by the rare execution of justice on the murderers, or whether the universal practice of carrying pistols and knives bears fatal effect, I cannot say. In the Eastern States of America, where the same habits and the same laws prevail, the average of murders is only eighteen to the million. In British Columbia, where the carrying of arms is the exception not the rule, and where men know that the loss of their own lives will be the penalty of taking another's, murders are of very rare occurrence.

The discovery of gold formerly brought to California the idlest and most reckless vagabonds in the world, and desperadoes poured in from all sides; the best of a bad lot flocking to the mines, the worst remaining in the city, to gain by gambling or thieving the money they were too lazy to earn by digging. Robbers and murderers then walked the streets in gangs, in broad daylight, and not unfrequently to the sound of music. But, at last, a movement took place among the better-disposed citizens; Vigilance Committees sprang up, justice was promptly administered, and the reign of terror was at an end. Would not the better and more certain administration of the law have a salutary effect in the present day in reducing the enormous amount of crime which is still abroad? But, in spite of the defects, which after all are natural to a young and richly-endowed State, and which time must remedy, San Francisco, to all appearance, is as well governed as any city in the Eastern States. The police are efficient; gambling is held in check; and the Fire Department is admirably organised.

The school system is good in a certain way, but more attention should be given to the solid branches of education. In a young country, where work is the element most needed for success, the public schools turn out little else than a lot of clerks, and book-keepers, and hundreds of young women who all want to be school-mistresses. At an age when in older countries young men begin to work, here they are left with some knowledge of arithmetic, a smattering of French or German, a little music and less geography; but are unable to drive a nail straight, or to do anything useful except add up long columns of figures and measure out yards of riband. What is wanted in California is a race of educated working men and women; and a practical course of study in the Labour Department of schools is one of the means for satisfying that want. There are evidences, however, of a high civilisation, and that the intelligent and moral element is in the ascendant. There are excellent libraries and reading-rooms, having a great number of members. The churches are well-attended; there are charitable institutions of all kinds, and a call to assist them is always liberally responded to; in a word, the general tone of the community is hospitable and sympathetic.

Of course California has its political jobbery, as well as other States, but she seems fortunate at present in having the right men in the right place. A Californian politician has no opinion of his own, but depends on that of the newspapers of his party. Whatever the majority says must be right. But then that is the opinion of the Americans generally; they much prefer being tyrannised over by a hundred to being quietly ruled by one. With them 'the majority' can do no wrong. I should like to know what they call the wholesale bribery and corruption of their political rulers! But who can explain American politics?

A black gentleman, at a coloured Convention held a few months ago at Sacramento, gave a good idea of the requisite qualifications for a Parliamentary career in America, when he said, in the course of a very amusing speech, 'If I only had privileges ekal to my cheek, I'd ha' bin in Congress long ago.'

The best men in America stand aloof from politics. And no wonder, if the ignorant gabble of many political speeches is a sample of the quality of the men who direct the fortunes of the nation. Ignorance in rags may be tolerable, but ignorance in broadcloth, even with the accompaniments of 'a beautiful cravat, sustaining a faultless dicky'—which a certain well-known clergyman of New York says ought to be worn by every true gentleman—is unendurable. Fortunately, the American people have acquired the art of governing themselves, and that is the only true road to a successful Republic.

Probably in no other city in America are the labouring classes in such prosperity as in San Francisco. Civilisation has there contrived a means to enable the labouring man to have a house of his own, and almost every mechanic has his house and garden. If a small shopkeeper or labouring man has saved sufficient to buy a small 'lot' of ground in the city or suburbs, and has not means to build his house, he applies to one of the Building Associations for a loan. When the society has satisfied itself of the soundness of the title and the value of the ground, it loans on a mortgage upon the property the sum required for building. The loan is payable in monthly instalments. The value of real estate is always increasing; so the loan is a very safe one for the company, besides being a very useful one for the recipient. The rate of interest paid is about ten or twelve per cent. per annum; and this is not much, considering what enormous profits are made in all branches of business.

The steady labouring men are not fond of mining speculations, but generally invest their wages in land, or deposit them in the savings banks. It is no uncommon thing for a hired man to own a valuable city lot, or a nice little farm in the country; and savings bank deposits accumulate very fast with interest at twelve and fifteen per cent. The annual dividends of the Savings, Loan, and Building Societies are a proof of the prosperity of servants and labourers, whose high wages ought certainly to make California a veritable El Dorado to them.

Californians are very generous and intelligent, as well as very energetic; and in spite of their tremendous exertions to make money, nowhere is money less valued than in their State. Of course, there are a few 'suddenly-rich' men who indulge in the most ostentatious extravagance.

'Shoddy' must show itself in a land where the general feeling is to estimate a man by his money. Consequently, you see, here and there, a diamond ring outside the glove, or a gorgeous coachman with a bad hat, and holding white reins attached to brass-bespangled harness. But these are the exceptions. Refinement and culture predominate; and a taste for natural beauty is seen in the quiet flower-decked home of the mechanic, as well as in the more magnificent country residences at Menlo Park and Oakland, where the artistic tastes of the proprietors are as evident in the interior of their houses as in the beautiful gardens which surround them. Some of these gardens are most delightful, and all are kept with the greatest care. It is a perfect treat to leave the dust of the city for a day and wander amongst the botanical treasures which abound in the grounds, and a visitor is always sure to receive a most hearty welcome.

I must say I was astonished—although perhaps so short a residence in California hardly gave me a right to judge—that the Western people, in spite of their intelligence, evinced so little interest in the subject of literature, and especially in that of home manufacture. Pollack, a poetical genius closely identified with the past and present of California, is almost unknown among them. His writings are uncollected, and his grave is not marked even by a slab to perpetuate his memory. Mark Twain had to go elsewhere to find people who could appreciate other things besides dollars. Joaquin Miller had to seek in England the just reward of his merits, and the fame of Bret Harte was made in the East.

The intelligence of the community at any rate supports a very well-conducted press, and two or three of the journals ought to be most lucrative properties, judging from the frequent paragraphs they contain about their enormous circulation. They may perhaps be influenced too much by a spirit of rivalry—in fact, it is war to the knife with some of the Western newspapers—but they discuss questions with plenty of ability and fairness, and there is not that eagerness to abuse England and the English which is so characteristic of Eastern journalism.

It is true that the contents of certain newspapers are very soiling, and of these Baron Hübner remarked, in 1871, 'Je n'ai vu nulle part des journaux quotidiens plus dépravés que ceux de San Francisco. En les parcourant je n'ai remarqué que récriminations inutiles, grossièretés qui feraient frémir un exalté de Belleville!' But these form the exception. Amongst the superior publications, the 'Overland Monthly' stands out preeminent for its refinement and good taste, and takes rank with the periodicals issued from the English press.

As a rule, the American press never loses an opportunity of abusing the English. If, once in a way, some scandal appears in an English newspaper it is immediately copied into the American journals—not once only, but three or four times, and each time with some new exaggeration. If it concerns the nobility, the joy of the journalist is supreme. The Canadian Pacific Railway scandal was a real godsend to them.

Some people condemn American journalism as a whole. It is narrow, they say, superficial, and abusive on every subject external to its own country. But this is too sweeping a judgment; considering that men like Woolsey, Charles Adams, Higginson, and others of the most scholarly writers in the country, are constant contributors to its newspapers, while nearly every American professional author, except Longfellow and Hawthorne, has at some time written for the press.

But even clever and accomplished literary men cannot help sometimes having a hit at the 'Britishers.' In a recent letter from the editor of the 'Louisville Courier,' he states, as his opinion, that the average British subject hates all Americans, and he goes to some trouble to explain the fact. I must say I think his explanation an utter failure; and his coarse letter could only have increased the ill-will between the two nations, if it had ever really existed.

And yet I hear that this man has been made a member of an influential club in London, and has most likely received that kindness and hospitality due to all strangers of merit—his bad humour is therefore difficult to account for.

The Americans generally are far in advance of us in the art of advertising, and the Californians carry it to the utmost limit of inventive power. The English papers often contain puffs, but they can be recognised at a glance. Not so in the San Francisco papers. In them the reader is led on with extreme artfulness through a long sensational story, or one of pastoral simplicity, in perfect ignorance, almost to the very last, of the real object of the narrative. The stranger the tale, the more cunningly is the *finale* led up to. Here is an example: 'Not long ago, in one of those old baronial halls for which England is so renowned, a strange drama was enacted. Sitting in the deep embrasure of a fine Elizabethan window, which was not the least charm of a beautifully-appointed boudoir, overlooking an old-fashioned pleasaunce, was a lady, evidently in deep distress. Her husband, a tall, handsome man, held in his hand an exquisitely carved pillar which had been broken off the door of a superb old oaken cabinet. This accident would never have occurred if it had been purchased from the celebrated stores of Messrs. Wall & Co., San Francisco. Their furniture never breaks.'

Again, what can be more striking or better adapted to raise tender emotions than the following effort from the muse of a provision shop?—

> "Oh, say not I love you because the molasses
> You purchased at Simpson's were golden and clear;
> The syrup, the sugar, the jelly in glasses,
> The crackers, the mack'rel, I know were not dear;
> But when you came to me with Simpson's smoked salmon,
> And showed me his samples of Limburger cheese,
> I felt that his claim to be cheap was not gammon;
> I loved you, and said so, dear Jane, on my knees."

Even great disasters are made use of—*vide* the following: 'In the fire which recently destroyed the Grand Opera House, in Paris, the scores of the musical library, dating from the days of Lulli and Rameau, were burnt. The losses sustained by the musicians were very, very serious. One of the orchestra lost a Straduarius violin worth 1,400 dollars. The harps alone were worth 4,000 dollars. But what the lessee grieved for more than anything else was a cask of Gerke Wine that had been sent to him from San Francisco! Frenchman as he is, he declared over and over again that the Gerke Wine, for dry qualities surpassed all light wines he had ever tasted.'

If advertising is necessary to success in trade, San

Francisco ought to be a most flourishing city. Houses, windows, and dead walls teem with advertisements, and even the pavements are made use of as places for puffing. I suppose the wooden side-walks are considered convenient for the purpose, because the boards which form them are so far apart that your stick or umbrella is constantly being torn from your hand, and whilst recovering it there is ample opportunity for studying the pictures or the writing with which it is sure to be surrounded. These plankings are like vast cribbage-boards. They tear dresses and trip you up, and their general appearance would disgrace a colony of Hottentots. But then you are not supposed to walk, or if you do, you are thought to have connections in the shoe trade; and in California that is not what they call 'high-toned.'

The street-cars of San Francisco have one great advantage over those of New York—you hardly ever hear of a robbery in them, while in the latter city the pickpockets look on the cars as happy hunting-grounds made specially for their convenience. The notices in street and railway cars are sometimes very curious. I remember one that struck me as particularly odd. It ran thus: 'No gentleman will occupy more seats than one at a time—unless he be twins.'

But it is time to leave San Francisco and its flowers and fruits; its spiritualists, mediums, and Veiled

Prophetesses, its advertisers, and interviewers—the latter always ready to interview anyone and anything, from an emperor to an earthquake—and proceed on my journey to Vancouver's Island and British Columbia.

SOUTH FARALLONE ISLAND.
The Ramparts, Tunnel Rocks, Hole in the Wall, and Pyramids.—Fisherman's Bay.

CHAPTER XII.

SAN FRANCISCO TO MOUNT SHASTA.

The Bay—Education of turkeys—The sparrow—Larks—Golden grain—Stubble—Bad farming—Fruit—Marysville—Bank robbery—A humming-bird fight—Staging—Companions—Highwaymen—Scenery—No grumbling—'You bet'—Making oneself popular—Grizzlies—Spiritualism—Castle Rocks—Soda Springs.

THE simpler mode of going to Victoria from San Francisco is by sea, but I had been promised some good shooting in Northern California and Oregon, and was also very anxious to visit the renowned Modoc country, especially as the recent capture of Captain Jack and his band had removed all danger from the expedition. I therefore determined on making the overland journey, trusting to Providence for accomplishing the terrible three hundred miles of staging without being jolted to pieces.

As it was necessary to return to Sacramento, and thence to take the branch line as far as it was yet opened for traffic, I crossed the bay to Vallejo, and got to Sacramento by a different route to that I had before travelled. Crossing to Vallejo gives you an idea of the wonderful capabilities of California, with regard to its natural highways. In this respect there is no State in America, perhaps in the world, better off than California.

It has the ocean in front and the great bay of San Francisco, opening into other bays, and including about ninety miles in length of deep water, while beyond, it has several hundred miles of river navigation. The voyage up the bay was delightful, with ever-varying views of the Coast Range and Mounts Tamalpais and Diablo. The road to Sacramento was hot and dusty, and, except in one particular—the immense flocks of turkeys in the fields—wholly uninteresting. The education of turkeys is carried on here to a great extent in some places. These birds will eat anything and everything they can swallow, and are therefore used to destroy the 'army-worm' and other insects that infest the sugar-beet plantations. I should think they might be employed with great effect in destroying the locusts which create such havoc in the country, and whose ravages have hitherto defied all the efforts of man to guard against.

The English sparrow has not, up to the present time, found its way to California; the thrush and the sky-lark are also wanting. Various opinions are entertained there regarding the merits of sparrows, some people believing that their introduction would be an injury to the farmer. It is true that sparrows will eat grain, but it must be remembered that they also destroy grubs, caterpillars, and insects of nearly every description that prey upon grain and vegetation in general. The fruit-raisers of the interior might object to them, because they would occasionally peck at the cherries; but it is probable that even in gardens in the country they would do more service than harm. What a feast they would have on the grasshoppers, too, which march across the country leaving not a blade of vegetation behind them! The sparrows would save many a crop from being devoured.

The introduction of this bird has proved a great blessing to New York. The trees in the parks are in a much more flourishing condition than they used to be, and where formerly the worms and caterpillars held high carnival, and scarcely a leaf was to be seen on the trees, there is now beauty of foliage equalling that of the country.

The only bird to be seen in the streets of Western towns is the pigeon, which subsists principally on the scattered grain it finds in the streets, and leaves the destroyers of vegetation to work out their pleasure. The sparrow would be a great benefit to the towns, in destroying the insects that attack ornamental trees, as well as the flies and fleas that infest the sand in the streets.

There are some people always glad of a pretext for destroying harmless birds and animals. I saw an article in a San Francisco paper—written by a gentleman of that place—inviting 'weary business citizens of San Francisco to the sport of killing meadow-larks.' The comparative ease with which the lark-fields could be reached was urged as a reason for preferring that sport to the more common one of shooting quails and hares. This individual had also made the discovery that the little bird was fond of eating grapes, and was therefore himself delicious eating, as well as an enemy to mankind.

The sentiment, 'It's such a beautiful day! let us go and kill something,' which is said to be implanted in the bosom of many an Englishman, must have been very strong in that of the lark-slayer. But, until a law is passed prohibiting the ruthless slaughter of robins, larks, and small birds in general, crops must suffer and ravaging insects reign supreme.

The farms and corn-fields in the Valleys of Sacramento and San Joaquin, as well as in the more southern districts of California, give the traveller some idea of the immense resources of that country. As I journeyed on to Marysville I saw the golden grain stretching over the plain, down the slopes of the ravines, over the opposite hills, and into the distant valley; and frequently not a tree or shrub disturbed the view. Such tall stalks, too, and long full ears! A farmer told me that on some of his land the product generally reached sixty bushels to the acre, and eighty bushels per acre are known to have been taken from some places. The machine used at harvest-time merely cuts off the heads of the grain and throws them into a large cart, which looks like a house moving by the side of it. I saw acres and acres that had already been cut. The stubble would have gladdened the eye of many a sportsman in England on the 1st of September —cover almost sufficient to hide a tiger, and forming a safe retreat for the fowls of the air.

The yield of wheat to the acre was formerly wonderful in California. But now, owing to poor farming, in many districts the yield as a rule has been brought down to twenty bushels per acre where it used to average from ninety to a hundred. The land receives neither rest nor manure; and even the straw is burned. What with 'volunteer crops,' turning cattle in to feed, and burning the land, many farms are ruined. A 'volunteer crop' is one that springs up of itself in an uncultivated field, from scattered seeds of the preceding year. These crops are often wonderfully rich, receiving no aid from human labour, and are much sought after by lazy farmers.

Wherever the land is properly cultivated the average yield is forty bushels. But, what with the improvident habits of the people and the almost total absence of real economy in farming, the grain-fields of California are in great danger of being laid waste and desolate.

It has always appeared to me that the farmers paid too much attention, or rather gave too much land to wheat-raising, instead of raising different crops, and pursuing the other occupations usually included in farming operations. At present, if rain fails at the usual season, or if locusts devastate the country, the farmer is often ruined, although he calculates that one good season will compensate him for two bad ones. But everything here is left too much to chance and the great fertility of the soil.

Fruit is so plentiful that no trouble is taken in growing it, and the best varieties are neglected; consequently, the peaches, plums, nectarines, and strawberries, although in wonderful profusion, do not equal the European fruits in flavour and quality. Cherries, apples, and pears seem to grow to much greater perfection, but in no greater quantities, than other fruits. An orchard I saw near Marysville was a perfect wonder, both in extent and the quantity of fruit. But with all the advantages of climate and soil, skilled labour is still greatly needed in California, both for farming and fruit raising, and for dairy-farming and wine-making. The art of making good butter and cheese, and still less the art of making good wine, has not yet reached the Pacific Coast.

On reaching Marysville I found the little town in a great state of excitement, owing to an attempt which had just been made to rob the Bank. In the broad daylight a man walked into the Bank, and levelling a pistol at the **clerk,** who was the only occupant **of the** room at the time, began **to** break open the desks. The clerk dropped **behind the counter** and contrived to crawl to the manager's **room.** Arming himself with a shot-gun, the **manager** boldly faced **the** intruder, who **made for the door,** and was instantly **shot down.** His confederate, who was waiting outside, and **was mounted,** galloped **off** on hearing the report. A hot pursuit ensued, **but without success.** However, from the description given of his accomplice by the dying man, **there** was no doubt about his ultimate capture—at least, so said the police. For my own part I doubted it greatly.

The gardens of Marysville appeared to be a favourite resort of the humming-birds. **They** literally swarmed with these beautiful little **creatures.** They were of two **kinds, but their** plumage was not so brilliant as that of the South American humming-birds.

In the little garden opposite my room I had frequently noticed one of these birds which had much brighter plumage than the others, and I had named him 'Ruby,' from **his glittering throat.** One morning he was attacked by two very plain-plumaged birds; **for what cause I could not make out,** except that he **was** so much handsomer than his assailants. They struck at one another with their long beaks, then soared into the **air for** a moment, darting down swiftly again amongst

o

the flowers. There was so much quiet grace in their movements that it seemed impossible they could really hurt one another; but suddenly poor Ruby fell fluttering to the ground. I ran out to his assistance, but he was quite dead when I reached him. I found that one of his eyes had been put out, evidently by a blow from the sharp beak of one of his murderers. They were still hovering near, but presently flew swiftly away—perhaps in search of another victim.

I had Ruby stuffed, that being the only kindness left me to show him. But nothing could bring back the grace and bee-like movements of the living bird.

The intense heat—it had been very nearly 100° in the shade for some days—made me look forward to the long staging with anything but pleasure; indeed, I may as well say at once that I think nothing would induce me to undergo the heat, or encounter the dust and the intensely painful jolting of that journey again. When I call to mind some of the eating-places, the beefsteaks cut from a boot-leg, the plates of cakes apparently made out of an old flannel petticoat, and the grumpiness of some of the proprietors, I cannot help feeling that Shenstone never alluded to this journey when he wrote :—

> 'Whoe'er has travelled life's dull round,
> Where'er his stages may have been,
> May sigh to think he still has found
> The warmest welcome at an inn.'

Redding was the name of the station where the railroad terminated, and our misery began, in the shape of rickety old stage-coaches with seats of wrought-iron, or something equally hard and agreeable to sit upon.

The train arrived at midnight, and the coach started at one in the morning. That hour was the usual one for starting all through the journey—that is, if the start was made at the appointed time. But whether the departure took place a few hours before or a few days after was apparently of no consequence whatever.

My travelling companions were two commercial travellers of the most snobbish description, two Celestials of the ordinary type, and an elderly female with a face like a water-melon, and who in answer to any and every remark that was made never replied otherwise than 'I guess so.' My *vis-à-vis* was a middle-aged lady, decidedly inclined to *embonpoint*—I think you might almost have called her stout. As we progressed by a series of bumps and jerks, she was sent flying into my arms at intervals of half-a-minute. At last I became quite expert in catching her whenever she was propelled towards me, and then she would apologise and flounder back into her seat. My style of architecture being somewhat bony and angular, I do not think she appreciated this game of ball as much as she might otherwise have done, and I could hear her groan whenever she came against any particularly sharp angle.

Towards daybreak I managed to get a seat on the box, and found we were surrounded by thick, darkling woods, through which our road lay for the greater part of the journey. The driver told me an amusing story of a robbery that had lately been effected near that part of the road we were passing, and where, as I have lately heard, the stage-coach has again been attacked and robbed by highwaymen. The driver's story ran as follows:—

A man, whose appearance was that of a miner, was travelling along the road, when he suddenly heard a great noise from amongst the bushes, which were thicker on one side of the path than the other. Thinking that robbers were there, he fired off a pistol, and the outcry ceased. On making his way through the bushes he discovered a man tied to a tree. 'Thank goodness you're come,' he exclaimed. 'I have been waylaid, and the ruffians were robbing me, but when they heard the report of your pistol they made off.'

'Have they robbed you of everything?' asked the traveller.

'No, only of my watch,' was the reply, 'as I had, fortunately, placed all my money in my right boot, and the villains hadn't time to search for it.'

'And couldn't you get loose?'

'No, they have tied me too tight.'

'Are you sure they are all gone?'

'Oh, quite sure,' said the poor man; 'I could hear them ride off on their horses.'

'Then,' said the other, 'as they're gone, I think I'll finish the job myself.' Which he did!

Stage robbing is quite a profession in the Far West, and it has this peculiar advantage for its professors—no one ever thinks of resisting. The coach, bearing most probably a box of treasure, belonging to Wells, Fargo, and Company, is stopped in the depth of the forest by the captain of the gang, who covers the vehicle with his repeating-rifle, whilst another of the robbers opens the door and requests the passengers to alight.

The search then begins; and after all the valuables have been taken a polite good night is bidden by the highwaymen, and the coach is allowed to proceed.

No one grumbles, and everybody understands what a 'six-shooter' means when pointed at his head. This non-protecting principle does not arise from want of courage, for a Californian possesses rather too great a disregard for his life; but as money is so easily come by, it is taken as a necessary evil that it may depart in a like manner. Besides, even if travellers carry arms they are pretty certain not to be ready for use when required—thus, everything is made as pleasant and agreeable as possible. Summary punishment is often inflicted on the robbers; for in spite of the masks they are frequently recognised, and the police are soon on their track. There is no summoning to surrender or parleying with robbers in California; the quickest and surest shot is the man who comes off best.

We were delayed for a few hours in our first day's journey by the bridge being broken that spanned a narrow ravine. The stout lady was terribly frightened, and asked the water-melon lady if she didn't think the robbers had broken the bridge on purpose. 'I guess so,' was the answer, and that was all the consolation she received. Eventually she put her money into her blue cotton umbrella, which she thought a good hiding-place, and for the rest of the journey she saw highwaymen in every thicket and robbers behind every rock.

If it had not been for the dust, which was far worse than even anything I had experienced on the Yosemite route, our first day's drive would have been delightful. Sometimes the road ran through miles of solemn pines, gloomy and still, and with no undergrowth, only level beds of brown moss dotted with dropped cones. At other times we passed through long alleys of buck-eye, manzanita, and red-woods, with here and there a gigantic cedar or sugar-pine; now and then we crossed a rushing mountain-stream, the banks of which, covered with ferns and fragrant lilies, were in charming contrast with the red rocks and silver-grey lichens. There seemed to be but few birds, with the exception of red-shafted woodpeckers; perhaps an occasional jay would fly screaming between the dark branches, but otherwise there was no sound of bird or beast to break the stillness, which was apt to become rather oppressive.

Generally in California the inns on travelled roads are very fair, but on this occasion we found some thoroughly bad specimens—the outside very pretentious, the inside totally neglected.

In California one never thinks of grumbling at public accommodation; consequently, no improvement is made until competition absolutely compels it. Public criticism would do a vast amount of good and correct many abuses in America, but it never occurs to anyone to write to the papers on the subject.

I think stage-drivers and the class of people met with on the coaches are fonder of betting than any other people in the world, not excepting Chinese and Indians. It is perhaps more in their peculiar mode of expressing themselves than in the actual stakes that their betting consists. No sentence is ever completed and no opinion ever expressed or answer given without, 'bet your life,' 'you bet,' or 'bet your boots.' The latter is the favourite expression; it extends all through the West, and, I am sorry to say, up into British Columbia, where they ought to have more command of language than to adhere strictly to one style of gambling exclamations. I asked a driver whether it was a Californian saying, and he answered, 'jest as much English as Californian, you bet your boots;' and he continued—alluding to the bagman inside—'**say,** mister; those chaps ain't high-toned, and no specimens of Californy, you bet your life.'

The same man told me that he was the best whisky-drinker thereabouts, and that he drank nothing else, as it made him popular. Now, **how whisky**-drinking could add to his popularity I am unable to conceive.

On the way, we stopped **at a** very neat little farm-house, at the edge of an almost circular cornfield. Nearly the whole crop had been trampled down and destroyed, and the owner informed us it had all been done by grizzly bears. These animals are very fond of sucking the ripe ears of corn, and will tread down acres in a single night. Of all beasts that walk the earth a grizzly is the most formidable, and it is a difficult matter to get even professional hunters to pursue them. The immense masses of muscle and fat **over their** vital organs render them exceedingly **difficult to kill** outright, and a wounded **one is a** terrible opponent. They can run as fast as a horse, and their prodigious strength enables them to crush a bull as easily as if he were a squirrel. However, they seldom attack man, unless they are **wounded or** have their cubs with them. They are then very dangerous and savage.

The rage for spiritualism, which is very strong in the large towns of California, had reached the wilds through which we were travelling, and we passed a small cottage, a dirty untidy-looking place, where the mother and daughter had of late taken to seeing ghosts and spirits. They had given up all work, being under the impression that mediums should be above attending to domestic duties. The consequence was that the husband and father, who considered spirits, except of a certain kind, as unnecessary to his social comfort and position, used the most forcible arguments against the spectres and their mediums, and the shanty was a continual scene of strife and wailing. The unhappy proprietor got into the coach, and informed the driver that there was another tea-party of spirits in prospect; and that he had made up his mind to leave home and never return to it. This threat, I found out, had been repeated so often, that now it was generally discredited; and when he descended at the next halting-place it was understood that the following morning would see him on his way back. Spiritualism as a religion is advancing with rapid strides in America.

One of the chief causes of its success is that it includes amongst the members of its Church everybody who in any way believes in the supernatural, and gratifies the tastes of its believers in any form most pleasing to themselves.

After crossing the wooded valley of Pitt river—or, as it is generally called, the Upper Sacramento—the road constantly ascended amidst brown hills covered with fine oaks, until, on reaching the crest, pine-forests again surrounded us and extended up the picturesque Castle Rocks, which reared their sharp peaks far off on our left. This range of granite and limestone rocks attains an elevation of about 3,000 feet, and extends along the Pitt Valley. The summit is broken into innumerable ragged **forms resembling** gigantic castles, with battlements and donjons, whose clearly-defined walls and angles stand out boldly against the bright blue of the California sky. The glare of the sun falling on the snowy limestone peaks is perfectly dazzling, and it is a relief to turn the eye towards the blue-grey granite cliffs and the shadows of the wooded crests below.

Sometimes the valley broadens into prairie breadths and plains covered with **rank** grass, surrounded by slopes clad with manzanita and cotton-wood, where the Pitt River Indians dwell and spear their salmon. Now and then **a settler's hut may be** seen, with a little cultivated land around it. But farming does not answer well; and though the land is light and easy to work, it is generally less easy to secure the crops.

Continually traversing woods of mountain-pines, we **at** length **caught a** glimpse **of Mount** Shasta ; its rugged snowy peak, standing like a sentinel at the entrance of the Sacramento Valley. Presently we arrived at 'Soda Springs,' and the heat and dust of the day rendered the water more delicious than the best manufactured soda-water I ever drank. The water of these springs, in which iron and soda predominate, is highly charged with carbonic acid gas. It effervesces strongly, and is extremely pleasant to the taste. Invalids often spend weeks at the inn, as the water has wonderful curative powers—it certainly creates a most voracious appetite.

I met at the Springs two travellers who were going to ascend Mount Shasta on the following day; and as they had no objection, I gladly joined them in their expedition, and was not at all sorry to say good-bye to the lumbering old coach for a time.

CHAPTER XIII.

MOUNT SHASTA.

Game—Foliage—Barrenness—Night—Morning—Clouds—The crater—Boiling springs—View—Sunset—Red snow—Sisson's—Play of colour—Packing—The trail—Our first deer—American deer—Destruction of game out of season.

MOUNT SHASTA is the most striking feature of Northern California. Its height is about 14,500 feet above the sea—very nearly the height of Mont Blanc. Mont Blanc is broken into a succession of peaks, but Shasta is one stupendous peak, set upon a broad base that sweeps out far and wide. From the base the volcanic cone rises up in one vast stretch of snow and lava. It is very precipitous to the north and south, but east and west there are two slopes right up to the crater. It is a matter of doubt whether Shasta is dead or only sleeping. Vesuvius slept calmly for centuries, and then spread death and desolation for miles around. The base of the mountain is magnificently watered and wooded, and forms a splendid hunting-ground. The woods are full of deer and bears; and now and then a mountain-goat, an animal very like the chamois

MOUNT SHASTA.—View from Sisson's, Shasta Valley, Cal.

of the Alps, is seen in the higher part of the mountain.

Well-provided with blankets and provisions, we started with a guide, and a man to look after the horses, at a very early hour, and rode through a beautiful forest of pines, silver firs, and cedars. Along the banks of the streams were aspens, willows, and the trees known by the name of the 'Balm of Gilead,' whose vivid green leaves were already changing to a rich orange or an apple-red—forming a beautiful contrast of colours with the glazed green of the cedars and the green-tinted white of the silver firs.

After an easy ascent to a height of about 8000, feet we reached the limits of vegetation. Thence our upward path lay over snow, ice, and lava—lonely, isolated barrenness on every side, relieved only by an occasional solitary dwarf-pine, struggling to retain life amidst fierce storms and heavy-weighing snow. Many of them were quite dead, but embalmed by frost and snow in a never-decaying death.

With a few loads of this fuel we soon made a splendid fire, the warmth of which was most welcome in the cold rarefied atmosphere. Scarcely had we finished a capital supper ere night descended, and great clouds and fitful fogs began to drift past. These in their turn broke, and the moon threw a weird light over the forest below; whilst above rose piles upon piles of pinkish lava and snow-fields, reaching far up into the sky, whose magnificent blue grew more sparkling and clear every moment.

Wrapping ourselves in our bundles of blankets, we crept as close as possible to the huge fire, and before long my companions were fast asleep and snoring. I could not sleep a wink, and mentally registered a vow never again to camp out without a pillow. No one can tell till he has tried it the difference there is between going to sleep with a pillow under the head and a stone or a pair of boots or saddle as its resting-place.

The deep silence, unbroken save by a most unromatic snore, was painfully oppressive, and I longed to hear even a growl from a bear or a deep whine from a Californian lion.[1] I listened intently, for it seemed as if the slightest sound, even a hundred miles away, ought to be heard, so still and frosty was the air.

But none fell on my ear, not even a murmur to soothe one to sleep, and I began to think bears and lions were snares and delusions, when, just as I was dozing off, I felt my arm violently pulled, and a voice called out that it was time for us to make a start. Hot coffee soon had a cheering effect, and long before daylight we left our warm camping-ground, and began the higher

[1] These so-called lions are a sort of panther, and abound in most parts of California and Oregon. They are very cowardly, and seldom attack a man, unless they can spring on him from a tree, and not often then.

ascent on foot. Broken stone and slabs of lava afforded pretty good foothold, far preferable to the fields of frozen snow, which we carefully avoided. After a couple of hours' hard walking we seemed to be just as far from the summit as when we started; but the views gradually became grander. From a rocky promontory we looked back over a sea of glittering clouds, the only land visible being the peaks of the Coast range, near the Pacific; all else was cloud, to which the moonlight lent an almost dazzling whiteness.—

> 'Far clouds of feathery gold,
> Shaded with deepest purple, gleam
> Like islands on a dark blue sea.'

When the sun rose and the mists cleared off, the scene was indescribably grand, and the gradual unfolding of the vast panorama unapproachable in its splendour.

After some hours of weary climbing over crumbling scoria and splintered rock we reached the crater. In the ascent to the summit overlooking the crater, we had to cross an ice-field. It had that blue tinge found in the ice of which glaciers are composed, and its slipperiness made it almost impossible to walk over it, the ice lying often in ridges resembling the waves of the sea.

The main crater covers several acres. It is hemmed in by rims of rock, and is filled with volcanic *débris*, covered with snow and ice. Numbers of little boiling springs were bubbling up through the bed of sulphur, and were suggestive of the subterranean fires which once threw their molten lava over the surrounding country. The view from the summit was most extensive, and fortunately there was none of the usual smoke from the forest-fires, so prevalent in autumn in Northern California and Oregon, to impede the range of vision.

Looking northward, far over into Oregon, we could see her lakes, valleys, and mountains. Southward, we could trace the Sacramento and Pitt rivers. The great boundary-wall of the Sierra Nevada lay to the east, and farther onward, the deserts and sparkling lakes of Utah could be distinguished. To the west, the sinuous outline of the Coast range was visible, and beyond, the broad Pacific shelved away to the horizon. Fertile valleys, rugged mountains, wood and water, all lent their aid to enhance the beauty of this unsurpassable scene.

The descent to our camping-ground was accomplished in a comparatively short time. On the way, we stopped to witness a most glorious sunset. Round the horizon ran a thin mist with a brilliant depth of colouring. To the east, a blue gauze seemed to cover each valley as it sank into night, and the intervening ridges rose with increasing distinctness. The lower country was flooded with an exquisitely delicate light, and a few fleecy clouds tinted with gold, pale salmon, and sapphire, passed over the empurpled hills of the Coast range. The great shadow of Mount Shasta spread itself, cone-like, across the valley; the blue mists were quenched; the distant mountains glowed like fairy hills for a few moments; and the sun, poising itself like a great globe of fire in the darkening heavens, descended slowly below the golden ridge to illumine another hemisphere.

During our descent we passed through some patches of red snow, which leaves a crimson track behind those who cross over it. This curious phenomenon is always avoided by the Shasta Indians when acting as guides or porters, as they say it brings death if you tread on it willingly and after due warning. We found a warm fire to welcome us on our arrival at the camp, and the exertions of the day made us very willing to turn in among the blankets, where we slept soundly till long past daybreak. The following day, when we arrived at our original starting-point, my companions resumed their journey to San Francisco, and I went on to Sisson's, a station on the stage-road, whence I was to start on a shooting expedition amongst the Castle Rocks.

Sisson's, so-called after the name of the proprietor, is a very delightful place to spend a few days at. The view of Mount Shasta, which is directly opposite the house, is magnificent; and Sisson himself is a capital sportsman and guide, and succeeds in making his guests very comfortable. Looking at Mount Shasta is occupation enough for some time. The play of colour on the mountain is extraordinary. The lava, which is of a rosy hue, often penetrates through the snow, and when the sun shines upon it the effect is most beautiful. The pure white fields of snow are diversified by great blue glaciers, and when the sunbeams fall with refracted glory on the veins of ice they exhibit wonderful tints of opal, green, and pink. The effects produced by the mingling colours of lava, snow, and ice, and the contrasting shadows of a deep violet hue are so varied, and the radiation of colour at sunrise and sunset so vivid, that it is difficult to keep the eyes turned from the mountain—for nothing seems worthy of consideration in comparison with Shasta.

I had heard at San Francisco so much about the great quantity of deer in the region whither we were bound, that I confess I was rather sceptical on the point; as it invariably happens that where good shooting is looked for upon mere hearsay the results are most deplorable. However, our little cavalcade, consisting of Sisson, his two hunters, and myself, set out early one morning for Castle Lake, near which we were to fix our first camp.

The pack-horse which carried our tent, cooking utensils, provisions, &c. seemed to possess a capacity for carrying as much as a luggage-van. When all had been packed on his back—and it was no light load—

there was still room for more, and he trotted off as gaily as our own less encumbered animals.

Considerable skill is required to 'pack' a horse well. Our load overlapped too much at the sides, and the consequence was, that in going through the bush and between trees the entire load was twice swept from the back of the animal, which gladly seized the opportunity to disappear in the woods on a foraging expedition.

We were soon in the depths of the forest, following an indistinct trail in Indian file, and keeping a sharp look-out for deer. The trail led into a tangled maze of bracken and rose-briar, with now and then long vistas into the green heart of the wood. Presently we descended a steep track into a wooded ravine, from the dark recesses of which issued the rushing noise of a mountain stream, which soon came in view, tumbling over loose rocks and stones in frothing white masses. Here and there were long deep reaches covered with foam-crested circles of sparkling water, sweeping downwards to other falls, and the more noisy rapids, and overhung by drooping cedars and mountain cypress. Beyond, the rocky pine-clad steep rose black against the sky.

A low whistle from Sisson, who was in advance, called my attention to a fine deer which was standing in the shade of the trees, hardly a hundred yards off, gazing curiously at us, and showing its alarm by a quick little stamp of the foot. In a second I was off my horse; I pulled the trigger of my rifle, and had the satisfaction of seeing our first deer disappear in the bushes. Sisson declared the bullet had struck the rock just over the animal's shoulder, and that it was a capital 'line shot.' But I determined to avoid 'line shots' for the future, however capital they might be. It was the only deer fired at that day, though we saw two or three more in the distance.

The American deer is very like the European red deer in size, but differs somewhat in the structure and shape of its horns. In colour it is generally of a reddish-brown, with white on the throat and chin. The ears are tipped with dark brown, and the tail is white beneath, a circumstance soon discovered by an indifferent shot. The killing of these deer has by law been restricted to five months—August to December, inclusive. In some counties it is lawful to shoot them only during September and the two following months. Laws, however, are useless so long as the spirit of the population is set against their enforcement, and the merciless and incessant war waged on every wild animal, bird, and fish, at all times and in all places, in season and out of season, will soon render hunting, shooting, and fishing in America sports of the past. The wanton destruction of the buffalo in the West (only last **November** over five hundred were slaughtered in two days, **near Denver, by** white **men**), the murdering of hundreds **of** moose in Canada, and the knocking on the head with clubs of thousands of deer in New York and other States, **by** men on snow-shoes, during the deep snows of winter, are examples of the strange perversity and folly of the white settlers of every part of America. Civilisation and culture have nothing to do with the decrease of game, as game increases in the same ratio as cultivation increases, if woodland is left of sufficient extent to afford shelter to the animals, and they are unmolested during the breeding-season.

But some people kill for the mere love of slaughter; and the destruction of forests by fire, the roasting of eggs in spring, the reckless annihilation of animals at seasons even when they are utterly useless, and with the sure prospect of a total extermination, are all nothing compared to a little present selfish advantage. It has been urged that it is quite impossible to institute game laws in a new State. But there are very few States in America which are not old enough by this time to comprehend what are their own interests; and the rigid enforcement of the laws, and the example of educated men who are settled throughout the rural districts, would soon produce some effect on the minds of the masses as regards the wholesale destruction of game out of season.

CHAPTER XIV.

CAMPING OUT.

A frying-pan—Castle Lake—Famine—Fishing—Dinner—A song—Fresh quarters—Deer-hunting—Ambush—Mountain-sides—Bears—Wild flowers—Home—Camp life—A duel—Woodpeckers—Maternal love.

Our course for the greater part of the day's ride ran up and down hills, having here and there delightful clumps of mountain oaks, and, clustering beneath them, groups of splendid tiger-lilies. It was almost dark when we reached our camping-ground at Castle Lake, but we soon found a capital place for a halt by a clear running stream, with plenty of grass growing near for the horses. A fire was soon made, and by the time some grouse and quails which we had shot on the way were ready for cooking, it was discovered that Sisson had quite forgotten to provide dishes or plates of any sort. Luckily he had remembered the frying-pan, and that for the next few days was the only article we had to cook in and eat out of.

The weather was so lovely that, although we had tents, we never used them during our ten days' expedition, but slept by the fire and beneath the bright stars and tall solemn pine-trees.

By daybreak **we were up** and swimming in **the lake**, which at that hour was almost too cold for much enjoyment; but the early morn being the **best** time for deer-shooting, we **were** obliged to be up before the sun. Castle Lake is far more picturesque than **Lake** Tahoe, and though much smaller it has far greater variety. Steep **wooded** hills slope down to the water's edge, **and** bare barren bluffs rise up perpendicularly **from the** lake whilst banks of wild flowers clothe the **low promontories** that sometimes jut out far beyond the steep banks.

The first view of the lake was very beautiful. The rosy light from the east was striking here and there on the grey rocks and among the deep pine glades; and now **and then across these** bright streaks a long-necked doe with her fawn would pass **and** repass, whilst down at the water's edge **a** fine fat buck was taking a long draught, quite regardless of the intruders into his sanctum.

Our first morning's hunt was most unsuccessful. We saw plenty of tracks of deer, but not one of the deer that made them. We therefore returned, after about six hours' **extremely** hard climbing and walking, **to our** camp for breakfast. As Sisson had calculated on our obtaining plenty of venison, he had provided no meat; or, as he said, 'nothing **but** bacon, and that I've forgotten.'

In the daytime it was too hot to do anything but lie under the trees by the side of the lake and wish for the evening; and as that time approached I began to have serious doubts about the bill of fare for our dinner, for we had eaten the last grouse at breakfast. If I had only been a fisherman I might have quieted my fears in the mysterious absorption of fishing. But I never had patience enough to become an adept in the 'gentle craft,' whose soothing virtues, neither poisonous, like opium, nor transient, like music, ought to be cultivated early. Nevertheless the cravings of hunger determined me to turn my mind to fishing. Sisson had brought his fly-book and lines; so we cut ourselves rods, and whilst the others whipped the waters with the lordly fly I contented myself with the more humble grasshopper. The lake was said to be teeming with fish; but after an hour's dipping and splashing, without the minutest result, I took my gun and rushed up the nearest hill. At dark I returned, without having fired a single shot, only to find that the others had not caught a single fish—owing, they said, to a ripple, but owing, I thought, to there being nothing to catch. Oh! that dinner! no fragrant stew, no grateful soup—nothing but a few potatoes and beans, washed down by oceans of tea. But we were all so very hungry that we made a hearty dinner—agreeing with Sancho Panza that 'the viscera upholds the heart, and the heart the stomach,' and that it was necessary to eat well to be ready for the hard work of the morrow.

Sitting round the fire, when the banquet was over, somebody suggested a song as a suitable conclusion to the festive occasion; upon which one of the party, evidently inspired with the idea that he held in his hand a silver goblet of wine—the reality being a tin cup of weak tea—struck up ' The Glorious Vintage of Champagne!' The third line of the first verse,

'When man has nothing left to stake,'

was so appropriate to our situation that it was enthusiastically encored, and the *refrain* sent us merrily to bed. The next morning we determined to shift our quarters to the other side of the lake, as it was evident the deer had collected over there. As there was no regular trail we had considerable difficulty in finding our way. The pack-horses, too, would every now and then rush between two trees; and if they would not give way, as was generally the case, why, the packs did, and then there was half-an-hour's delay in tying them on again. On our way we shot a deer—so the provision enigma was solved for the present, much to our delight, but to the sorrow of the old pack-animal, who thereby had his load considerably increased. Having reached the other side of the lake, we crossed the mountain and soon established our camp in a beautiful valley, which looked **as if** it ought to be a perfect home for wild game.

Driving is the mode of deer-hunting most generally practised in America. The shooters are placed round a certain tract which is beaten by men and hounds. But it is a dull stupid business for those who do not happen to be in a lucky position; even then there is not much pleasure in discharging your gun or rifle at a great timid animal which has been driven up to within a short distance of you, where he **stands trembling,** and with imploring eyes seemingly begging not to be shot. But the **worst** practice of all is that **of** lying in ambush near some 'lick' or spring, to which the deer comes down to drink, and shooting him down in cold blood, without either difficulty or excitement.

Indians are extremely fond of this mode of killing; but then they do it from necessity, to supply themselves with food, not for sport. Our hunting-ground was much too rough and hilly for horses; and not caring about 'lying in ambush,' we always started two and two in opposite directions **at** daybreak, and shot what we could by steady walking. We certainly had no cause to complain of scarcity of game around our new camp; for on the second day after reaching it one of the hunters was sent **home with** eight deer, and with orders to return as soon as possible with the forgotten plates and dishes.

In the early morning the hills were alive with deer; and it was no unfrequent occurrence to meet with one before we had left our camp five minutes. It was very hard walking up the mountain-sides, as most of the ground was covered with loose angular rocks, which turned over when trodden upon. The brush too was so thick as to be almost impenetrable. But the quantity of game would have compensated for many more difficulties than we had to encounter. One morning we counted no less than twenty-seven deer, singly, or in groups of two or three. We saw also two or three black bears, and once had a long shot at one; but did not manage to kill him. Sisson was very confident that we should meet with others, as the woods were full of all sorts of berries, of which they are extremely fond. One morning we found the tracks of a bear round our camp. One of the hunters had heard him, but it was too dark to see the brute, and bears are very methodical in their movements. We laid in wait for some hours, near a path along which bruin had lately travelled, but never got a glimpse of him. His keen scent had probably told him of our whereabouts.

Our valley would have been a rare spot for a botanist. Some of the wild flowers were most beautiful

—one kind particularly so. It opened only at sunrise, and had an exquisite lilac tint, its leaves glistening with dew like a diamond spray. Mountain-lilies looked up from the dry grass, from the crisp bracken, and from the arid hill-sides, each petal richly variegated and resembling the plumes of a pea-fowl. There were open glades green with herbage, and bright with many-hued blossoms; and in the centre of some of these oases were little sparkling springs, surrounded with hundreds of pitcher-plants, which we made use of as cups. This curious plant is an admirable fly-catcher. There were always several dead flies and other insects at the bottom of the long stems. Sometimes, a bunch of forget-me-nots, with a few wild columbines, and honey-suckle clustering round the briar-roses, recalled to mind many a home-scene, and lilies, pitcher-plants, strange ferns, and the wild deer would be all forgotten at the sight of the well-remembered shrubs and familiar flowers. At such moments one is apt to feel a great longing for home and rest; yet it is wonderful how naturally we take to camp life. Its freedom and simplicity, with the earth for a bed and the sky for a ceiling, are very captivating for a time. Then there are the glorious wild haunts into which it leads us; the awakening in the fresh gray of dawn; the delicious bath in the mountain torrent; the appetite acquired by healthful exercise and appeased by trout and venison (when you can can get them) cooked on the glowing embers; the pursuit of game up to the high mountain-tops, and at night the ruddy watch-fire, round which we gather and talk over the day's events, or tell stories of the most heartrending description.

One of the most horrible stories I ever heard was told us by a hunter who had recently arrived from Texas. It related to a duel that was fought in July last, and of which he had been an eye-witness.

The duel was of so atrocious a character that I should hesitate to record the particulars of it did I not know that they are strictly true. They show too what tragedies are still enacted in some parts of America, and before a crowd of eager spectators.

A man of the name of Anderson had killed another, named M'Cluskey, in a drunken fray. The brother of the murdered man determined to be avenged, and at length found Anderson at a place called Medicine Lodge, in the Indian Territory. Both men, one a Texan and the other from Kansas, were well-known desperadoes, as utterly reckless of their own lives as of others'.

A duel was quickly arranged, and seconds chosen. Revolvers and bowie-knives were the weapons. At sunset they met in the presence of a number of trappers, hunters, railroad surveyors, gamblers, and Indians.

They were placed back to back at a distance of twenty-five paces, and according to previous arrangement were to wheel round and fire at a given signal, and after that to conduct the fight as each thought best. They fired almost at the same instant. A pause ensued—each combatant closely scanning the other, to observe the effect of the shot.

Across Anderson's cheek was a deep furrow, from which the blood trickled down and told of the sure aim of his antagonist.

M'Cluskey remained standing; to all appearance unharmed. But those near him saw a sudden contraction of the nerves and his face blanched to a death-like pallor, but none knew where the ball had taken effect. At the second fire M'Cluskey anticipated his opponent, and taking a deliberate aim broke his left arm. Anderson uttered a sharp cry and sank on one knee, but quickly recovering himself, returned the fire with dreadful effect. The ball passed through M'Cluskey's mouth, carrying away several of the clenched teeth and lodging in the base of the skull. He staggered forward wildly, made desperate efforts to steady himself, and with wonderful courage continued to advance. Anderson, in his crippled state, wished to avoid a hand-to-hand encounter, and fired another shot, which broke M'Cluskey's left shoulder. As if this was not enough, he sent another ball after it, which striking him full, caused him to fall heavily on his face.

M'Cluskey, now mortally wounded, and growing

weaker every moment from loss of blood, still retained his grasp of the pistol and fired at his antagonist. Anderson had been closely watching for this, and tried to save himself by dropping on the ground. Too late, however, as the bullet struck him in the abdomen, and he, like M'Cluskey, was now a dying man. By a last supreme effort M'Cluskey drew his knife, and feebly tried to crawl in the direction of his enemy. The latter managed to raise himself to a sitting posture, and prepared to meet him. Both had dropped their revolvers, and Anderson was unable to move any portion of his body except his right arm. With this he raised his knife, and as M'Cluskey crawled up within reach dealt him a terrible blow in the neck, half-severing the head from the body. The great effort caused him to pitch forward on his face, leaving the knife sticking in the wound.

Everyone supposed that the blow must instantly have killed M'Cluskey, yet before falling he twice plunged his own knife into the body of Anderson. The dead bodies, firmly locked in each other's embrace, were taken to a house and laid out side by side on a gaming-table, and in a few hours after were removed for burial.

We found in the valley two woodpeckers' stores. The red-headed Californian woodpecker has a great talent for carpentering, and may often be seen busily engaged boring holes in the bark of a pine tree and afterwards filling them up with acorns. The holes are generally at an equal distance from each other, and just the right size for the acorn. As these birds do not eat acorns the reason for their stowing them away is not very clear. Though the storing takes place in the autumn yet a thorough inspection and critical examination of the larder goes on all the year round. It is most amusing to see one of the birds gravely examining the holes, as if he were not quite satisfied that the distance between them was correct. The old stump of a tree, called ' Stock im Eisen,' which is still to be seen in Vienna, and into which travelling artisans on passing through that city used to drive nails, in order to bring luck, is very like a large woodpecker's larder.

On our last day in the woods we saw a striking instance of maternal affection and courage in a doe. Having killed all the deer that we wanted, we were taking a stroll with our shot-guns, when a doe and fawn suddenly jumped up quite close to us. The hound that was usually held in a slip-knot happened to be loose, and at once gave chase to the fawn, which he very soon would have caught, had not the mother diverted his attention by running **close to him** whenever he closed on her child. I followed as fast as I could, and had not the poor frightened creature run in a circle I should not have been able to save it; **as it was, I got up just as** the dog caught it, and the mother actually came to within twenty yards of us, bleating most pitiably. Bret Harte's lines were very applicable to this scene :—

' And she looked me right in the eye—I'd seen nuthin like it before—
When I hunted a wounded doe to the edge o' the Clear Lake shore;
And I had my knee on its neck, and jist was raisin' my knife,
When it gave me a look like that, and—well, it got off with its life.'

CHAPTER XV.

FROM YREKA TO THE LAVA BEDS.

Eaten by a bear—Forest fires—A desert—Sage-hens—Mountain-sheep—Modocs—Indians—Belief—Cost of Indians—A liberal Government—Indian agents—Present policy—Reservations—Issuing rations to Indians—Santanta and Big Tree—Red Cloud—War Department.

From Sisson's a forty miles' jolt on the old stage-coach, through forests, up and down hills, and finally across a broad cultivated valley—along one of whose mountain sides ran a 'flume,' conducting water for a distance of over seventy miles—brought us to the little town of Yreka. From this place I was to branch off to the Modoc country and the Lava Beds—a distance of about a hundred miles. Yreka is a small but flourishing mining town, with a temperature, when I was there, exactly that of an oven. I was therefore very glad to set off to the mountains, in company with two gentlemen to whom I had letters of introduction.

The first part of our journey was between brown, dry, and barren-looking hills, which in spring are covered with herbage, and afford capital grazing for sheep. Leaving these, we crossed a valley yellow with stubble and dotted over with farm-houses, and then began the long mountain ascent. The low red rock, hard foot-hills and hillocks, spiked with straggling oaks and pines, were very picturesque, but reflected the heat of the sun in a manner uncomfortably suggestive of sunstroke; that evil, however, is of rare occurrence in California. Presently we reached a sheep-ranch, where a few weeks before a poor boy, who had gone up the mountain in search of stray sheep, was killed by a bear —at least such was the supposition, as the people who sought for him found nothing but his cap, but saw the tracks of a large bear, evidently from the marks, in pursuit of some one running away. The track had been followed as far as was possible, and Indians skilful in following the faintest trail, had been brought to assist, but nothing more had been discovered.

After leaving the ranch we came to a splendid stream, which rushed out of the bare rock after running underground from its source near the top of the mountain. The dense forest into which we soon plunged afforded a most welcome shade, and we remained there for the next two days—camping luxuriously in the most delightful spots, but troubled now and then by swarms of mosquitoes. On the other side of the mountain we passed large tracts of forest on fire, sometimes stretching for miles, and giving a charred, dismal aspect to what would, otherwise, be a beautiful woodland scene.

But the flames looked magnificent at night, lighting up snowy Shasta with great effect.

In the west and north-west these vast fires rage all through the autumn, their smoke covering the hills and plains. And yet they appear to have very little effect on the immense wooded regions in which they prevail.

In former times, the Indians used to encourage these fires, that they might more easily hunt game and gather the roasted acorns. But now, there are severe laws against firing the brush and underwood. Yet careless travellers and woodmen still leave their camp-fires burning; thereby often causing great damage to settlers, and seriously affecting the water supply. Lakes that once had water all the year round are now dry, except, perhaps, in the spring-time, and streams disappear long before they reach the lands through which they once used to run.

Our last day's journey, before reaching the ranch near which we intended to pitch our camp for a week's hunting, was across a most forbidding district. For miles and miles, nothing was to be seen but low sage-brush and heaps of rock, with a few juniper trees scattered among them. Now and then a villainous-looking *coyote* would sneak across our path, making his way to some distant spring, and ready to pick up any sage-hen or rabbit foolish enough to come near him. Rugged volcanic peaks towered in the distance, and all around was desolate and arid. The very juniper trees increased the idea of thirst, as they grow only where there is no water and hardly soil enough to support their roots; but they afforded a little shade from the blinding sun, so we were grateful even for their melancholy shadows. Sometimes a snake hissed from the scorching rocks and glided into the brown, dry, interminable brush—adding to the loneliness of the vast solitary desert:

> 'Here silence reigned with lips of glue,
>   And, undisturbed, maintained her law,
> Save where the owl cried, "Whoo! whoo! whoo!"
>   Or the hoarse crow croaked, "Caw! caw! caw!"'

The hours occupied in crossing this waste seemed days, and our horses were as glad as we were ourselves when we reached a small stream, whose banks we followed for some distance until we arrived at our camping-ground.

The following day, we amused ourselves by shooting sage-hens and prairie-chickens. The former are big birds, something between a pheasant and a barndoor fowl. They were there in great numbers, but afforded very little sport, and, as we afterwards discovered, were very sagey, ill-flavoured birds.

One morning some Modoc Indians came to our camp with venison for sale. One of them, who could speak a few words of English, told us that in the mountain above us there was a band of wild sheep. These animals are exceedingly shy, and difficult to approach; but as I was very anxious to obtain a head for stuffing I set off the next morning to try if I could meet with them. An eight-mile tramp of the most heart-breaking description brought me to the top of the mountain, on the north side of which I spent the day, without seeing a living animal of any sort. I then returned to the camp, and found that my companions had killed a deer, greatly to the **disgust of the Modocs**; who had refused to accompany me, because, as they said, **they did** not like climbing after the sheep, but in reality because they were too lazy to care **for** any shooting but that **obtained by** lying in ambush. On this occasion **my** friends had followed **the** example of the Indians, but had chosen their ambush in a more fortunate place.

I made two more attempts to get at the sheep, and finally succeeded in coming suddenly upon them on the south side of the mountain; just where the Indians had said they would not be. I had not time to pick and choose, but fortunately the head of the one I did get was a very fine one with magnificent horns, and it was no light work carrying it into camp.

The mountain-sides were tangled with thick chapparal and all sorts of wild berries, such as huckleberries, thimble-berries, currants, and a sort of cherry. Some of the ravines were composed of masses of loose flints, down which I slided that evening, regardless of my rent garments, and clutching at flimsy wisps of grass, which parted at once from the inhospitable soil that had long ago pinched off the roots in its iron grasp. But more often I was brought abruptly to a stand-still, or rather sit-still, by thorny shrubs, dead, perhaps, but in full possession of their prickly powers.

On arriving at our camping-ground I found that my companions had arranged with the English-speaking Modoc Indian, who was called 'Miller's Charlie,' to guide me on the following morning to the Lava Beds. They had visited them before, and did not care to repeat the visit, as it necessitated a ride of over thirty miles and across a wretched country without any shade whatever. The Modocs who were camped near us were all known Indians. Only one of them— the one who was to be my guide—had taken part in the late war, and he only because compelled to it by Captain Jack and his men. Still it was a matter of surprise that they had been allowed to remain there. The settlers would have been very glad to have got rid of them.

It may not be out of place here to say a few words on the rights and wrongs of the Indians, and to give a brief outline of the Modoc War.

There are altogether about a quarter of a million of tribal Indians now remaining. Some are partly civilised, **but most of** them are in a state of utter barbarism. **The** Cherokees are the most civilised tribe, **and have** their own written language, laws, churches, **and schools.** The good qualities attributed to the red men are, patient endurance, dignity of feeling, and self-**control. Yet, as a** rule, they are treacherous and proud, bloodthirsty, dirty, lazy, and ready to steal, beg, or scalp, as it may suit their purpose.

When in need of anything, they can be humble enough, **and** 'Red Clouds' and 'Spotted Tails' then **swarm into** Washington and try to gammon and overreach the 'Great Father.' The wild Indian still holds **to his** ancient belief, that the white man is a poor weak **creature** who can be humbugged and cheated at every opportunity; and the shifting policy and bad manage**ment of** the American Government does not tend to lessen that belief.

The cost of these Indians, what with agencies, army appropriations, presents, and pensioning, is about eighty million dollars. The mismanagement of the Legislature with regard to the Indians is proverbial, and **a different policy** will be necessary before an end to continual wars and outrages can be expected. The **great** Indian question is said to be, ' White man, got **any rum?'** But that **is** looking at it more from a social than from a political point of view.

It is not because the Government is parsimonious

that the Indians rise up in hostility against the whites; for the Government is generous, and appropriates very largely for the benefit and support of the Indians. But it is because the Government is most indiscreet in its selection of agents to carry out its compacts with the Indians. The Government treats the Indians like men and brethren, and makes all sorts of promises, contracts very formal treaties, and when the big chiefs appear at Washington for a 'pow-wow' sends them back to their hungry tribes with promises of beef, beads, and blankets. It then furnishes unprincipled agents with the necessary goods and provisions, and they for their own gain at once set to work deliberately to swindle and cheat the Indians. While the Indian agent has the opportunity he generally makes the most of his chances, and robs the Indians without let or hindrance—'Cheat the Indian while the contract lasts,' is his motto.

There are some men who have never betrayed the trust reposed in them, but such is not the case with the Indian agent generally. Recent investigation has shown that some contractors used to cheat the Indians out of seven of every eight dollars appropriated for their support by the Government. A very 'elastic currency' is that in which the Indian agents transact their dealings, and may well be called 'Indian robbery.' The record of American legislation with the Indians has been a history of robbery, murder, fraud, and profligacy.

Who can wonder, therefore, that the Indian, driven from his home and hunting-grounds, breaks forth into acts of reprisal, of robbery, and even murder, under the idea that it is a duty, a right and necessary thing to do, even though he be killed for it, and that he ought not to submit tamely to the wrongs inflicted by the white men? How can the Legislature arm the Indian, load his rifle, feed him on beef, and expect that he will not shoot, whilst allowing its agents to cheat him right and left?

The United States Government is firm in its determination that the Indians are neither to be exterminated nor abandoned, but are to be helped and protected. In 1872 President Grant wrote as follows: 'If the present policy towards the Indians can be improved in any way I will always be ready to receive suggestions on the subject; but if any change is made it must be made on the side of civilisation and Christianisation of the Indians. I do not believe our Creator ever placed the different races of men on this earth with the view of the stronger exerting all his energies in exterminating the weaker.'

Even 'reservations,' which it is self-evident are necessary for restricting the depredations and tribal fights of the Indians, present great difficulties to the perplexing character of the Indian question.

No 'reservation' can be large enough to herd buffaloes. The red man must hunt or plough to keep himself alive, and cultivate the ground he will not. The manner of issuing rations on these 'reservations' has not tended to civilise the red men to any great extent.

The agent furnishes the tribe with between one hundred and fifty and two hundred head of cattle at a time. The Indians then drive all but twenty or thirty into an inclosure. Three or four of the copper-coloured wretches then take their rifles and revolvers and commence firing on the herd, taking no aim, but just banging away promiscuously—their great object being apparently more to maim and torture the poor animals than to kill them. The wounded cattle soon set up a bellowing that the red-skins listen to with a delight that could only be excelled if the cries were those of 'pale-face' victims. After the massacre is finished the Indians jump into the corral, and there is then a strife for securing the tongues and other parts of the animals, which eaten raw are very choice to the red man's palate.

Afterwards they turn their attention to the animals reserved for a hunt. These are stampeded across the prairie, and are pursued by the Indians on horseback with lances and revolvers, *à la* buffalo hunt—their tormentors uttering those hideous yells for which they have long been famous.

By means of spears and pistols, the miserable brutes (I refer to the cattle) are so lacerated that they are soon exhausted by loss of blood and the frantic pace at which they have tried to elude their pursuers. When one falls, the Indians try to urge it on, by goading, to another race; but when they fail in this, they stand over the fallen beast and torment it until death ends its miseries. The squaws are then turned out to get the carcases into camp and cut them up. There are sometimes frightful contests among them for choice portions of the animal; and a couple of them may frequently be seen hacking at each other with knives over a tender sirloin. When the last animal is killed, the Indians return to their lodges; their bloodthirstiness whetted to such an edge that the only wonder is that they can be restrained from massacring the entire post.

The Indian Department still does the most extraordinary things. Very lately, two chiefs, named respectively, Santanta and Big Tree, both vile Indian murderers, were captured and imprisoned, instead of being hanged. After some correspondence between the Governor of Texas and the Indian Department, in which the latter almost begged that the prisoners should be released, Santanta and Big Tree were restored to their miserable tribes. And now news has arrived, as might have been expected, that Big Tree has shown his gratitude by leaving the 'reservation' and going again on the war-path—robbing and murdering wherever he can. Western men all agree that there is but one policy to be adopted towards the red man, and that policy consists in the use of the rifle and the revolver. 'Scalp 'em fust and talk to 'em after,' is the sentiment. The Indian Commission lately wanted the Sioux Indians to abandon their reservations in Nebraska and Wyoming. Red Cloud, their chief, had the impudence to demand eleven hundred stand of arms, and one hundred choice white women for squaws. The commissioners offered some arms, but declined to give the women, although it was thought at the time that it would be a fine opportunity for getting rid of the female suffragists. The chances are, they would have received a lesson on 'woman's rights' which they would not easily have forgotten.

There are in all ninety-two reservations, and the tract known as Indian Territory is so extensive that it would hold 250,000 Indians, giving 150 acres to each man, woman, and child; but they care not for acres without buffaloes.

Even the best Indian agents lack the force and power which savages alone respect. At present, if an Indian suffers wrong he is much more likely to go for redress to the officer commanding the nearest military post than to his agent. In the one case, he sees with his own eyes evidence of a force to compel obedience, whereas, in the other, he sees nothing of the kind. **They do not know what influences direct the so-called policy of the Government, and they see** in its shiftiness only **inefficiency.** This brings about the question, why is not the Indian Bureau under the conduct of the War Department, instead of under **that of** the Department of the Interior? Such men as General Sheridan and other able military officers would soon **sweep** away the race of Indian agents and save the country **many** a life, as well as many a dollar.

It **seems** evident, while **the policy** is pursued of treating the Indians as nations or tribes of a character sufficiently independent to entitle them to the right of making treaties, while they are yet to be supported more or less by the Government, that they should remain in the charge of that branch of Government to which the country looks for the enforcement of the terms of the treaty on the part of the Indians; and that branch is the War Department. The military forces are stationed on or near the frontiers, where they can most securely keep in **check the raids and forays of the red men;** and it is right that they should have some voice in preventing needless Indian warfare, which is more fraught with hardship and danger than **any other,** and affords less of that opportunity which is the soldier's highest incentive, and which confers his truest reward.

CHAPTER XVI.

THE MODOCS.

Treachery—Treaties—War—Murders—Modoc success—Peace Commission—Captain Jack—An interview—Warning—Murder of the Peace Commissioners—Marvellous escape—Lower Klamath Lake—The camp—The Lava Beds—Panic—Savage squaws—Warm Spring Indians—Surrender—Execution—Pelicans—Graves—After dark.

THE Modocs are an offshoot of the Klamath Indians, a tribe which has always evinced a quarrelsome and warlike spirit. During one of their insurrections a chief of the name of Modocus broke off with his followers from the rest of the tribe, and established an independent nation.

In 1864, some horses having been stolen from the white settlers, a war was commenced against the Modocs. In the course of this war numbers of emigrants were waylaid, tortured, and slain, and in consequence a company of white men proceeded to the Modoc country to avenge these wrongs. After first trying poison, and failing, they got the Indians to agree to a 'peace-talk.' The Indians arrived at the appointed meeting-place and laid down their bows. Upon a signal being given, the whites, with a treachery only equalled later by the murder of the Peace Commissioners, opened fire on the Indians, and forty out of forty-five were slain. In the same year a treaty was made with Schonchin and Captain Jack, chief and sub-chief of the band, in which they agreed to take up their residence on the 'reservation.' After a short time they got tired of their new quarters and returned to the old ones. Several unsuccessful attempts were then made to get them to return to the Klamath reservation; and in 1869 the Superintendent determined that if possible Captain Jack, who had then become chief, should, with his followers, be sent back. A message was dispatched, asking him to meet the Superintendent half-way. The answer returned was to the effect, that if the Superintendent wished to see Captain Jack he must come to him.

The Superintendent then visited the Modocs, and found the chief surrounded by seventy or eighty warriors. A feast was proposed, but declined—for Jack well remembered the poisoned banquet of 1864. Finally, however, he consented to return to the Klamath reservation, on condition that he should be allowed to choose his own dwelling-place. But the 'medicine-man' objected to this, and, drawing his revolver, said that they would not go there at all.

After some discussion, Jack retired to his camp to hold a council, at which, as was afterwards found out, a proposal was made to assassinate the white party. Whilst the latter were anxiously awaiting the result of the council, a detachment of soldiers arrived. The Modocs were disarmed, and removed on the following day to Lake Klamath. But Jack had escaped to the Lava Beds. Messengers were sent to him, and he agreed to come in, provided that the Klamath Indians should not be allowed to taunt him with being a coward.

This was agreed to, and the Modoc band was handed over to the care of the agent. Jack now made up his mind to remain on the 'reservation,' but after a time the Klamaths began to insult him; and having appealed to the agent, he was provided with a new home. The same thing happened again, and at last he declared he would no longer remain in a home that was no home to him at all, and accordingly he left the 'reservation.' Towards the end of November 1872 the newly-appointed agent sent orders to place the Modocs on their 'reservation' peaceably, if possible, but by force if necessary.

The Indian camp was surprised, and one man refused to surrender. He was disarmed; a fight ensued, and the Modoc War was begun. The news immediately spread to the settlers, who organised themselves, and operations for attack and defence were conducted with ardour. Fourteen settlers were killed, and many

R

more would probably have been murdered but for timely warning given by friendly Modocs who had received kindness from the owners of some of the ranches scattered about the district. Volunteers were organised; 400 soldiers were sent up, who at the first battle near Lost River retreated under cover of a brisk fire. This victory gave great encouragement to the Modocs.

The feeling against the Indians on the part of the settlers was most bitter, on account of the numerous murders that they had committed; and although Captain Jack was willing to make peace, the majority opposed him, and they determined to fight it out.

Great preparations for war followed the first defeat; troops were concentrated, and the Modocs, who had gradually retreated to the fastnesses of the Lava Beds, sent out emissaries to all the tribes on the north-west.

At this time the Peace Commission was resolved upon, and in February it succeeded in opening communication between head-quarters and the camp at the Lava Beds. Terms of peace were continually proposed, and were at first accepted, then rejected by the Indians. But at last, on April the 2nd, 1873, the Commissioners met the Modocs about half-way between the stronghold and the Lava Beds. After the usual preliminaries the talk began, and Captain Jack stated his grievances. He said he had always advised his men not to fight, and that all he wanted was a home on Lost River. As this could not be conceded the meeting was adjourned; and when the Commissioners returned to the camp they felt that they had narrowly escaped with their lives, and determined to trust the Modocs no more.

However, two days after, Captain Jack sent a message asking Mr. Meacham, one of the Commissioners, to meet him alone. This was thought very dangerous; but Mr. Meacham, who had had considerable experience of the Modocs, bravely determined to accept the invitation.

The report of the meeting is as follows:—Captain Jack said: 'I was born free. I was not made for a slave. I will not ask any man where I can go. I am not a boy. I am no woman. God gave me this country. He put me here first. The white man found me here, but now wants it all. I only want a small place for my people. I want to live like a white man. I never beg or steal. I pay my debts, and no man can say I ever cheated him. I do not want the President to give me anything. I can take care of my people, if you will take the soldiers away.'

Mr. Meacham then asked that the men who had committed the atrocities on Lost River should be given up.

'Who will try them,' Jack asked, 'whites or Indians?' 'Whites,' was the reply. 'Will you give up the whites who killed the Indians?' was Captain Jack's next question. He was answered 'No.' Upon which he said that the law was all on one side; but the meeting terminated amicably, and Jack abandoned his claim on Lost River.

Three or four days elapsed before another meeting could take place, and in the meantime a Modoc squaw, belonging to a half-breed who acted as interpreter, returned from a visit to the Lava Beds, and said that she had been told that the white men must not go there any more, for they would be killed.

At the first meeting, on April the 2nd, it had been agreed to hold another 'talk' at the Peace Commission tent on April the 11th. By the terms of the meeting, five unarmed men on each side were to discuss the points in question.

The Modocs said that if the Commissioners would show their confidence in them in this manner, they would have like confidence, and would all come in and surrender.

The terms were accepted by Doctor Thomas, by the advice of General Canby; but Messrs Meacham and Dyar opposed the views of General Canby and Doctor Thomas, feeling sure, after the warning received, that something was wrong. At length, having great reliance on the experience of General Canby, they consented to keep the appointment. As they were setting out, the squaw who had before told them of their danger held Mr. Meacham's horse, saying, 'Meacham, you no go; they kill you.'

A consultation was held, and in spite of Mr. Meacham's utmost efforts to prevent it they determined to keep the engagement with the Indians. Doctor Thomas was strong in his faith that God would protect them.

On reaching the ground the party found Captain Jack and his warriors already assembled. The first few minutes were passed in what was evidently manœuvring for position; the Indians continually making changes, so as to bring the Commission party near together, and as far from themselves as possible. At last Hooka Jim, one of the Modocs, went up to Mr. Meacham's horse and secured it with a rope. He then slowly and quietly put on Mr. M.'s coat, and this action confirmed the belief of all, except Doctor Thomas, that treachery was intended.

General Canby made a short speech, and then asked Doctor Thomas to talk. The Doctor in a few words informed the Indians that he and the others were sent there by the President of the United States, and that no more bloodshed was wanted. When he had finished, Jack rose to his feet and stepped to the right of General

Canby, and Schonchin moved to the side that Jack had left.

Jack then made a short speech, and while Riddle was interpreting it two warriors were seen approaching from ambush, each with an armful of guns. The party all sprang to their feet, with the exception of the squaw, who threw herself flat on the ground.

Mr. Meacham said to Jack, 'What does this mean?' He replied by drawing a pistol and calling out that all was ready. Many pistol-shots were fired, one of which struck the General in the face. He retreated, pursued by Jack and another Indian, a distance of forty yards. At last he fell on the rocks, when Jack stabbed him in the neck, and the other Indian shot him through the head with a rifle, and stripped him of his clothing. After the first shot, Doctor Thomas was taunted with not believing the squaw when she told him of the danger, and was almost immediately shot dead by Boston Charley. Schonchin was to have been the executioner of Mr. Meacham, and he approached him with a revolver and knife. The first shot grazed his shoulder, the small pistol that Mr. Meacham had drawn probably spoiling the Indian's aim. Mr. Meacham's pistol missed fire, and he ran towards a small ridge of rocks amidst a shower of bullets, one of which struck him on the temple, another in the arm, a third on the head and rendered him unconscious. The Indians then proceeded to strip

him, and Boston Charley began to take his scalp with a
blunt knife, and had lifted five or six inches of skin,
when the cry of 'Soldiers! soldiers!' was raised, and
the work was left unfinished. The Indians then retreated to the Lava Beds, and war was resumed.

And now let us take a look at these Lava Beds,
where the Modocs for so long baffled all the efforts of
the United States troops in their attempts to dislodge
them.

The ride thither from our camp was over a wild
desolate country of rock and sage-brush. We skirted
Lower Klamath Lake—a vast sheet of muddy water,
fringed with tall rushes, from the midst of which rose
numerous herons and cranes. After crossing several
rocky ridges and levels of brown brush, scantily stocked
with sage-hens, we entered a long narrow valley, flanked
by low steep hills on our right, and on our left by a
stretch of mountain, level at the top and bearing the
name of 'Table Mountain.' Riding along the line of
dust that ran through the valley of brush, and over the
alkali plains, was wearisome in the extreme, and the
heat was almost unbearable, there being no water fit to
drink in those parts—even the horses declining the
stagnant pools of Lower Klamath Lake. Turning
abruptly off to the left, we gradually ascended till we
reached the high bluff where the camp of General

Gillem was pitched, and below us, spread out at our feet, lay the far-famed Lava Beds.

The Lava Beds must be about three miles long and about a mile broad. They are bounded on one side by Tule Lake, on the other by mountains and hills, and throughout are covered with natural fortifications. The principal part of the Modoc camp was a large opening in the ravine, of about an acre in area, and on all sides of which rises a wall a hundred feet in height, forming a bowl with sloping sides. A flat surface of lava extends back for more than a mile from the summit of the wall, and this flat has numerous holes with small openings, which widen downwards into large caves. The caves communicate with one another and with the camp. Huge rocks, two and three hundred feet in height, rise from the earth almost perpendicularly, and sometimes a narrow path leads to the top of them, the summit being defended by a breastwork of rock.

One man could keep a hundred at bay in these volcanic caverns.

A small body of troops advanced a considerable distance on one occasion amongst the beds of lava, and were resting in what they considered a perfectly safe position, when suddenly they were surrounded on all sides, and hardly one of them escaped. It was afterwards discovered that two men of this party had been only wounded, and had managed to hide themselves; but as soon as it was dark the Indians came out of their caves to scalp the dead, and the two men were found and dragged to the camp, where the squaws beat them to death with clubs.

The successes of the Modocs in their stronghold led to a complete change of tactics with the Americans and to a change of commanders, and such efforts were then made to dislodge the enemy that four of the most redoubtable of the Modoc warriors, perceiving that the pursuit was going to be relentless and lasting, threw down their arms and surrendered. They even offered themselves as scouts, and turned States' evidence against their comrades. They were notoriously the most bloodthirsty and dangerous of the band, and certainly deserved the same punishment as was afterwards awarded to Captain Jack; but General Davis having accepted their services and promised them protection as a reward for the capture of the murderers of the Peace Commissioners, the gallows was cheated of some very deserving subjects.

Nettled by disasters, and roused by the cry of vengeance from all parts of the country, the troops redoubled their efforts; the Modocs were hunted from stronghold to stronghold, from ravine to ravine, and finally, at the beginning of June, Captain Jack gave himself up. A few days later the last of a band that had spread terror throughout the settlements of Northern California and Southern Oregon, and had for a long time defied the whole of the military force sent against them, also delivered themselves up, and the war, unparalleled for its ferocity and murderous success on the side of the Indians, was ended.

The execution of Captain Jack, Schonchin, Boston Charley, and Hooka Jim, in October, at Fort Klamath, was the last act in the Modoc drama. The three last-named died with Indian stoicism; but bravely and courageously in comparison with their acknowledged chief, Captain Jack, who was utterly broken and unnerved. When they ascended the scaffold, a mournful wail from the 500 Klamath Indians who had assembled to witness the execution filled the air. A few moments later, and the spirits of Captain Jack and his three companions departed to the happy hunting-grounds.

To return to our expedition to the Lava Beds; we descended the steep trail of the bluff, wending our way towards the lake, with the hope of finding the water fit to drink; but to our disgust it was perfectly poisonous, and the air was tainted with the odour of myriads of dead fish which were floating on the lake, having been killed by the great heat.

Hundreds of pelicans and wild fowl of various descriptions rose up as we approached, and my Indian guide gave me a sample of his skill, by firing at a string of pelicans as they flew over his head, and missing them all; much to his dismay, as he had tried to make me understand that he was wonderfully expert with his carbine.

After tying up our horses we visited the Lava Beds on foot, passing on our way a small enclosure filled with the graves of many poor fellows who had fallen in the late conflict. Captain Jack's cave and headquarters and other curious hollows and natural fortifications were next inspected; but as it was getting dark, and we had a tedious return journey to make, I could not devote much time to the examination of the different points of interest in these strangely desolate regions.

The country round was full of rattle-snakes. I managed to kill two, and was afterwards very careful where I put my foot when walking on the sage-brush.

Long before we reached the camp the deep rose-purple of the eastern hills had faded away, and so dark a night set in that even the Indian gave up the attempt to follow the trail. But, fortunately, the unerring instinct of our horses enabled them to find their way in the darkness as well as in the light.

By midnight we were home again, and the following week I said farewell to my hospitable friends, and in company with an American artist and a German traveller crossed the Klamath river into Oregon; and from Jacksonville set out for the Mystic Lake, in the beautiful Klamath Land.

CHAPTER XVII.

FORT KLAMATH TO THE MYSTIC LAKE.

A custom—Fort Klamath—The agency—Dead Indian country—The Lake of the Woods—An Indian workshop—A cañon—Snow-fields—The crater's rim—A snow-camp—An alarm—O-po-co-ninne—Mystic Lake—A canoe—The medicine man—The island—Law of death—Midnight—Internal fires—Surmises.

THE national American custom of drinking at 'the bar' admits of many forms of invitation. At San Francisco the latest mode of expression was 'Will you go on a bond?' When we arrived at Jacksonville we found that the form used was much more expressive, and 'Stranger, let's irrigate,' was the one most constantly in use. There is a pastoral suggestion in that invitation which is not possessed by any other, and you feel, when thus addressed, as if a proposal were made to extend a benefit over the country in general, as well as on yourself.

It certainly was excessively hot at Jacksonville, which may have accounted for the perpetual dryness which seemed to prevail there. If the farmers of that part of the country would but irrigate their lands as well as they irrigate themselves there would surely never be any cause to complain of scanty crops and dry weather.

Jacksonville had few inducements to detain us, and as soon as we could obtain horses and a guide we started for Fort Klamath, which we reached on the third day.

There we saw the unfortunate Modoc prisoners, and afterwards started on some delightful expeditions into the Klamath country.

The Indian Agency and the military fort occupy a beautiful position on Great Klamath Lake, which lies close under the mountain shadows. Above the lake a lovely prairie reaches to the mountains which enclose the valley on three sides. The Indians call it the 'Beautiful Land of Flowing Water,' and it deserves the name. Streams of the purest water rise from the hillsides; and the water is so clear that the smallest pebble is visible at a depth of ten or fifteen feet. These rivulets wind amongst beds of willows, through green meadows and clumps of evergreens, and at last flow into the lake. From the Agency, which is distant about five miles from the fort, the view is most romantic. The distant snow-peaks encircle the valley with their white walls, as if guarding the home of the Klamaths. To the north, Mount Scott rises to a height of 10,000 feet; to the left, Mount Pitt looks down on the valley from an altitude of 11,000 feet; and nestling at its southern base is Glacier Lake, which is supplied by the melting snow, and whose shores are bordered by pine forests and fine grazing lands.

Towards the west is discerned the 'Snowy Chester,' a circle of twelve snowy peaks, enclosing a lava bed twenty miles in circumference, and dotted with small circular lakes, probably the craters from which the peaks were thrown up long before the Indian made it his favourite resort.

To the east lies Dead Indian Country, and beyond it there is a beautiful sheet of water, called the 'Lake of the Woods,' enclosed by a forest so dense and dark that the sun's rays cannot pierce and brighten its gloomy depths. Near this lake, we were shown what must have been the spot used by Indians in olden times as a manufactory for arrow-heads and spears. The remains of a log-hut, and a few circles of stones, evidently fireplaces, from their blackened litter, were all the signs of an Indian camp that we could see. But our guide told us that numbers of chipped arrow and spear heads and the rough rocks on which they had been sharpened, and some pieces of flint and obsidian, had been found there a short time ago.

Now, of course, the Indians use firearms, and when they want arrow-heads and spears they buy metal for the purpose from the white men. But it is not so very long ago that they chipped the agate, jasper, and chalcedony, and laughed and sang in the pine woods by the quiet lake—knowing nothing of the pale-faced race, and living on in the happy thought that the home of their ancestors was to be their own for ever.

One bright morning we mounted our ponies and started for the Mystic Lake, in the Cascade Mountains, distant about twenty-five miles. The trail ran through a gently rising thickly wooded country, fragrant with the laurel and pine, and abounding with wild flowers. Sometimes the tall grass in the narrow meadows swept up to our stirrups; sometimes no trace of vegetation was to be seen—save the stunted hemlock growing amidst lava boulders and pumice-stone rocks.

As fast as possible we made our way till we reached an elevation where undergrowth became scarce, and we then found ourselves on the brink of a splendid cañon whose walls were supported by basaltic columns several hundred feet in height. A foaming torrent dashed through the gorge, and many thread-like waterfalls tumbled into the deep abyss amidst a luxuriance of madrona and manzanita bushes.

Our artist companion was very anxious to make a halt for the purpose of sketching the scene; but it could not be, for the sun was already sinking, and we had miles of snow yet to cross. Taking the snow-field, we pressed up the mountain-side towards the black line above us, which the guide told us was the rim of the crater.

Soon we entered a belt of dwarf hemlock, whose

tops had been cut by the strong winds to an even height, thus giving it the appearance of a well-clipped hedge.

We crunched over the snow without hindrance; for it was so hard in most places that the horses' hoofs made no impression, beyond sending myriads of frozen particles flying from the hard crust and sparkling like diamonds in the light of the afternoon sun. Occasionally, in more exposed parts, the animals would flounder in through the yielding surface, and we had to zigzag upwards to avoid the swift torrents fed by the melting snows and descending the narrow ravines. At last, after crossing an open stretch, we reached the black line on the ridge that forms part of the wide circling rim of the Mystic Lake, which lay fifteen hundred feet below us. But the dark shadow of the mountains already covered it when we arrived at the summit, and nothing could be distinguished in the sombre depths beneath. We therefore busied ourselves in preparing our camp for the night.

In a small ravine sheltered by snow-walls we kindled a huge fire of the broken boughs of hemlock and pine; then we cut or scooped out a cave in the hard congealed mass, in which we spread our blankets. After supper we turned in, and found our snow bedroom as snug, comfortable, and warm as a brick walled chamber, and decidedly more picturesque.

The night was bitterly cold and the winds swept

mournfully around us, but we slept the sound sleep of 'tired nature' after our long mountain ride; our surroundings of snow and fire shielding us from the cold blasts. Towards midnight we were suddenly awakened by a hoarse hideous yell, which echoed from every peak and crag of the neighbouring mountains. The warwhoop of a hundred wild Indians close upon us could alone be likened to it. The profound stillness that followed made us doubt whether we had not been dreaming; when suddenly the light of a very bright moon revealed to us a dark creeping object stealing round the shadowed corner of a steep rock, and before we could well distinguish its outline another burst of music told us that 'O-po-co-ninne,' our pack-mule, or rather donkey, had broken his tether, and was about to pay us a visit. In a few moments he had found out our whereabouts, and was enjoying the warmth of our big fire, sublimely unconscious of the confusion and alarm he had created.

One of our poets (Coleridge, I think) says of the donkey—

> 'Poor foal of an oppressed race,
> I love the languid patience of thy face;
> And oft with gentle hand I give thee bread,
> And clap thy ragged coat, and pat thy head.'

When he behaves himself, I do the same, but when he awakes me in the middle of the night, and then, after stumbling over my feet and kicking me, finally settles himself down across my legs, just too as I am dozing off into a comfortable sleep, why, it is necessary to use means more forcibly striking than 'a pat on the head' to bring him to his senses. At the first gleams of daylight we were up, ready to welcome the sun when it should light up the dark waters of the lake with its cheering beams. A marvellous sight is the Mystic, or Crater Lake, as it is sometimes called. It is about ten miles long and seven or eight broad, and the mountain wall which surrounds it is a sheer cliff rising from fifteen hundred to three thousand feet. The height we reached was about 9,000 feet above the level of the sea. The walled-in waters look up to grey cliffs edged with ragged pinnacles of red lava.

At the water's edge is a rim of boulders, but no beach, no friendly shore—the solid smooth basalt closely encircling the deep blue water.

By-and-by the sun's rays glimmered on the crest of Mount Scott, throwing a shadow half across the lake; then other peaks shone out, and a little later the rim of the crater was struck, and in about an hour the waters below were sparkling and gleaming in the full glow of sunshine. Gazing down we saw the perpendicular walls reflected in those waters of unknown depth. The mountains and shrubs appeared as distinct below them as above. It was impossible to say where the land ended and the lake began, so mirror-like was the surface of the water. So still, too, so unruffled, almost death-like in their calmness, were these azure blue waters lying at the base of the steep grey rocks, and forming, with the surrounding lofty mountains, whose snow-covered sides and peaks towered high above us, a grand, strange, and most impressive scene —the haunt of the Nereids below, the abode of the Snow King above.

On the south-west side of the lake an island juts up, formed of volcanic rock, and having a crater on its summit. The cone of lava is nearly two hundred feet in height, and the sides from a distance looked smooth and symmetrical. Suddenly, near the island, a little speck appeared, and

> 'O'er the water floating, flying,
> Something in the hazy distance,
> Something in the mists of morning,
> Loomed and lifted from the water,
> Now seemed floating, now seemed flying,
> Coming nearer, nearer, nearer.
> Was it Shingebis the diver?
> Or the pelican, the Shada?
> Or the heron, the Shuh-shuh-gah?
> Or the white goose, Waw-be-wawa,
> With the water dripping, flashing
> From its glossy neck and feathers?
> It was neither goose nor diver,
> Neither pelican nor heron,
> O'er the water floating, flying,
> Through the shining mist of morning,
> But a birch canoe, with paddles,
> Rising, sinking on the water,
> Dripping, flashing in the sunshine.'

The guide knew an old Indian trail leading down to the water's edge; we therefore agreed to descend and persuade the occupant of the canoe to take us to the island. The trail was partly covered with brushwood and small pines, which proved very useful in aiding our descent. The glaciers and the snow-walls which overhung the cliffs made our journey rather a perilous one; but we reached the water's edge safely, and there found a hideous old Indian, just about to land—the trail down which we had come being the only road to and from the lake. The guide understood from the Indian that he was a 'medicine man,' and had come there 'to hear the whispers of unseen beings borne on the breath of the wild winds that swept over the waters, and to talk with the Great Spirit who lived on the shores of the dread lake; that, when he had concluded his business with Manitou, and had seen the fairy canoes sailing over the goblin waters, and had given his messages to the departed spirits who bathed in its mystic depths, he would return to his tribe with a charmed life and possessed of supernatural powers.'

As the canoe could only hold two persons, and that with great difficulty, the artist and our guide remained on shore, and the German and myself, after a couple of hours' paddling, reached the island, and landed on the lava beach. We found the cone, which had looked so smooth from a distance, rough and rugged, and aided by the hemlock which grew over the surface we soon climbed to the top. There we found a crater about a hundred feet deep and over two hundred feet across.

On one side there were traces of steps cut into the **lava,** but so broken and dangerous as not to invite a descent. This island seems to have been the last effort **of** the volcano, when the mountain had nearly burnt itself **out, and** from its base a ridge of lava reached for a long distance towards the western shore. The depth of the lake is unknown, but it is said to have been sounded unavailingly to the depth of one thousand feet.

We reached our camp that evening very hungry **and** tired, and were greeted **by** 'Opo-co-ninne' in his best musical style. As we intended to have a moonlight view of the lake we kept ourselves awake **by** giving an impromptu entertainment, consisting of stories, singing, **and** recitations, to the wandering spirits who chanced to be floating around.

One of the poems recited **by** the artist, who was an admirable elocutionist, had been read in many a deso**lated house** in Memphis during the dreadful yellow fever pestilence which had lately depopulated the town.

At my **request he wrote it** out, and it runs as follows:—

THE LAW OF DEATH.

BY JOHN HAY.

The song of Kilvany—fairest she
In all the land of Savatthi.
She had one child, as sweet **and gay**
And **dear** to her as the light of **day.**

She was so young and he so fair,
The same bright eyes and the same dark hair;
To see them by the blossomy way,
They seemed two children at their play.

There came a death-dart from the sky—
Kilvany saw her darling die;
The glimmering shade his eyes invades,
Out of his cheek the red bloom fades;
His warm heart feels the icy chill,
The round limbs shudder and are still.
And yet Kilvany held him fast
Long after life's last pulse was past;
As if her kisses could restore
The smile gone out for evermore.

But when she saw her child was dead
She scattered ashes on her head,
And seized the small corpse, pale and sweet,
And rushing wildly through the street,
She sobbing fell at Buddha's feet.

'Master! all helpful! help me now!
Here at thy feet I humbly bow;
Have mercy, Buddha! help me now!'
She grovelled on the marble floor,
And kissed the dead child o'er and o'er;
And suddenly upon the air
There fell the answer to her prayer:
'Bring me to-night a lotus, tied
With thread from a house where none has died.'

She rose, and laughed with thankful joy,
Sure that the god would save the boy.
She found a lotus by the stream:
She plucked it from its noonday dream,
And then from door to door she fared,
To ask what house by death was spared.
Her heart grew cold to see the eyes
Of all dilate with slow surprise.
'Kilvany, thou hast lost thy head;
Nothing can help a child that's dead.
There stands not by the Ganges' side
A house where none hath ever died.'

Thus through the long and weary day
From every **door** she bore away
Within her heart, and on her arm,
A heavier load, a deeper harm.
By gates of gold and ivory,
By wattled huts of poverty,
The same refrain heard poor Kilvany:
'The living are few—the dead are many.'

The evening came **so still and fleet,**
And overtook her hurrying feet,
And, heart-sick, by the sacred fane
She fell and prayed the god again.
She sobbed and beat her bursting breast:
'Ah! thou hast mocked me! Mightiest!
Lo! I have wandered far and wide—
There stands no house where none hath died.'
And Buddha answered, in a tone
Soft as a lute at twilight blown,
But grand as heaven and strong as death
To him who hears with ears of faith:
'Child, thou art answered! Murmur **not!**
Bow, and accept the common lot.'

Kilvany heard with reverence meet,
And laid her child at Buddha's feet.

At midnight the view of the Mystic Lake was not merely grand, but perfectly fairy-like in its weird splendour. The crater-peak of the island rose like a silver pillar from a mass of molten gold—so magical was the effect of the moon's rays as they fell on the still lake. The shadows of the high cliffs mingled with the moonbeams, and everything floated in a silver haze before us. Nothing seemed real. The crags and snow pinnacles stood out with distinctness, but as if seen through silver gauze. The stars looked down from the steel-blue sky, like great eyes gazing into the deep waters, from whose clear depths they were reflected back with a brilliancy scarcely less than their own; whilst the cold glittering moon shed a mysterious light over the silent volcanic region, and gave to it that appearance of eternal death which is said to reign in her own exhausted bosom. Once only, as we watched and listened, a gentle moaning wind swept over the broken tops of the gnarled pine trees around the rim of the vast crater, and after rippling the smooth surface of the lake into golden ladders died away as gradually as it had arisen.

Nothing would have seemed more natural than to have beheld fairy barks gliding over the deep lake waters, and urged on by unseen hands to the music of the spirit voices; nor would it have appeared strange to have heard issuing from the silvery vapour clear familiar tones, whispering the prayers that perhaps were uttered far, far away.

Silently we turned from the too-bewildering scene; and having looked our last on the Mystic Lake, with a sense of relief we threw ourselves down on our rugs by the pine-fire and talked till we fell asleep.

There is little doubt but that ages ago there stood here a vast volcanic mountain, higher perhaps than any in the world, the clustered heights and peaks around us forming but a small portion of its cliffs and spurs, and reaching only a comparatively short distance up the original central cone.

Where the vast sheet of water forming the lake comes from is an interesting question. There is no visible outlet, but it probably finds an underground passage leading to the waters of the Rogue River, which rises near the western base of the mountain, and to Wood River, which feeds the Klamath Lake, on the south-east.

The waters of the lake do not rise or fall, and their depth is unknown. Where the waters go to, may be surmised, but where they come from, who can tell?

The Western Land furnishes many memories of grand and striking scenes, but none awaken such feelings of solemn wonder as those of the Mystic Lake.

CHAPTER XVIII.

FROM JACKSONVILLE TO THE COLUMBIA RIVER.

Oregon forests—The Umpqua Cañon—A poultry fancier—A female hermit—Willamette Valley—Eugene City—The Three Sisters—The Mackenzie River—Oregon City—Falls of the Willamette—Portland—The Columbia River—Scenery—The Multanomah Falls—Castle Rock—Cape Horn—The Cascades—A portage—Coffin Rock—Dalles—A Sahara—Catching salmon—Great Salmon Falls—Fish eagles—A crane story.

FROM Jacksonville to Rosebury is only about a hundred miles, and there, thank Heaven! good-bye to the old coach.

After crossing Rogue River—a splendid stream, and full of fish—we entered the Umpqua mountains. In Oregon the size of the forests is much greater than in California. The trees themselves too are larger. Firs are more numerous than pines, and the splendid madrona laurel gives the country a semi-tropical appearance. Birch, balsam, spruce, and other trees of more Northern climes grow everywhere, and the oaks spread themselves almost as grandly as in Northern California. There, they grow in groups or clumps, and preserve just so much distance between each other as allows of their full development, at the same time presenting a mass of foliage of **great beauty** and fine form. A rare maple, called **from** its curious grain the ' **curly** ' maple, is **also found** in Oregon. When polished, it is one of the most beautiful woods I ever saw.

The Umpqua Cañon was formerly an ill-omened pass for travellers. It is the resort of the Rogue Indians, who infest the country, and are very quarrelsome and dangerous. When an emigrant train was approaching, the Indians would send a party on in front **to form** an ambuscade, **and others** would follow the doomed waggons **into** the melancholy cañon, where nothing but bleached **bones would** remain to tell the murderous tale to the next travellers. Numbers of little wooden crosses still point out the spot of many a ruthless **slaughter.**

At one of the small farms where we stopped **for** dinner—or rather supper, as any meal after breakfast is always called—we were regaled on fowls (not chickens) in all **sorts of** disguises, but in one respect all alike—their extreme toughness. Our driver afterwards told me that the proprietor of the farm was a little mad on the subject of poultry, and **that** it was generally supposed **he** fed the fowls on sawdust instead of corn-meal. There was a story, he said, of one strong-minded hen **having** laid a nest-full of bureau-knobs, and **that after sitting** on them for three or four weeks she had hatched a complete set of drawing-room furniture.

There was certainly an immense number of aged hens running about, and each had her name—to which, by the way, she never answered—thereby causing much sorrow to the proprietor, who seemed to me to pass his time in chasing the unfortunate birds about the grounds and throwing sticks at them.

He reminded me of a strange character who lives at a place called Oak Bluffs—an old woman of ninety —tall, crooked, and with a grim face surrounded by unkempt grizzly hair. In her youth she had been jilted by her sailor lover, whereupon she vowed to retire from the world, and has since lived alone at the above desolate dreary spot. Her dwelling is a low wooden shed, surrounded by old haystacks, and near a wood of brush and oak trees. A red cow and about a dozen hens are her only companions. To these she has given the most extraordinary names, and she sings and talks to them as if they were human beings. A graveyard is set apart for her favourites, and tombstones mark their graves.

She is called a poetess, most of her effusions being in blank verse.

Not long before our visit one of her chickens was carried off by the ' pip,' upon which she composed a pathetic lament, concluding with ' Then the Lord thought best to take her from evil to come.'

She has also written a lengthy treatise on ' Doctoring

Hens,' which with her 'poetry' she sells to visitors. She must have made a nice little sum by this time, as all who visit the neighbourhood go to see her.

Oregon is a grand country for sheep, and Oregon wool is celebrated for its fineness and flexibility. At one place a farmer told me he had that season sheared a Spanish merino sheep whose fleece weighed twenty-three pounds.

Roseburg at last! The shrill scream of the iron horse betokened that we were once more in civilised regions; and soon after we were on our way to Portland—about two hundred miles distant by rail. Leaving Roseburg, we entered a most charming gorge, thickly clothed with dark pines, silver cedars, and magnificent laurel trees. Grand rocks, softened by mosses and clinging vines, towered far above us; and at our feet a swift, bright stream ran through groves of azaleas and golden willows. From the number of tents and waggons we passed, the greater part of the population from the adjacent villages must have been camping out in the ravine, and it certainly looked most cool and inviting. A lovely spot indeed to sojourn in, if one could only be satisfied with the delights of mountain scenery and clear blue waters dancing in the sunlight!

Following the banks of the Willamette River, we arrived at Eugene City, where the snow-clad summits of the 'Three Sisters' loomed in sight. The Indians believe that these three peaks were three giantesses who had rebelled against their husband, Manitou, and were in consequence turned into stone. They rise from a range of volcanic hills, and are of an exact pyramidal form and of equal size.

A broad belt of forest encircles them and extends to an altitude of 6,000 feet. Above this belt, untrodden snow lies in broad glittering fields.

The Mackenzie River flows through the plain, and is singularly beautiful. Great blocks of basalt come sheer down to the water's edge, and are divided naturally with great exactitude into huge segments. Their yellow and brown colours are reflected with wondrous effect on the surface of the stream. After a few most pleasant days, passed in the neighbourhood of Eugene City, I went on to Oregon City, and there remained to visit the Falls of the Willamette.

The river narrows near the town, and the water, rushing very swiftly, is precipitated down a fall of about 50 feet. The rocks on either side are of deep black basalt; and these huge walls, when viewed from the south, are extremely grand. It is only when they are seen from below that the mind is fully impressed with the magnificence of these falls. They have been worn into a horse-shoe form by the action of the stream, and the river plunges into the depths below in great curves and sweeping currents. Masses of broken basalt show their heads amidst the rush of foaming waters, and altogether there is noise, mist, and confusion enough to justify the Oregonians in their pride of their miniature Niagara. Formerly, these falls were the only obstruction to the free navigation of the river, but now it is overcome by the construction of locks, which have been built in the most substantial manner. The scenery of the river is very picturesque and diversified, and a lovely panorama of hill and dale, water and forest is continually passing before the view.

Portland had lately been nearly destroyed by fire, consequently I had not a good opportunity of judging of the town. It is, however, beautifully situated on the Willamette River, and is surrounded by magnificent forests. There are some delightful drives through the woods, one especially to a place called the White House, through a succession of glades and glens full of splendid trees and sweet-scented shrubs, and with views of peculiarly quiet loveliness.

The Willamette runs into the Columbia River about twelve miles below Portland; so, taking the morning steamer, I prepared to ascend that river, which for grandeur of scenery is not surpassed by any river (with the exception, perhaps, of the Fraser) on the American continent.

We started so early that a grey fog swallowed up

VIEW ON THE COLUMBIA RIVER.   P. 273.

everything, and the only objects visible were the paddle-boxes and the funnel.

We steamed very slowly and cautiously down the Willamette, and as we approached the junction of that river with the Columbia the mist lifted. As it slowly crept back to the shores and up the hills and away to the north, mountains sky and river came out with intense brilliancy and colour under the rays of the rising sun.

Wonderful forests extended from the far distance down to the very edge of the river. Beeches, oaks, pines, and firs of enormous size formed a sombre back-ground, against which the maple and ash flamed out in their early autumn tints. On the north, the four stately snow-crowned mountains, Rainier, St. Helen's, Jefferson, and Adams lifted themselves, rose-flushed, high up in the heavens; the great river flowed rapidly and smoothly between mountain shores, from a mile to a mile and a quarter apart, and the bold rocky heights towered thousands of feet in the air.

These mountains line the river for miles. When occasionally a deep ravine opens you catch a glimpse of distant levels, bounded, in their turn, by the never-ending chain of mountains.

There is a rare combination, too, of beauty about these mountains; vegetation and great variety of colour heightening the picturesque effect of the huge masses of bold bare rock.

Now and then the cliffs impeded the flow of the river, which then ran, disturbed and dangerous, between rocky islands and sand-bars. Often the agitated waters became gradually calm and formed long narrow lakes, without any apparent outlet, until a sudden turn showed a passage through the lofty walls into another link of the water-chain.

Sometimes a cataract of marvellous beauty came leaping down the rocks from a height of 200 and 300 feet.

The Multanomah Falls in particular are most beautiful, possessing both the swift resistless rush of the steady downpour of water and that broken picturesque outline which is the principal charm of a fall.

Castle Rock, a huge boulder with basaltic columns like those of Staffa, stands out grandly and alone from a feathery mass of cotton-wood, whose golden splendour rivals in beauty that of the spreading dark green boughs of the pines, whilst the contrast of colour heightens the effect of each brilliant hue.

On the crest of the rock a fringe of pine-trees, growing out of the bare stone and dwarfed to insignificance, shows the vast height of this rifted dome.

And now we are approaching Cape Horn, whose

ramparts rise sheer and straight, like a **columnar wall, 800 feet high.**

This majestic portal forms a worthy entrance to the **cascades.** Fierce seething rapids extend for six miles up the river, and the track of the 'portage' runs near the **water's edge for** the entire **distance.** The river is **narrowed here by lofty heights of trap rock,** and the bed itself is nothing but sharp gigantic rocks, sometimes hidden by the water and sometimes forming small islands, between which the foaming torrent rushes with tremendous uproar.

Near where the 'portage' begins, a relic of Indian **warfare,** in the shape **of** an old block-house, stands **under** the fir-trees.

A small party of white men held a very large body **of** Indians at bay there for several days in 1856; and as the provisions ran short, a grand attack was made on the red men, **who** were totally routed with great **slaughter.**

The scene in this gorge is wild in the extreme. Passing Rooster Rock, the mountain sides approach **each other, and** the river flows faster and fiercer; the pillared **walls rise** sometimes to a height of nearly 3,000 feet, **and the wind** roaring through the ravine beats up huge **waves and adds to the wild** grandeur of the view. Whenever **the mountains** recede to the **South,** Mount Hood **fills the horizon. Rising 14,000** feet, its snow-covered head shines **out magnificently against the** blue sky, **with** unvarying **grandeur and a** strangely attractive **form.**

Soon we pass an Indian burial-ground called Caffin **Rock,** a bare desolate slope, covered with rude monuments of rock and circular heaps **of** piled grey stones.

Dalles City, where we now arrive, ranks **as the** second **place of importance in Oregon. It takes its name from the** 'dales,' **or** rough flag-stones, which **impede the river, making** narrow crooked channels, **and thereby causing** another **'portage'** for a distance **of fifteen** miles. Above the town **the scene** changes; the cliffs disappear, and from splendid forests and mountains **we** pass into a region of sand and desert. One tall **pillar of** red rock, overlooking the sandy waste, stands up forlorn and battered, as if it were the last fragment **of a giant** peak; and numbers of birds hovering over it seem to regard it as their special observatory.

Hot white sand is everywhere, and the wind scatters it about in a **most uncomfortable manner,** covering the **track and half-stifling you in its blinding** showers. The river scenery is **very fine all along this passage,** the Dalles being **a succession of rapids,** falls, and eddying **currents.**

Although it was late in the season hundreds of salmon were still ascending, and on the flat shore-rocks were several Indian lodges; their occupants busily engaged in spearing and catching the fish.

Their usual mode of catching salmon is by means of nets fastened to long handles. They erect wooden scaffolds by the riverside among the rocks, and there await the arrival of the fish—scooping up thirty or forty per hour. They are also very skilful at spearing them; rarely missing a fair mark.

At one of the falls we saw a most treacherous contrivance. A large tree with all its branches lopped off had been brought to the edge of the river and there fastened, with its smaller end overhanging the foaming fall. A large willow basket, about ten feet deep and over twenty feet in circumference, was suspended at this end. The salmon in its efforts to leap the fall would tumble into the basket, and an Indian seated in it would then knock the fish on the head with a club and throw it on shore.

This mode requires relays of men, as they soon get almost drowned by the quantity of spray and water. Very often, between two and three hundred salmon are caught in a day in this manner. We saw about twenty, averaging in weight from five to twenty pounds, caught in the hour during which we watched the process. But the hook-nosed salmon—coarse, nasty fish—were the most abundant. They always appear in the autumn, and are found everywhere.

The salmon are in their greatest perfection in the Columbia River towards the end of June. The best variety is called the 'chinook,' and weighs from twenty to forty pounds. This species is generally accompanied in its ascent by a smaller variety, weighing on an average about ten pounds, and which is also extremely good eating. Gradually, as the salmon go higher and higher up the river, their flesh changes from a bright red to a paler colour until it becomes quite white. There are such enormous quantities of them that they can be easily jerked on shore with a stick, and they actually jostle each other out of the water. It is estimated that over 500,000 salmon were taken out of the Columbia River during the year 1872.

There is a perfectly true story told of a traveller who, when riding, had to cross a stream running from the Cascade Mountains, at a spot where the fish were toiling up in thousands; and so thickly were they packed as to impede the progress of the horse, which became so frightened as almost to unseat his rider.

When the salmon are caught, the squaws cure them by splitting them and drying the pieces upon wickerwork scaffoldings. Afterwards they smoke them over fires of fir branches. The wanton destruction and waste of these fish is terrible. In the season the Indians will only take the fish in the highest condition, and those that do not satisfy their fastidious tastes are thrown back mutilated and dying into the water. Even when they have killed sufficient to last them for years, they still go to the falls and catch and spear all they can, leaving the beautiful silvery salmon to rot on the stones.

Salmon ought certainly to have 'Excelsior' for a motto. Always moving higher and higher, they are never content, but continue the ascent of the river as far as it is possible. They go on till they drop, or become so weak and torn from rubbing against the rocks and against one another, that they are pushed into shallows by the stronger ones and die from want of water.

Out of the hosts that ascend the rivers, it is generally supposed that a very small proportion indeed ever find their way back to the sea.

Just below the Great Salmon Falls the whole volume of the stream rushes through a channel hardly one hundred and fifty feet in width.

At the falls themselves the river is nearly a mile across, and pours over a rocky wall stretching from shore to shore and about twenty feet high. It is fascinating in the extreme to watch the determined creatures as they shoot up the rapids with wonderful agility. They care neither for the seething torrent nor for the deep still pools, and with a rush—and with clenched teeth, perhaps—they dart up like a silver arrow, and defying rock and fall, are at length safe in the smooth haven above.

Sometimes a speckled beauty, too weak to take the grand leap, falls back into the rapid—wounded by the sharp stones and dying. This is the opportunity for the great white-headed fish-eagle, which is as fastidious in his tastes as an Indian, and prefers a fresh-killed, or rather dying fish, to any other. With one fell swoop he seizes the victim in his talons and carries him off. Now and then a tall crane may be seen standing on a rock or in the shallow water, and out of mere spite pecking at a poor exhausted fish.

I never see a heron or crane fishing without thinking of the clergyman who sought every opportunity to impress upon the mind of his son the fact that God takes care of all His creatures. Happening one day to see a crane wading in search of food, the good man pointed out to his son the perfect adaptation of the bird to his mode of getting his living. 'Look!' said he, 'how his legs are formed for wading! What a long slender bill he has! Observe how nicely he folds his feet when putting them in or drawing them out of the water! He causes no ripple, and is thus able to approach the fish without giving them notice of his arrival. My son,' continued he, 'it is impossible to look at that bird without recognising the goodness of God in thus providing him with the means of obtaining his subsistence.' 'Yes,' replied the boy, 'I think I see the goodness of God as far as the crane is concerned; but, after all, father, don't you think the arrangement a little hard on the fish?'

With the Salmon Falls my trip up the Columbia ended, and I returned to Portland, to resume my journey to Victoria—the chief town of British Columbia, and situated on the southern extremity of Vancouver's Island.

CHAPTER XIX.

KALAMA TO VICTORIA.

A tedious journey—A terrible threat—An epithet—Olympia—Puget Sound—Snokomish City—An Indian cemetery—Flat-heads—Use of Indians—American diplomacy—Washington Territory—Salmon not taking a fly—San Juan—Victoria—Dull times—Terminus—A view—Climate—Roads—Esquimalt harbour—Sport—Indians—A red admiral—Superstition—Hospitality.

DOWN the Columbia for some miles to Kalama, a little village, in Washington Territory; thence, by the new Northern Pacific Railway for fifty miles, to Sinino. I think we must have been over five hours doing that fifty miles. In some places the trees were so near the newly-laid line that it was like pushing one's way through a growth of brushwood, and now and then the removal of a branch, or perhaps the whole tree, fallen across our road, would afford pleasant occupation for half an hour or so. It was, in fact, a primeval forest, thick with cedar, spruce, arbor vitæ, and firs; the trunks covered with orange-green moss, the branches hung with brown Spanish moss, and the marshy ground brilliantly coloured with yellow and purple flowers.

Our journey was enlivened by a brief wordy warfare between an irascible old gentleman and a man whom he accused of having taken his seat in the carriage. After an exchange of very doubtful compliments the elderly gentleman produced a little pistol, saying, 'Do you see that? Now, don't speak to me, or touch me, or even look at me again, or I'll blow your head off.' Upon which the other coolly retorted, 'Do you see that umbrella settin' thar? Now, you touch that umbrella, or even look at that umbrella, and I'll ram it down your throat—and then I'll spread it.' This terrible threat had the effect of somewhat appeasing the old gentleman, but not before he had vented his wrath on an inoffensive clergyman who had endeavoured to assuage his anger, and whom he effectually silenced, after a round of abuse, by designating him 'an ecclesiastical old pelican.'

From Sinino a pleasant drive of fifteen miles brought us to Olympia, a small town, situated at the head of Puget Sound. Great dissatisfaction and anger reigned there, because it had just been decided that Tacoma, instead of Olympia, was to be the terminus of the new railway. The Olympians poured down their wrath on the railway, the new site, and on everything and everybody outside their own domains. Such 'a storm in a tea-cup' could never have been witnessed before!

Puget Sound is one of the loveliest sheets of water

that can be imagined. It is bounded by forests sloping down to its very edge, and hundreds of islands are dotted over its surface. The view of Mount Rainier from Olympia is magnificent, the vast mountain, apparently, being snow-covered from base to peak. The mountain views all down the Sound are delightful, and the whole journey as far as Snokomish was like sailing on a lake in the midst of high woodland. The water, very deep and transparent, rippled into gleams of gold away to the bases of the glorious mountains, which are shaded from the deepest purple softened off to the clearest grey, and their rounded contour varied by many a dim rift, wooded glen and slope.

Snokomish City is decidedly a 'one-hoss settlement,' as an Anglo-American, whose acquaintance I made on the steamer, expressed it, and 'biled' shirts are looked upon as quite out of place. The hotel accommodation was not, strictly speaking, good, and those who were effeminate enough to like washing had to take their turn at a tin basin, with a cake of musty yellow soap and to dry themselves on a fortnight-old towel, hung from a broomstick in the bar-room. However, as I was able to obtain ponies, Indian guides, and provisions for a ten days' shooting expedition into the interior, in search of elk, the aspect of the collection of wooden huts denominated a 'city' did not matter. The country through which we passed was replete with picturesque beauty, and the mountain streams were stocked with trout, which furnished us with many an evening meal.

The weather was so beautiful that we took no tents; but, as it was very cold at night in the mountains, we were provided with blankets. Our ponies were poor creatures to look at, but they were hardy, and willing to go any distance. On the third day one of the Indians refused to go any further. We were approaching, he said, the territory of a hostile tribe, who, he asserted, would kill him. On that day I shot two deer, lots of grouse, and a wolf. On the fourth day we arrived at a small lake, near where the elk were supposed to be; and as the Indians found some of their tracks I went to bed in the expectation of having a shot at one the next day. Before daylight we were up, and started with two other Indians who came into the camp with an offer of their services, and after a long and hard walk we reached the north side of the lake. I was stationed in a beautiful wood, while the Indians were beating in an opposite direction, and had not been there half an hour when I heard a crackling in the bushes, and out walked a fine elk. He did not see me, and as he stood still at about a hundred yards' distance I had only to take a deliberate aim, and down he fell. He was not very large, but his horns were remarkably fine, and, being still in the velvet, considered quite a curiosity. The head was stupidly cut off too near the ears to look well when stuffed. To my disgust we met with no bears; but I shot a beautiful golden eagle, measuring nearly nine feet across the wings, and in splendid plumage. I came near him only by creeping on my hands and knees, for about two miles, up and down the sides of mountains—for whenever I got almost within shot he would sail off for a few hundred yards and wait until I again nearly reached him; then off he went again, though I do not think that he really saw me. I had a long shot at another much larger elk, but unfortunately missed him.

In one very lonely spot we found an Indian burial-place. These Indians—' Flat-heads '—have a peculiar way of depositing the remains of their dead The corpse, dressed out in its best apparel, which usually consists of a bit of old blanket, one leg of a pair of trousers, and a feather, is placed in a box about three feet high and long, and about two feet wide. The knees are thus brought up level with the head, in about the same position as the deceased would adopt when sitting by his camp-fire. The box is then fastened high up in a tree, out of the reach of wild animals, and his weapons and any little knick-knack—such as an enemy's scalp-lock, an old boot, a beaver hat with no crown—in fact, anything of which he was particularly fond, are then hung around it. Under one of these boxes we saw the remains of a canoe, and from the signs of luxury shown by other articles hanging about—the barrel of an old musket, the skeleton of a dog, a paddle, half a panther's skin, and what was once a blanket—it was conjectured that it must have been the tomb of a great chief. The 'Flat-heads' derive their name from their custom of bandaging their children's heads between two flat pieces of wood as soon as they are born, one being placed on the forehead, the other at the back of the head. This bandage is kept on night and day until the child is nearly three years old, by which time the head has acquired the desired beautiful shape which it afterwards retains. They are the most hideous and repulsive-looking Indians I ever saw. The 'bandaging system,' I hear, is dying out with them, or rather, the tribe is dwindling away, as there are not many of them left.

It is difficult to imagine for what end Indians were placed upon the earth. Perhaps they were merely intended to live with wild animals amidst wild vegetation and enjoy their wild life, until races of greater capacity were ready to occupy the soil. A succession of races, like a rotation of crops, may be necessary to turn the earth to the best possible account, and consequently the Indian must be removed to make room for others.

Returning to the Sound, some distance north of

Snokomish, we coasted down, **then crossed to Fort Townsend, and took the steamer to Victoria.**

Soon we sighted the Island **of** San Juan, lately handed over by us **to the United States, in** accordance **with** the decision of the Emperor of Germany.

This island and Washington Territory are examples, on the North-West of America, of the unscrupulousness of the Government of **the** United States and the superiority of its knowledge to that of ours. The **clauses in** the ' Rights of Fishing' treaties, on our **Eastern shores,** exhibit a **like** capacity.

The Emperor Napoleon said truly, ' America is a fortunate country. She grows **by** the follies of our European nations.'

Regarding Washington Territory, surely the Columbia River is the natural boundary; therefore, why in **1846, when** Oregon was ceded by Great Britain, was not this **river** considered the rightful limit, instead of the **imaginary line** (the **49th parallel**) which now constitutes the **southern** boundary **of** British Columbia ? Simply because **American** diplomatists knew the value of their claims, and **British diplomatists** knew nothing about it.

It is not easy to conceive what reasons for claiming **the country** north of the Columbia could be urged by **the United States** Government. But they knew the prospective **value of the** magnificent inland waters of Puget Sound, and acted upon that knowledge. With the possession of that grand inlet, British Columbia could easily compete with California and Oregon; without it, it becomes a difficult matter to do so.

Whether there is any truth in the story told of a certain naval officer who at the time of the dispute was stationed on the Pacific Coast, and who wrote home to his brother, the then Prime Minister, that the salmon in the Columbia wouldn't take a fly, and that the country was not worth making a fuss about, I do not know, but at all events the story has obtained popular credence in British Columbia.

The Island of San Juan commands everything British on the West and North; and though its military occupation by the British would be utterly useless, yet in the hands of the United States it becomes a perpetual menace to us, and places the command of the Straits in American hands.

It is only fair to say that, according to the *wording* of the treaty of 1846, the island does belong to the United States, but according to facts and the *spirit* of the treaty it certainly does not.

We soon crossed the Straits of Fuca and passed into the harbour of Victoria. Its entrance is narrow and crooked, and it only accommodates vessels drawing about 18 feet of water; but dredging is constantly going on when funds permit.

Men-of-war always lie in the harbour of Esquimalt, which is about three miles from Victoria.

A walk through the streets of Victoria impresses the traveller with the idea that more than half the population is Indian, and the remainder composed of every nationality under the sun. The town itself is a pretty, cheerful, bright place, and looked business-like enough when we saw it; but, on enquiry, we were told that everything was at a stand-still and 'times were never so bad.' It is a remarkable fact that go where you will, no matter at what season, 'times were never so bad' within the memory of the oldest inhabitant as they are sure to be at that very moment when information is sought on the subject.

Victoria, like Mr. Micawber, is 'waiting for something to turn up,' and that something must be the railroad. This 'waiting' retards the growth of the city, and is hardly in accordance with the true spirit of trade. The railroad will doubtless be of immense service when made. But, at present, men hold on to 'business lots' and 'real estate' near the town, in the uncommercial but hopeful spirit of making large sums in the future at one stroke; or they demand such a high price for their land as discourages emigrants and intended settlers.

The position of Victoria indicates a bright future in store for her.

The products of China, Japan, and Australia must all converge towards that terminus whose line of railway will ere long extend from the Pacific to Newfoundland, passing through the splendid provinces of the North-west, and forming the quickest and surest route to European markets.

The harbours of Vancouver's Island and the inlets of the mainland are many and deep. The wealth in minerals, forests, and fish in British Columbia, is unlimited; and there is no reason why the Straits of Fuca should not form a commercial highway of vast importance, and eventually become another 'Golden Gate' between the Old World and the New.

The town of Victoria slopes gently up from the water's edge, and the view from the church eminence overlooking the harbour is strikingly beautiful. Across the straits the snowy range of the Olympian mountains rises abruptly from the shore.

Towards the Gulf of Georgia masses of rock of singular form, bare and rugged in some places, clothed with shrubs in others, contrast in the most picturesque manner with the calm and lovely scene over the harbour. The blue waters run far up into the undulating country, in deep fiords, bays, and inlets; and these innumerable indentations of the rocky shore are fringed with luxurious vegetation. Here and there are scattered beautiful little islets, amongst which the

Indian canoes glide stealthily about. A little farther off, hills broken by misty glens, the haunts of the wild deer, slope gradually away, backed by the dim outlines of graceful mountains, towering tier above tier, and flanked by purple and gold-tinted headlands rising from the sea. Over all there floats a soft dreamy haze, a charmingly effective finish to a landscape so suggestive of peace and rest; so soft and harmonious, that many a spectator must have turned away with a tightening of the throat and a misty gaze not altogether the effect of the atmosphere.

The climate of Victoria is delightful. It is a crisp invigorating climate—a climate of elastic lungs and rosy English cheeks. Fruit and flowers grow with a Californian luxuriance. The flowers especially have an extraordinary brilliancy of colour; but, unfortunately, labour is so scarce that a well-kept-garden is very seldom seen, and the suburbs do not present that cultivated appearance which might be expected with the advantages of such splendid soil and climate.

The town and the environs are blessed with most capital roads; and if the state of the highways is a test of civilisation, Victoria must be far advanced indeed. Beautiful drives and rides extend in every direction, and it is quite a luxury to walk on the roads, so free are they from dust or mud.

A very pleasant walk of three miles along one of these

fine roads or by a path through the woods brings you to Esquimalt. The first view of this harbour is of magical effect. The road runs through a diversified country of rock and forest, with the sea on the left. Suddenly, a break in the rocks on the right reveals an apparently circular lake, on which three or four men-of war are lying sleepily at anchor. This harbour is a perfect gem; it is surrounded by thickly-wooded hills, has excellent anchorage, and is almost landlocked.

Plenty of sport, too, all around. Grouse and deer abound in the woods, and the popping of guns may be heard all day, in the shooting season; and, alas! out of it too. There is also capital trout and salmon fishing; but the great drawback to this amusement is that the fish will not take a fly.

Now and then you hear of somebody having had a successful day's fly-fishing; but the 'spoon bait' is most generally resorted to, and with dire effect. In the morning, canoes full of salmon may be seen entering the harbour. The price of a big fish varies from a 'bit' up to half-a-dollar, but the latter is considered an extravagant price. The Indians, however, are getting too lazy even to fish, and many of them prefer buying a salmon from a white man to paddling out a short distance in their canoes and catching as many as they want.

I think the Indians—or '*Si-washes*,' as they are called here, a name derived from the French *sauvage*— of Vancouver's Island are, with the exception of the Diggers, dirtier and wilder-looking than any I have seen; but they give very little trouble, and are quiet and contented, so long as they have a coloured blanket to dress in. I used to be much amused with one of them, whose ideas were evidently far grander than those of his neighbours, as he always paraded up and down the streets in a full suit of naval uniform, including a cocked-hat and feathers. Both the uniform and the hat he had embellished with more gold lace than could possibly have fallen to the share even of the Lord High Admiral in the days of Queen Elizabeth; but it added considerably to the respect he inspired among his tribe. His proud martial appearance was, moreover, heightened by floating streamers of red riband with which he decorated his long black greasy hair, and which at a distance gave him the appearance of a drunken recruiting sergeant, who had dressed himself in the wrong uniform, and hung himself out as a scare-crow.

The Australians have a superstition that boring the ears of children is sure to give them large and beautiful eyes. The Indians, I think, must have the same idea, with the addition that boring their noses will give them large and beautiful mouths.

They have undoubtedly succeeded as far as size goes, but their beauty may be questioned, and I do not think anyone who has ever seen these people could answer the question, 'Who can tell where the lips end or the smile begins?'

Victoria, and indeed British Columbia in general—that is, as far as my very limited experience goes—is most hospitably inclined: everybody seems glad and willing to do the honours of the country to strangers, and you are seldom at a loss for pleasant companions for shooting excursions and trips of all sorts up the coast and across to the mainland. One of the pleasantest expeditions we made was up the Fraser River. But I must reserve that for another chapter.

CHAPTER XX.

UP THE FRASER.

New Westminster—Stumps—Halcyon days—Fishing—A panther—Ferns—Sal-lal—Burrard Inlet—Steam saw-mills—Up the Fraser—Anonymous gifts—Providence—Wood-cutters—Hope—A silver-mine —Rapids—Yale—Hudson's Bay Company—Christianised Indians— Missionaries—A waggon-road—A trail—Fatal accident—Hell's Gate —Suspension-bridge—Scenery to Boston Bar—Indian larders—Salmon —Fishing establishments—Boundary line—Haro Straits—The Driard House—British Columbia.

THE Gulf of Georgia, which we had to cross before reaching the mouth of the Fraser River, is flecked all over with lovely islands, thickly wooded, and in many places affording rich pasture-land. The beauty of this archipelago is best seen when coasting up Vancouver's Island towards Nanaimo and Comox, an excursion we were to make after our return from the Fraser. The angle at which we crossed the Gulf made the distance about fifteen miles; and as a strong wind was blowing and there was a heavy swell, the passage bore a most unpleasant resemblance to that between Dover and Calais.

The entrance to the Fraser is graced by immense mud-flats, which are connected with rich bottom-lands extending far into the interior, and forming a delta of great agricultural importance. New Westminster, the capital of British Columbia, and the only town on this delta, is situated very picturesquely at a distance of about twenty miles from the mouth of the Fraser and seventy-five from Victoria. It was dark when we arrived; so we could, therefore, form no opinion of the merits of the town till the following morning. Then the feeling was forced upon us that a more desolate, forsaken-looking place we had never seen.

The site is a splendid one: a magnificent stretch of the river, with gently sloping hills rising behind the town, and covered with fine forests. But close round the town the huge cedars and pine trees have been cut down or burnt, and the huge blackened stumps give it a very dismal, neglected appearance. These stumps are left standing in every direction, in the straggling streets, around the church, and in the ill-kept gardens. The houses for the most part are empty, and ruin and decay are the chief features (besides the stumps) of this now 'deserted village.'

Once it was a gay, flourishing little town, with plenty of society and amusements; but that was in the 'golden days,' when the Government House was occupied, when sappers and Marines filled the little barracks, and nuggets rolled down from the mines of Cariboo. The energy and varied talents of one man alone keeps New

Westminister from fading away into utter oblivion. He is magistrate, captain of the Volunteers, general authority on Government matters, school inspector, and town-councillor; he plays the harmonium in the church, attends to church business, manages the school feasts, rings the church bells,[1] and in fact is the presiding genius of the place. He put his house at our disposal as headquarters during our visit, and turned what would otherwise have been rather a melancholy sojourn into an extremely pleasant one. There are only two walks in New Westminister; one goes to Burrard Inlet, and the other follows the bank of the river to an old rifle range, and crosses the Brunette, a small stream that runs into the Fraser. In this stream we one day saw a number of large trout and white fish; so a day's fishing was arranged, which resulted in a perfectly empty bag, the fish, as usual, declining a fly, and even the ground-bait which we temptingly displayed. We were gratified, however, by the sight of a big panther which walked out of the wood and across the road close to us. It would have been a capital shot, as it moved along quite slowly and gracefully, never even turning his head to look at us; but, of course, I had not my gun with me, and if I had had it I should most probably have seen a fish walking across the road.

[1] This peal of bells was originally intended for the church in Victoria, but by mistake it was sent from England to New Westminster, where it has remained ever since.

Burrard Inlet is reached from New Westminster by a very good corduroyed stage-road nine miles long. The entrance to the inlet from the Gulf of Georgia is fifteen miles north of the mouth of the Fraser River. The drive thither was a most pleasant one. A collector of ferns could have gathered a charming variety from the banks and dells on the road-side. There were various sorts of shrubs, too; one, called the sal-lal, with a berry like our berberry, only much larger, and edible, struck me as being very suitable for English woods, as it is very hardy, and would make a most splendid cover for pheasants. At all events, I shall make an attempt at growing it, and its failure, I think, will be very improbable.

When we arrived at the Inlet we found a tiny steamer ready to take us across to the large steam saw-mill on the opposite side. A beautiful sheet of deep water is this Inlet. It is twenty-five miles long, with an average breadth of over a mile.

Three natural divisions form three distinct harbours, the middle one narrowing at both extremities—thus making an outer and inner harbour. Vessels of the largest size can enter, and there is safe anchorage for 500 ships. The woods all round the shores are stocked with deer. The usual way here of hunting them is to send dogs into the forest to drive the animals down to the water's edge, where they are shot.

Forests, as a means of wealth, are perhaps the greatest resource of the country, and our visit to the saw-mills gave us an insight into the lucrative business of 'lumber-making' from an almost inexhaustible supply of the most splendid material. There are two steam-mills on the Inlet, and although they run night and day, yet their proprietors are compelled to refuse numerous orders.

The mill on the south side of the Inlet is the more picturesque of the two. The white workmen live in what look like very comfortable little houses, and are evidently well cared for. The workmen represent all nationalities, Whites, Chinese, Sandwich Islanders, 'Si-washes,' and negroes. The natives cannot be depended upon for work, for as soon as they have made enough money to keep them in idleness for a time they withdraw their services, and return to their dirt and squalor until necessity drives them back again.

The houses of the aborigines are the most complete ' whited sepulchres ' one can imagine. The fronts, facing the harbour, are generally clean-looking and well whitewashed ; but the backs, the sides, and the interiors are filthy beyond description.

We left Burrard Inlet thoroughly well up in the intricacies of ' lumber ' and edified by a most interesting visit.

The next day we started for Yale, which is the

head of the navigation of the Fraser, and about ninety miles from New Westminster. The course of the Fraser is full of dangers and difficulties. The extreme swiftness of the stream and under-current renders a capsize almost certain destruction, as the river is as full of 'snags' and 'sawyers' as the Mississippi.

Our flat-bottomed vessel, the 'Onward,' had a first-rate captain, who knew all the snags and rocks in our course, and was able himself to take the wheel in any of the bad parts of the river.

The voyage at first was rather monotonous, but as the dense woods were putting on their autumn tints there was always plenty of colour to relieve the dulness of the low overhanging banks. Sometimes we stopped at new settlements, consisting of about two or three houses; at other times at places where there was no appearance of a house at all, on which occasions a box, a parcel, or whatever there was to leave was deposited on the bank, and we resumed our journey. These articles, I presume, were destined for some person in particular, but it rather looked as if they were intended generally for anybody who chose to appropriate them, and that if a Robinson Crusoe or a man Friday should happen to be wandering that way he might accept the consignment as a Providential gift. By the way, how is it that the hand of Providence is always apparent in that which pleases us, never in that which displeases?

For instance, how constantly we hear the expression, 'Providentially saved,' but never 'Providentially lost;' yet calamitous results, I presume, are as much permitted by Providence as fortunate ones.

'Wooding up' was a cause for continual lying-to, the appetite of the furnace being insatiable.

Wood-cutting and rail-splitting are regarded here as the last resource for a living that a man can descend to; but from the good price paid per foot, and the enormous quantity of wood used, I should have thought them very profitable occupations. The loneliness and utter isolation of the life of the woodcutter must be their chief drawbacks, and the possession of a squaw wife, and the accompanying blessings, are perhaps not likely to conduce to a high state of civilisation.

As soon as night came on the boat was tied up to a convenient tree, and there we remained till daylight. As we approached Hope the scenery became much grander; high mountains sloped down to the riverside, and sand bars, from which melancholy miners were endeavouring to extract gold, were frequently met with. Hope is a pleasantly-situated little settlement. We stopped there to visit a silver-mine which had lately been discovered in the mountain above the town. We could trace one seam of silver ore for two hundred feet up and for about one thousand feet along, with a breadth of from four to eight feet. This mine has raised **great** expectations; and if they are **justified** by the results, the companies ought before long to **be** in a **very** flourishing position.

Between Hope and Yale there is a point where the stream **runs** so swiftly that for two or three minutes the vessel seems standing still, and it requires a considerable rising of **the steam-gauge and many** extra heaps **of** resinous wood to be piled on the furnaces, to enable the panting boat to stem the current and glide **once** more into comparatively still water.

Yale has a **thriving** appearance, and the scenery in the neighbourhood is superb. Hills **rise in wooded** slopes for nine and **ten hundred feet**, then **bare** rocks and **crags** shoot **up for** another thousand feet, and streams dash down **in cataracts and falls from** the distant mountain-heights.

The Hudson's Bay **Company** has a very nice house here, in which we were most hospitably entertained. **But where in America is there** a Hudson's Bay post where travellers are not welcomed and received in the kindest possible manner?

Since this wonderful **old** English company **first received** its charter, in 1670, **times** have indeed changed; **and the policy of the** company has also changed. Instead of keeping the country closed, as in **former days**, their efforts are directed to opening it up as much as possible.

This change has perhaps been forced on them, now that they are no longer the rulers of the North-West; but they have gracefully given way to existing circumstances, and still carry on their trade with the skill which characterised it in former days. The old outcry against the company, accusing them of sacrificing colonists for the sake of minks and silver foxes, had no foundation. The company attended to its own business; and if the real value of the country was not known, it was not for the H.B.C. to destroy its own prospects by pointing it out.

At Yale we attended service at the Indian church one Sunday morning. The impression left on my mind by the deportment and the apparent general feeling of the congregation was of a mixed character.

The outward tokens of a religious ceremony were manifest, but there seemed to be a mere parrot-like rendering of the devotions, which excluded—at least according to my view of the matter—any idea of the true sentiment of Christianity being either felt or understood by the Indians. The good pastor, however, assured me that they understood and appreciated all that was said. The service was of course conducted in the Indian tongue, and, certainly, a hymn, one of the 'Ancient and Modern,' was sung in a very creditable manner; yet I have strong doubts as to the efficacy of the ceremony. I certainly saw many of the congregation indulging in their favourite vices a few minutes after leaving the church, yet wearing the same sanctimonious expression they had assumed during the service. But the missionaries themselves know best whether their labours are well rewarded or not; those whom I have met have been satisfied with the past and are sanguine for the future. The world cannot judge of the value of missionary labour; it must be judged from a far higher standpoint, and the reward of many earnest men, whose lives have been passed in preaching the Gospel to a few poor Indians, will not be found wanting when good works are summed up in the balances of eternity.

The waggon-road from Yale to Cariboo is hardly surpassed on the continent for the engineering skill exhibited in its construction; and considering the infancy of the colony that undertook the work, it is a perfect marvel.

Formerly, an old Indian trail alone led to the mines of Cariboo, 300 miles from Yale. This trail wound up and down steep mountains, crossed rivers and gorges, and in one place led over a ravine by a bridge not two feet wide, over which the traveller had to crawl with his heavy pack, and with the sure knowledge that if he slipped he would fall over perpendicular rocks nearly 2,000 feet into the Fraser below. Now, a fine but dangerous-looking road runs the whole distance. It has been hewn out of the rocks and cut through them, and is built up with masonry and wood, sometimes running at a height of 1,200 feet above the Fraser, and sometimes descending almost to its edge. The chief danger consists in the fall of rocks, and in landslips occasioned by heavy rains or the melting of snow; but the road is so narrow and the rocky wall so perpendicular that loosened rocks and stones generally fall clear of the road and descend into the foaming river.

The least want of care in driving, or the horses shying, would instantly hurl the waggon down a steep of several hundred feet on to the rocks below.

Strange as it may appear, fatal accidents seldom happen. The only one that had occurred for years took place the day before we reached Yale, and within a quarter of a mile of the town. One of the stage-drivers had driven his wife and child for a short distance along the road; on returning, the horses shied at a wheelbarrow by the road side, and the carriage was immediately thrown on to the rocks, which at that place stretched out below the road and over the river. The drop was about twenty feet; a few yards further on or further back, and all would have been dashed from those precipitous heights into the river. As it was, the poor mother died on the following day, but the father and child escaped with but few injuries. One of the horses was killed on the spot; the other kicked itself free and fell over into the river.

The scenery of the Fraser between Yale and Boston Bar, a distance of about five-and-twenty miles, is grand in the extreme, and I think even excels that of the Columbia River. At 'Hell's Gate,' about ten miles above Yale, the river rushes through a channel only about fifty yards wide, the rocks on either side being perpendicular. The difference between the height of the river in summer, at the melting of the snows, and in the winter is not less than ninety feet, as may be seen by the high-water marks on the rocky walls.

Rugged and inaccessible mountains rise to a height of several thousand feet, and are so precipitous that a feeling of giddiness is experienced when looking up at their snowy summits. A very pretty suspension-bridge crosses the river about ten miles above Yale, and makes a picturesque break in the stupendous character of the scenery. Just imagine grand cañons and giant cliffs, along whose rugged sides the road runs, and whence the swift-rushing river, far far below, looks like a mere silken-thread; wild heights, sometimes bare, sometimes pine-clad; snow-capped peaks, rising above ranges of lofty mountains, the narrow pass dwarfed by the altitude of the towering rocks on both sides, and you have some of the ingredients of the Fraser scenery.

All along the road were tiny houses high up in trees, round the trunks of which were pieces of tin and iron, turned over at the tops, to prevent animals from climbing up. These houses ('*cache*') are the Indians' larders, and contain quantities of dried salmon ready for the winter's consumption. The salmon in the Fraser are as numerous as in the Columbia, and between Yale and Boston Bar the atmosphere was often quite tainted by the smell of the dead fish. Spearing and netting were going on everywhere, although the season was far advanced. A very delicious little fish, called the 'eulachon,' is caught in the Fraser at certain seasons in immense quantities. The season lasts for about a fortnight, and during that period they appear in such shoals that they are actually raked into the boats; buckets, nets, and all sorts of queer contrivances being put into requisition for their capture.

A short distance below New Westminster there is a large establishment for canning and barrelling the salmon, but there is room enough and plenty of occupation for many more fisheries, without causing any diminution of the salmon; for the fish swarm in every portion of the river, and they often vary their course according to the state of the weather. On warm calm days they play along the shore, and when it is cold and rough they seek the mid-channel or shelter under the bluffs and rocks.

Three systems are in use for fishing—gill-net fishing, the 'weir,' and 'dragging the seine.' In the former, nets are used with a mesh of sufficient size to allow the head but not the body of the fish to pass through. This mode of fishing is employed on dark nights. The net is thrown into the channel which the fish generally take, and the current carries it down for three or four miles. It is then hauled into the boats, the fish being killed by knocking them on the head with clubs. The salmon caught in these nets are larger than those procured in any other way, as the small fish can pass through the meshes.

The weir is simply a large trap made of twigs and poles. The catch is often enormous, four and five hundred salmon having been caught in a single haul. Fishing with a 'seine' is done by day and on moonlight nights. The net is placed in the stern of the boat, a man on shore holding on to a rope attached to it; the boat then pulls out on the river, paying out the net as it goes, and when it meets the current it is swung round until it reaches the shore again when all is paid out. The 'seine' is then pulled ashore at both ends and emptied of its spoil.

The Fraser did not seem to me to offer so good a site for fisheries as the Columbia. Nevertheless, most profitable establishments might be erected in many places; as near the salt water as possible, that the fish which are of the finest quality might also be in the best condition.

As we returned to Victoria we caught a glimpse of the boundary line between the United States and British Columbia. This boundary line cuts through the forest from east to west, parallel with 49° of North latitude, and extends from the Gulf of Georgia (where a pillar marks its commencement) right across the continent to Manitoba, and then inclines southward to Lake Superior. For several hundred miles a broad distinct cutting, which has a very singular appearance, has also been made through the thick woods. The sail through the Haro Channel presents a combination of water, island, and mountain scenery that for variety and beauty cannot easily be surpassed. On the mainland there is the long line of the Cascade mountains, from which we had just descended by the Fraser. The grand Mount Baker, the principal feature in the landscape, stands out, in its snowy covering, monarch of all the surrounding heights. Further south, Puget Sound stretches far inland, while the Olympian range extends towards the sea, sheltering the island of Vancouver from the rough winds of the Pacific.

On returning to Victoria harbour we again established ourselves in our quarters at the 'Driard House'— a comfortable hotel, but unfortunately at that period employing a most execrable cook, who, I trust, has long since entered on his proper occupation in the Shoe-black Brigade.

The accounts given of British Columbia are so various and contradictory, and the country has been so praised by some and run down by others, as it has suited their different interests, that it might be pictured either as a Garden of Eden or a howling wilderness by those who have never visited it.

The little that I saw of the interior of the mainland does not warrant my saying much about it; but from what I beheld myself and gathered in conversation with people who lived there, the following remarks may be received as facts.

The climate, although a few places suffer from the extremes of heat and cold, is on the whole exceedingly healthy and pleasant. The vast extent of the mountain ranges forms an almost insuperable barrier to great commercial intercourse.

A sparse population and difficult intercommunication, which is in fact solitude, give the conditions of barbarism; and until good roads and highways are constructed the colony cannot make much progress.

The lands in the interior where cultivation has been employed are wonderfully rich and fertile; wheat and oats, with straw six feet long, and producing seventy bushels to the acre, grow with comparatively imperfect culture. As a fruit-garden it equals Oregon. Its grazing regions are immense, and would be of enormous profit, if there were average means of transportation; but at present, timber, the fisheries, and mining offer the richest prizes to capitalists, whilst the very high rate of wages that labour commands soon places the working classes in comparatively affluent circumstances.

The delta lands of the Fraser are of great extent and richness, and they are at present occupied only by a few farmers. The future prosperity of this part of British Columbia will doubtless depend to a great extent on its ditches and dykes. Those lands situated on the Lower Fraser are subject to overflow at certain seasons.

The work of dyking looks formidable at first for individual effort, but in reality is much easier than clearing away forests. Land, too, that has been subject to inundation is twenty times more valuable than forest land.

But it is to the Government we must look for large and important works of reclamation by dyking. And when these are begun, and the sound of the locomotive is heard in the land, they will attract thither a multitude of steady and permanent immigrants. The present state of torpor and inactivity will then give place to the energy and business-like habits necessary for the development of the industries and resources of the country. British Columbia will then be advanced to the front rank of the Dominion, as a vigorous and prosperous province.

CHAPTER XXI.

RETURN TO NANAIMO.

Miners—Difficulties and dangers—Good and bad luck—Gulf of Georgia—Calculating birds—Nanaimo—Duck-shooting—An Indian guide—The beaver dam—Fishing—A river—Stars—Merit—An entertainment—The coast.

DURING our absence from Victoria the town had had an influx of visitors. New gold-mines had lately been discovered on the Stickeen river, and hundreds of men stricken with the 'yellow fever' were on their way to the north-west of the Territory—men of all classes, all ages and occupations; men of refinement and education, and others who had never opened a book; desperadoes and law-abiding men of all nations and creeds; and all wearing the same weary, anxious, and care-worn look alike habitual to the steady and the improvident miner.

> 'There is an order
> Of mortals on the earth who do become
> Old in their youth, and die ere middle age,
> Without the violence of warlike death;
> Some perishing of pleasure, some of study,
> Some worn with toil, some of mere weariness,
> Some of disease, some of insanity,
> And some of wither'd or broken hearts;
> For this last malady is one which slays
> More than are number'd in the lists of Fate,
> Taking all shapes, and bearing many names.'

The difficulties and dangers encountered by miners on their way to new diggings are of no common order. Very often—as in the case of the Stickeen miners—no trail exists along which even an animal could pick its way. Obstacles that would stop an engineer have to be faced and overcome. You must trudge, with your provisions on your back, up and down mountain precipices, over rocks and snow, through a country probably infested by unfriendly Indians. When hungry you must cut wood before you can cook and eat. In wet weather you must remain moist and chilled till it is fine again. Your hands and clothes will be torn to pieces; and if you are unfortunate enough to possess a tent, it will probably be only just large enough to crouch in, besides adding considerably to the weight of your pack.

And the difficulties do not diminish when your destination is reached. 'Prospecting' is a work of incredible toil in a mountainous region covered with thick forest; and though gold may be everywhere, it must be found in large quantities to enable the miner to live. Provision-dealers and hucksters of all kinds, who, with gamblers, &c. follow close in the wake of the army of gold-hunters, will only sell their goods at fancy prices, consequently the greater part of the earnings goes into their pockets.

Two or three may make fortunes in less than a

fortnight, and a few may by degrees accumulate large sums, but hundreds will only just make sufficient for a living, and tens of hundreds nothing at all. Mining is like any other kind of gambling—once taken to, the difficulty then is to leave off. The excitement of knowing that at any moment, by a 'lucky hit,' a fortune may be grasped, acts like a stimulant and urges on to exertion long after expectation is dead. Success in mining depends on 'luck,' and therein it differs from success in the ordinary affairs of life. In the latter case good luck is a man of pluck, with sleeves turned up to meet difficulties, and working to make things come right; while bad luck is a man with his hands in his pockets and a pipe in his mouth, looking on to see how things will come out.

In Calaveras County, California, an instance of really bad luck came under my observation.

The original locator of a claim worked for years running a tunnel through the hard rock. After he had bored a distance of about 800 feet his pecuniary affairs became so involved that he was obliged to give up the mine before reaching gold. Broken down in health and spirits, he was nevertheless obliged to seek employment, and again went to work at the tunnel for wages, the new proprietor having determined to continue the boring. He had been employed there about a fortnight, when he struck through to gravel, from which unprecedentedly large returns have been obtained; so that after labouring for years the poor man was obliged to relinquish work just as wealth was within his grasp.

Once more in the beautiful Gulf of Georgia! but this time coasting up the island over a smooth sun-lit sea. Every mile discloses some new charm in the beautiful landscape. The numerous islands are composed of rock and sandstone, and the action of the sea has worn the soft material into caves, hollows, and many curious and fantastic forms, all of which are overhung with luxuriant vegetation, while above thick woods extend to the summits of the undulating heights. Winding through the straits and among the countless islets requires good steering, not only on account of the narrowness of the passage, but because of the almost invisible shoals and the swiftness of the current. Wildfowl of all sorts abound in these waters—the uneatable species fluttering lazily about close to the vessel, widgeon, teal, and mallards keeping carefully just out of gunshot.

It is extraordinary with what nicety birds can calculate distances. They even appear to know what weapon is to be used against them, and will keep their distance accordingly. With an increased range of rifle or fowling-piece, birds adapt themselves to the circumstances, and contemplate their enemy from just outside the limit of his range, and no more. It is the same force of instinct, I suppose, which enables birds of passage to strike their exact destination in precisely the calculated period.

For a yachting man, the Gulf of Georgia would be most attractive, as, irrespective of the scenery, deer and grouse are in abundance on most of the islands, and the bays, inlets, and natural harbours afford most ample anchorage.. A sketch-book, too, might soon be filled with innumerable 'bits' of charming effects of colour and formation.

Our course was past the farming districts of Saanich and Cowichan and other smaller settlements, at each of which we stopped to deliver letters and freight, and towards evening arrived at Nanaimo, where we intended to remain for some days.

The whole coast of Vancouver's Island and a great part of the mainland of British Columbia is a series of magnificent bays and inlets, and the scenery of Nanaimo is of the same character. The town itself occupies a most picturesque site, and the view overlooking the bay from the residence of our extremely hospitable host and hostess was charming. Although a coal-mining village, Nanaimo possesses but few of the unpleasant features common to such places. The neat little white cottages are scattered about in pleasant nooks and on rocky crags ; often they are surrounded by shrubs, trees, and patches of cultivated land, not very neat, perhaps, or well-tended, but still garden-like and pleasing.

Wild ducks frequent these parts in great force ; and we determined one day to visit them at their head-quarters—a beaver dam, situated a few miles from the inland extremity of the bay. The Indians paddled us over in canoes, and after a short walk we arrived at the entrance of the narrow valley, at the top of which was the dam. My two companions posted themselves in the valley, down which the ducks were obliged to come when disturbed, and I started off to the dam with one of the Indians. This individual was a most ludicrous object. He had got himself up for the occasion in his Sunday best, which consisted of a striped blanket worn like a toga, one boot, covering a lame foot, and a piece of blue linen wrapped round his head. He had given his face an extra bright coating of vermilion, and had softened the colour by a few white lines across his forehead. His countenance was melancholy in the extreme, and as he hopped on his lame foot over the marshy land his appearance was something between that of a flamingo and a disappointed heron.

After a long walk we arrived at the dam—a large square swamp, surrounded on three sides by high rocky hills covered with trees. The dam itself was so covered with willows and treacherous little islands made of sticks and rushes, which afforded no footing, that it was an admirable stronghold for the wild fowl as well as for the beavers. No dog or human being could swim or walk inside it, as the former would inevitably have been drowned by entanglement with the weeds, loose sticks, and brush, and the latter have immediately sunk over his head in the yielding mud and quicksand. The consequence was no ducks could be gathered except those that fell on shore. I made my way as well as I could along the dam-bank which ran across the valley, and when I had got as far as I could I raised a shout. Instantly the air was alive with hundreds of ducks and teal, and as they flew over my head on either side of me down the valley I banged away to my heart's content. This went on for about ten minutes, until the ducks—many of which kept circling round backwards and forwards—got tired of the sport and took their departure. All this time plenty of shooting had been going on at the entrance of the valley, and I was sure a capital bag would be the result. Unfortunately, numbers of my ducks fell into the dam. I had a very good retriever with me, and he made one attempt to get a duck that fell within a few yards of us; he was unsuccessful, and very nearly got drowned. As for old Flamingo, he was well acquainted with the dangers of the deep, and I could not induce him to make the slightest effort to retrieve.

So we picked up those that fell on land, and after many a regretful glance at the dozen or so we had to leave, returned to see what the others had done. Nothing is so annoying as losing dead game; clean missing your shots is nothing, but not being able to gather what you have killed is terrible.

My hopes of a large bag were not to be realised, as most of the ducks had flown so high that they were out of shot, and our total only numbered about fifteen or twenty head after all.

The following day we passed in salmon-fishing (spoon bait) on the other side of the bay, and in less than two hours we had caught about twenty very nice fish. An Indian who had been fishing all day came in the same evening with between forty and fifty.

The Nanaimo river is a very beautiful one, and to be paddled up the stream lying on soft mats stretched at the bottom of the smooth-going canoe, only rising now and then for a shot at some wild fowl, or occasionally landing for grouse, of which there are innumerable quantities all over the island, is a most deliciously lazy way of passing a day.

The stream winds tortuously through luxuriant meadows and wooded hills, past overhanging rocks, at the base of which many species of ferns and wild flowers grow. Sometimes the stream flows swift and deep, and often so shallow that paddles have to give place to long **poles with** which **to** push the canoe up the rippling rapids.

Now and then rich vales appear among the rolling hills, unoccupied save perhaps by an **Indian hut,** while in the distance the prospect is bounded **by the** giant **forms of** the mountains.

In such amusements we occupied the daytime, nor was there a want of entertainment for the evenings. Programmes had lately been posted about **of a perform-** ance **to be given by a star of** the first **magnitude.**

It is a fact that directly any third, fourth, fifth, or sixth rate actor or singer sets foot in the West he or she is at once changed into a planet, or even a whole constellation, and becomes invariably either the 'admitted rival of the great Queen of **Song**' or the quintessence **of** every talent that has ever endowed the chief artistes of the theatrical world.

Success does not always follow merit **in** any country, but in America **there cannot** possibly **be any** success without gigantic 'puffing,' **by which means** an average street-singer is **made to** rank as a prima donna, and every clown **as a Grimaldi.** The performance in question, though hardly up to our expectations, was nevertheless very creditable, especially considering the circumstances under which it was conducted.

At the appointed hour our party **of four** arrived at **the hall.** As we had the room entirely to ourselves we found we had mistaken the time. Nobody else appearing, we strolled out for half an hour. Presently we heard a great noise of drums and tin-kettles, with which, as we afterwards discovered, a number of boys had been engaged by the manager to beat up spectators. But as not the slightest attention was paid to this invitation the performance at last commenced, and was gone through before an audience of about ten people, including the band, whose services were remunerated by a free admission.

I never wish to be the tenth part of an audience again, however admirable the performance may be.

The reason given for the wretched attendance was, first, that so many professors, operatic stars, and wizards, all coming under the head of 'humbugs,' had visited the town, that the people were determined not to be taken in again; but the second reason, and the likelier of the two, was, that it was the beginning of the month, and the miners had not the money to pay the entrance fee.

The manager and company left Nanaimo at daybreak on the following morning, and proceeded in canoes to New Westminster, where I hope a better reception awaited them.

The scenery all along the coast north of Nanaimo differed very little from that which we had already passed through. Everywhere beautiful islets abounded shimmering in green. The reflection of these wooded islets in the calm deep blue water was often as perfect as the reflection in a mirror, but sometimes a silvery spray from the swell—almost unfelt within the estuary—would suddenly shoot across their shadows and raise a white ripple along their shores.

Afar off, the slopes and mountain ravines displayed a thousand bright tints of velvety blue, grey, and green, enamelled with variegated wild flowers, while the fervid heat of the sun spread a diaphanous vapour over the dreamy picture indefinite as

> —— 'The twilight that surrounds
> The border-land of old romance.'

CHAPTER XXII.

BRITISH COLUMBIA.

Game in British Columbia—Grouse—Mud Bay—A day's shooting—Raccoons—No woodcocks—Summer ducks—Bears—Indians of British Columbia—Carving—Canoes—Chinook—Indian houses—Burials—Door-posts—Smuggling—Civilised and Christianised Indians—The 'Prince Alfred'—The coast—Grumbling settlers—A Bohemian—Sunset—The Golden Gate.

THE shooting in Vancouver's Island and on the mainland of British Columbia is excellent—bears, panthers, elk, deer, grouse, quails, and wild-fowl everywhere. Mountain-sheep, prairie-chickens, and fool-hens are also found on the mainland. The fool-hen simply sits up in a tree and allows a noose to be put round its neck. The grouse are not much more sensible, for after a short flight they generally perch up in the branches, and there remain until shot or frightened away by a volley of stones and sticks.

The grouse are of two sorts, the blue and the common or spruce grouse. The blue take to the mountains about October. When the grouse are found in the open the cold weather sets in and the leaves are off the trees. They afford capital sport, as their flight is very swift and they take a good deal of killing. The Indians bring them into Victoria by the hundred. Their method of killing them is by sitting under the trees to which they come for the berries, and then shooting them through the head; for when the bird is shot only in the head a much better price is obtained for it. The only time an Indian is at all picturesque is when he is so covered with grouse that he himself is invisible. I once counted forty-six brace on one man; they were hung on poles across his shoulders, and they formed necklaces and chains down to his feet—in fact, he was draped in grouse. The same thing may be seen every morning, and I daresay the number I saw is often exceeded.

Towards November the flocks of wild-fowl which congregate on all the waters is perfectly marvellous. Snipe cannot be depended on, for where there are thousands one day there may be none the next.

But ducks, teal, widgeon and both the blue and green-winged geese are always to be found in great abundance. At Mud Bay, near the mouth of the Fraser river, between two and three hundred shots per diem may be had without the slightest exertion. You have simply to lie concealed, and the birds flock down in scores. Of course this is not such sport as walking them up, but on large level flats you must suit yourself to the occasion, though there are many places where you can walk all day and enjoy splendid sport.

We drove out once to a swamp about ten miles from Victoria, and after shooting away all our cartridges—and we had taken a good many, too—at snipe, ducks, geese, &c., towards evening we had the mortification of seeing flight after flight of teal coming in everywhere around us, and all we could do was to look at them.

Our game-bag was very varied on that occasion, as we shot two raccoons. These animals are terrible poachers, and destroy enormous numbers of eggs as well as birds.

A friend of mine was out duck-shooting once near San Francisco, and after knocking down a great number of ducks it appeared to him and the man who was with him that they disappeared as fast as they fell. Watching very closely, they presently saw a little black thing moving slowly towards a dead duck, which presently vanished. They then rowed over to a small island near to which most of the ducks had fallen, and there they found numbers of ducks with their heads bitten off, and innumerable remains of others. On searching they discovered a quiet family of seven raccoons, one of which was of very large size, and actually showed fight.

There was no doubt then how the ducks had disappeared, and probably for years these animals had been fattening on canvas-backs and other ducks. Floating quietly down the stream, with only their black noses above the water, they would seize the unsuspecting bird, drag it under to the land, and after eating their favourite bits return for another fat duck.

Their greediness at length brought them to grief, as the whole family was destroyed.

It is curious that the woodcock is never found in British Columbia, nor, I believe, anywhere on the continent west of the Rocky Mountains. The woodcock, of all birds, loves a moderate climate, and it is very strange that it is never at any season met with in those parts where one might expect to find it perennially. The beautiful summer or wood duck is occasionally found in British Columbia, but is there regarded more as a curiosity than as the familiar bird so well known in the United States.

In a country where all sorts of unlikely birds perch on the trees, this duck—which is the only one of the duck family in America that roosts and spends the greater part of its existence among the branches—ought, one would think, to be met with more frequently. The beauty and glossy splendour of the plumage is so great, and the birds are so domestic in their habits, rarely moving far from their native haunts, that it is wonderful they are not more often seen on ornamental water.

In appearance they are to other ducks, with the exception of the Mandarin, as superior as the golden pheasant is to the rest of his species.

The black bear is the commonest in British Columbia; and as they are not dangerous, the Indians kill a great many of them in the winter in the following way:—Bruin prepares for the winter by making himself a nest with about a cartload of leaves, ferns, &c. in some sheltered place, and covers it with boughs and sticks, leaving an air-hole. The snow then gives it an outer coating, and the proprietor passes a comfortable warm winter, sucking his paws being his sole amusement—a ceaseless one with bears. The Indians find out where they are by the air-hole. A blank cartridge is fired, and Bruin then comes out to see what is the matter, and is immediately shot through the head.

Before leaving British Columbia let us take a glance at the aborigines. There are twelve nations, consisting of about twenty-eight thousand Indians. The Indians in the interior are far superior to those on the coast, the natural depravity and corruption of the latter being augmented by contact with the lower grades of white men. Many of the tribes are cannibals, and also eat dogs; and at the great medicine feasts they kill and devour slaves. Gambling is their favourite occupation.

Their commercial instinct is very keen. They will

steal anything they can lay their hands on; and whenever they can take the scalp of a white man they fail not to do so. Where education has been pushed they exhibit great mental capacity, and some of them, particularly the Hydaks, show great skill in wood and stone carving. They also make tasteful jewellery out of coins and pieces of gold.

Their canoes are very graceful and accurate both in design and workmanship. It is said that the lines of the first clipper built by an eminent shipbuilder in Boston were taken from a Nootka canoe. Their canoes are made from large cedar logs, which they scoop out and steam. The proper shape is secured by putting in stretchers, and after a little painting and carving the canoe is complete.

The language spoken by the Coast Indians has a most dreadfully guttural sound; but in the interior it is softer and more liquid. Chinook is a sort of language corresponding in some measure with the 'pigeon English' spoken in China. It was first introduced by the Hudson's Bay men, and is now generally spoken all through British Columbia. A few words of it go a great way and make a great show.

The Indians have very remarkable winter quarters; we saw a few of them along the Fraser. A deep hole is dug in the ground; a strong pole is then stuck in the centre, and the hut is built up with logs in conical form, from the ground to nearly the top of the pole. Sufficient space is left at the top, not only for the smoke to issue, but also to allow of the ingress and egress of the family; and strong cross-bars are fastened to the centre pole, thus forming a ladder by which they ascend and descend.

As it is troublesome work to climb up and down, the inmates leave their hut only three or four times in the winter; and as their dogs live with them, and when once in cannot get out, the filthy state and suffocating odours of these habitations may be imagined. Often fever and other diseases make a sweep of the entire family, whose grave is thus ready-made.

Amongst other strange modes of burial they have the following:—They cut down a cedar tree, and in the thick end they make a hole, in which the body is placed. They then reverse the tree, planting the thin end in the ground. It is curious that a cedar will look fresh and green for ages after this operation.

The Hydak Indians cut down trees for a different purpose. After felling a tree sixty, seventy, or eighty feet in height they carve it the whole way up in quaint figures and devices, and with great correctness. They then set it up again and cut out a hole for the door, and this forms the entrance to their huts, which are built out behind. Smuggling is carried on to a great extent amongst the Indians, and hardly a canoe goes up the coast that does not contain whisky, or what is called whisky. The liquor law prohibiting the sale of intoxicating drinks to the Indians does not appear to be a very wise one.

Indians will have liquor, and like getting it all the better on account of the prohibition. It is worse than useless to make laws that cannot be enforced. The vilest liquor is sold to the Indians, yet they are willing to pay for the best that can be obtained.

The bad liquor maddens them, and crime is the consequence. If they had to pay high prices for their liquor it would be an inducement to them to work, in order to obtain the necessary money. A law prohibiting a drunken Indian from approaching within a mile of a white settlement, and the enforcement of severe penalties on its infringement, would be very effective, and could easily be carried into execution.

In spite of all their faults, the Indians of British Columbia who live near settlements and have come under the influence of civilisation and Christianity are quiet and industrious. They find plenty of employment, sometimes fill places of trust, and are often employed as messengers and trusted with large sums of money. The conduct of the British Government, aided by the Colonial authorities, in protecting the property and persons of the Indians, and in punishing any who may wantonly injure them, is the principal cause of the satisfactory state of affairs among the Indians of British Columbia.

The influence, too, of clergymen and missionaries, both Protestant and Roman Catholic, is very great with these people; and the fruits of the religious training, so perseveringly persisted in, already warrant the belief that the moral life of the Indian will improve as he advances in civilisation. Some philosopher has well said : 'There are two men in every man; it is childish to see only one; it is sad and unjust to look only at the other.'

Of all vessels calling themselves mail steamers the 'Prince Alfred,' in which I returned to San Francisco, must certainly be the most wretched. Her accommodation is indifferent, her food supply bad, and her engines are of no power at all.

There was little to see on the voyage down, although we were in sight of land a great part of the time. It is curious that between Puget Sound and San Francisco there are no indentations on the coast, with the exception of the mouth of the Columbia river, at which place Astoria makes but an indifferent harbour.

This absence of inlets was all the more conspicuous after the splendid inland seas we had lately visited. Most of the passengers were men who had gone up to British Columbia with the idea of settling, but had left with the impression that false representations had been used to induce them to go there. Many of them, however, had not gone farther than Victoria; and having found that they could not be allowed to buy up Government land, which had been set aside for the public use and benefit, had left in disgust. I remember one case in particular which occurred when I was at Victoria, in which an intending settler had been very much offended because he was not allowed to settle on Beacon Hill.

Beacon Hill is an eminence commanding charming views over the Sound and the surrounding country, and is the public park of Victoria. The race-course runs round it; the cricket and foot-ball ground is included in its area, and it is the general afternoon place of *rendezvous*.

As this individual could not obtain so desirable a site, he departed and spent some time in writing letters to the newspapers, abusing the Government in particular and British Columbia in general.

There was one very clever agreeable Englishman on board, who had led a Bohemian life for some years; mining, sheep-farming, and trying all sorts of employments. He was an Oxford man, and among his other accomplishments was an admirable draughtsman. He showed me several very beautifully executed drawings. Marvellous to relate, he had cultivated his artistic talents all through his wild life; and I doubt not that it was owing to the refining influences of art that he yet retained such unmistakable signs of a graceful culture of mind and manner, so unusual amongst those who have passed much of their life amid such rough scenes and amongst still rougher companions. He had lately been struck down with mountain fever, a malady often fatal, and never very easily recovered from. Perhaps it was in some measure due to this disease that he had acquired an almost morbid dislike to returning to England. He said he had no friends there who would care particularly whether he returned or not; and if he had not been advised, on account of his health, to go back to his native land, he would much rather have remained at the Cariboo mines.

I had just finished reading one of (I think) Miss Thackeray's works, and amongst a hundred other charming passages was the following:—

'People who have been through trouble, and who have necessarily been absorbed in themselves, sometimes feel ashamed when time goes on and they come back to some old home and discover what faithful remembrance has followed them all along, and a love which perhaps they never expected.'

I gave him the book; and afterwards, on meeting him in San Francisco, where he was obliged to wait a few days for the vessel which was to take him home, he seemed quite reconciled to his return, and even anxious to start. I do not know whether the happy touching words had anything to do with the change in him, but it is pleasant to think that perhaps they had.

His sketches had brought him a very considerable sum, and there was no doubt that his future as an artist would be more profitable to him than his farming and mining career had been. I have a little water-colour of his, a sunset on the Pacific, quite Turneresque in its glorious misty colouring—one of those scenes when the day is stealing away to the other side of the world, all the colours of the rainbow melting into each other; above, a broad deep violet belt, from whose centre the radiating streaks of fire shoot upwards, as if from God's lantern from below the sea.

After five days of the smoothest possible passage we passed through the 'Golden Gate,' and very soon were again on shore in San Francisco.

CHAPTER XXIII.

SAN FRANCISCO TO THE GEYSERS.

The race for the blue riband—'Coasting'—Games in America—To the Geysers—Calistoga—The Petrified Forest—Foss—The summit—Speed—The Geyser Hotel—The Devil's Cañon—The Witches' Cauldron——The Pulpit—Indian legend—Indian duns—The Indian bath—Quicksilver mines—Quails—Return.

I FOUND on arriving at San Francisco that the only topic of conversation was a great race for 20,000 dollars which was shortly to come off. The race was open to the world, but the interest centered on two horses, one called 'True Blue,' the Eastern champion, from New York; the other called 'Thad Stevens,' a California bred horse of much renown, and consequently the Western favourite.

The excitement was not confined to San Francisco and the West, but extended all over the United States to the eastern verge of the continent. Crowds of men came from New York and other great cities in the East, and on the eve of the race San Francisco was as full as London on the night before the Derby. Races in America, either trotting or running (the latter is the term applied to a simple horse-race), do not flourish, to use the mildest term; but this race was undoubtedly the most important that had ever been run in the United States, and was one in which it was felt that each competitor would really do his best to win. The distance was four miles and repeat; and the Ocean House Driving Park, situated some miles from the town, was the scene of the race. The day was hot, the dust stifling, but the whole of San Francisco turned out to see the fun.

The road to the course, indeed, the whole of the intervening country, was alive with the usual accessories of a great race. From the millionaire's magnificent turn-out—which competed in a struggle for the front place with the pedlar's donkey-cart—there was every kind of vehicle, down to a hand-barrow; and the fast trotter, the winner of many a hard contest, had to accommodate his pace to the more dilatory movements of a dray-horse. On ordinary occasions it is painful to see a true American handling the reins, he drives so fast and pulls so hard. Holding the reins in both hands, and with his legs well stretched forward for leverage, he pulls as if he intended to pull the head off the horse. What a waste of labour there must be before a horse is properly trained to this!

But to return to the course. 'Thad Stevens' did not give one the idea of being able to compete successfully with first-class racers; but his condition was everything that could be desired. 'True Blue' looked a perfect racehorse, and was greatly admired for his beauty and grace of form. Four horses started; the winner might, therefore, have to travel twenty miles—the heats being four miles each. The first heat was run in seven minutes forty-five seconds, and was won by a horse called 'Daniels'; the second, in eight minutes eight seconds, was won by 'True Blue.' In the third heat poor 'True Blue' strained the tendons of his off hind leg and broke down, this heat being won by 'Thad Stevens' in seven minutes fifty-seven seconds.

As it was then almost a certainty that 'Thad' would win the next heat, and consequently the race, the excitement was intense, the California spirit rising to boiling-point. From the first 'Thad Stevens' took the lead and maintained it throughout, winning in eight minutes twenty and three-quarter seconds. He was so little distressed at the conclusion that he looked ready to start on another sixteen-mile race.

The announcement that the Californian horse was the winner caused a scene of the wildest enthusiasm. One man was so excited, and tossed up his hat in the air so often that at last he lost it, when he relieved his feelings by throwing up those of other people. Finally he was seized by two men who had lost their hats by his reckless enthusiasm, and after receiving a pommelling which must have greatly cooled his ardour, he was kicked out of the Park.

'True Blue's' accident was by some people thought to have been caused by the sandy soil giving way with him in a badly prepared part of the track; but others affirmed that he was intentionally struck by 'Thad Stevens.' However it may have been, the beautiful creature was crippled for life, and probably just in the moment of victory.

This unfortunate occurrence diminished in some degree the interest felt in the result of the race, but did not lessen the high merit and wonderful staying powers of 'Thad Stevens,' the winner of the blue riband for California. Whether sixteen-mile races can be indulged in with impunity is a question which others better acquainted with horse lore than I am must answer.

I have at last discovered the use of the steep hills which abound in San Francisco. 'Coasting' could not be indulged in without them; and 'coasting,' as far as I have observed, is the only popular amusement—with the exception of an occasional game of base-ball in a sand-field—amongst the juvenile portion of the population. And it is a game much enjoyed by the three genders, masculine, feminine, and tom-boys, whose ages vary from three to about fifteen. A 'coaster' is a small sledge on wheels, on which you sit while you glide down the wooden side-walk, from the top to the bottom of the hills. The best performer is he who, when approaching a cross-road, can most adroitly turn the corner without getting upset. Sometimes a string of perhaps half-a-dozen of these 'coasters' comes down upon you with the speed of a fire-engine as you are ascending the hill; but they are more generally encountered when turning a corner, and then the meeting is disadvantageous to some one.

What a difference there is between an American youth and an English one! At a time when the latter is accustomed to cricket, foot-ball, racquets, hare-and-hounds, &c., the former is amusing himself with his marbles and tops, skating a little or playing at base-ball—which is merely a game of 'rounders' deprived of half its fun—but 'coasting' a good deal, and fitting himself for anything rather than vigorous and sustained bodily effort. The apathy displayed towards our splendid English games may perhaps arise from the want of opportunity of witnessing and understanding them; for it is difficult to imagine any boy, who has once been accustomed to play cricket not entering heart and soul into that and the various other athletic games.

The Harvard men may row on for years, row on for centuries, but they will never win a race from English University crews, until American habits accustom the youth of the country to downright hard work long before the time arrives for entering the college-gates.

No one ought to leave California without seeing the Geysers. I started one morning with some friends to make the excursion. We crossed the bay to Vallejo; then we went on by train as far as Calistoga Springs, passing through Nassa Valley, which is one of the most fruitful of the many beautiful valleys in the State. Calistoga is a most unattractive-looking place. It consists of a group of small houses in the middle of a hot dusty plain, on which there is only some very scanty shrubbery, affording no shade; and trees will not grow on the hot sulphurous soil. Enormous sums have been spent by the proprietor of the hotel on the grounds and baths, in order to make it the Saratoga of the West; but from appearances I should think the attempt has turned out a failure.

From Calistogo we drove to the 'Petrified Forest.' Picture to yourself a vast wood of stony trees in full leaf, petrified shrubs with petrified flowers; petrified pines covered with petrified cones; birds' nests with eggs, all in a state of petrifaction; ferns and bracken which break when you try to gather them; here and there a petrified bird, perched on the hard branches, and whose song may have been petrified as it issued from his throat. Imagine all this—still you will have no conception of the Petrified Forest.

The drive there was pleasant, more on account of the lovely weather than the beauty of the scenery. We passed two or three deserted houses, in front of which dangled an old hoop-skirt, a gaiter, and an odd boot or two, which our driver informed us were the inevitable signs of the family having moved. Perhaps, we thought, they were afraid of being petrified too. When, at last, we arrived at the forest we found it consisted of a few scattered old stumps, of the most uninteresting description. The only curiosity in the collection was a large petrified pine-trunk, out of which was growing a fine young tree, which somebody remarked 'was like Lot's wife, with a live baby in her arms.' We did not linger long in the so-called 'Petrified Forest,' and we left it with a keen sense of having been taken in. The next morning we drove to the Geysers, over the hills some twenty-seven miles away.

Foss, the part owner of the six-horse stages which run between Calistoga and the Geysers, is renowned throughout California as being the first whip in the State, and probably in the world. He is a large man, with immense power of arm, chest, and shoulders. There is a look of mastery and will, such as is not often seen, in his hard face and firm jaw; and younger drivers, who have mostly been trained by him, regard him as the unapproachable king of the coach-box. His driving impresses you with a feeling of confidence in his great power and skill; and even when going at his terrific pace down the steep hills, it seems to be impossible that any accident should happen.

The drive, after leaving the main road, was full of enjoyment. It lay along a wild winding lovely mountain track. The hills were covered with brushwood and shrubs about half-way down, and then sloped away into the valley. They were decked with what in the spring had been great crops of wild oats, but which when we drove by was merely a mass of close-cropped yellow stubble. For many miles we toiled up the mountain-sides till we reached the summit, the view from which, at sunset, eclipsed everything I had seen in California. It strongly reminded me of that almost unequalled view from the garden of the monastery of Camaldoli, near Naples.

The Russian River Valley took the place of the Solfatara and the region towards Baiæ and Cumæ; a dark sombre lake supplied the place of Lake Avernus; and Naples, Pozzuoli, and the Mediterranean had their counterparts in San Francisco, Vallejo, and the Pacific.

The Russian River Valley is diversified by dark groves of noble oaks and huge lava-like eminences, in some parts covered with vegetation, vividly green, in others bare and bleak.

The beauty of the golden yellow plain, through which the course of the silvery river can be traced, was enhanced by the white farm-houses and ranches which peeped out from the crimsoned foliage of the changing maple; whilst here and there the dark cypresses heightened the colour of the red trunks of the graceful madrona.

Our descent to the Geyser Hotel was performed in a most reckless style. A mountain-wall on one side, a precipice on the other, and continual curves of such sharpness that the leaders were frequently on one side of the chasm when the coach was on the other. For the whole eight miles, the road twists and winds and crosses brooks and ravines. The horses, which had been eagerly listening ever since their arrival at the summit for their orders to 'Shake out,' dashed down the narrow road as only Californian horses can do, and completed the entire distance in about twenty minutes.

The Geyser Hotel we found remarkable for nothing except its extremely bad food, a circumstance quite inexcusable, considering the great number of visitors it receives in the season.

We heard afterwards that a lawsuit was pending about the ownership of the property, and till it was settled the people who rented it would not improve the place or make it even moderately comfortable, as they might be turned out at any moment. They were therefore content to gain what they could during their reign. A dirtier or worse-looked-after domain I never saw ; but, fortunately, the interest of the spot lies in its natural phenomena, and not in the hotel.

The hissing and roaring of steam, which sounded through the night, was sure evidence of our proximity to the infernal regions. Everything about the place is connected with the Devil in some way—at least by name— whereas, names designating the properties of the numerous springs would be rather more appropriate and equally euphonious. The first view of the Geysers is very striking.

From the verandah of the hotel, which is just opposite to the Geyser cañons, the whole scene can be viewed at once.

Clouds of steam issue from the earth in a hundred different places in the cañons and from the sides of the sloping hills. Pluton Cañon, which is crossed at right angles by the Great Geyser, or Devil's Cañon, lies at our feet. The whole country is mountainous, and the steep hill-sides are covered with oak, manganita, madrona, and buck-eye. Even among the sulphur springs vegetation flourishes, and shrubs and flowers peep out from the most unlikely spots. Far into the distance, hills succeed hills, and the 'Hog's

VULCAN'S STEAM WORKS.—From Pluton Creek. P. 346.

Back,' celebrated in old coaching days for the perilous character of its precipitous grades, forms a bold background.

Our first duty was to explore the Great Cañon; so, crossing the wooded ravine which separated us from the hot district, we entered a mysterious gorge, running up into the mountains directly from the river.

A small stream of water which rises at the head of this cañon flows through its entire length—pure and cold where it issues, but gradually growing hot and medicated as it receives the waters from the springs along its banks. The first part of this ravine is exceedingly picturesque, and trees and shrubs overhang the deep shady pools, in which many a delightful bath can be enjoyed. 'Proserpine's Grotto' is a charming retreat among the rocks, surrounded with the fantastic roots and tangled branches of the madrona and bay-trees, and roofed in by luxuriant foliage.

Gradually, the sulphurous odour becomes stronger and the puffing noise of underground engines increases; springs bubble and boil in every direction, and clouds of steam roll through the gorge, wetting you through, and making it difficult to distinguish the boulders, upon which you have to hop to avoid the boiling water of the stream. The subterranean roar becomes almost terrifying. You fear every instant that the thin crust of hot mineral deposits over which you are walking will give way, and your Geyser trip end in a visit to black Tartarus.

Carefully picking your way, and almost stifled, you arrive at the brink of the 'Witches' Cauldron,' a black opening in the solid rock, about eight feet in diameter, and of unknown depth. This Plutonic reservoir is the grandest of the Geyser springs, and its roar is like that of Vesuvius. It is filled with a bubbling surging liquid of intense blackness, and throws up its dusky spray to a height of three or four feet. Mr. Muybridge, the artist photographer of Messrs. Bradley and Rulophson, of San Francisco—whose photographs, as well as those of Mr. Watkins, are world-renowned—grouped three ladies about this cauldron in the attitude of the witches in Macbeth, and made a very telling picture—

> 'Double, double toil and trouble;
> Fire burn and cauldron bubble.'

Leaving the boiling well, we crossed endless living, dying, and dead geysers, and climbed a rocky height called 'The Pulpit'—the Devil's, of course. It is just above 'The Cauldron,' and opposite 'The Steamboat' geyser, whose shrill scream can be heard above all other sounds. From it there is a splendid view of the cañon, and the steaming and boiling fountains around. So numerous are they, it seemed marvellous that we had been able to thread our way through them up to 'The Pulpit.' Some enthusiastic pilgrims had planted the Stars and Stripes on its summit; but we found the flag on the ground and the pole broken, his Satanic majesty having thus resented foreign interference in his affairs.

Passing over the 'Mountain of Fire,' we were attracted by a loud whistling noise. This we found came from a small pipe that had been placed over an aperture, whence, with terrific screeching and screaming, issued volumes of steam. Leaving the 'infernal regions,' our pathway crossing strata of sulphur, magnesia, alum, Epsom-salts, &c., we made our way down the mountain-side back to the hotel.

The cañon is a large laboratory, and the ground is strewed in all directions with a great variety of mineral deposits and chemical compounds. The waters are impregnated with acids and salts, and the number of highly-charged springs is enormous. Amongst others there are the 'Alkali,' the 'Eye-water,' the 'Boiling Alum,' the 'Iron,' the 'Red,' the 'White,' and the 'Black' Sulphur Springs. The 'Devil's Inkstand' is a small spring, from which flows a liquid which has the quality of being indelible, and is a very good subtitute for ink. An earnest request is always made that visitors will taste the different waters. To comply with it would be almost as agreeable as trying the contents of the bottles in a chemist's shop-window. The healing properties, however, of some of the springs have been proved, and many cures have been effected by the waters. It is said, that the Indians first discovered the value of them as baths in the following manner.

A wandering tribe happening to pass near this cañon, and one of them being very ill, was, with the customary Indian kindness, left there to die, a little dried meat being all the provision thought necessary for his sustenance. Finding it cold, and seeing the vapour issuing from the ground, he crawled towards it and laid himself down there to sleep. In a few days this vapour-bath cured him, and he was able to rejoin his tribe. Previous to this, the cañon itself had been carefully avoided by the red men, as they thought the Devil was always lying in wait there, because he had once been made a fool of on that spot by an Indian.

The tribe being encamped on the other side of the cañon, the Devil called one day on a wicked '*brave*' and told him that his time was come, and that he must accompany him to the unhappy hunting-grounds of the bad Indians. 'All right,' said the *brave*; 'but first I have a little business to transact, some money to collect,[1] and a game of poker to win. If your

---

[1] The Indian has a peculiar mode of reminding a debtor that he has a claim on him. He never duns him, but cuts a number of small sticks and paints a rim round the end of each; these he throws into his debtor's wigwam, and forthwith, without speaking a word, goes his way. The hint is generally taken, the debt paid, and the sticks destroyed—for

majesty will go over to the opposite cañon I will join you as soon as the sulphurous vapour has passed away.'

As the vapour has never ceased ascending the wicked '*brave*' has never appeared, and the Indians say that the ' bad spirit ' is still waiting and watching there for his victim.

The rude ' sweating-booth ' at the old Indian Spring was just as luxurious as the bath-house over the river. The latter place was in keeping with the inn, and was far more likely to impart disease than to expel it.

Edwin Forrest, the great tragedian, was cured of rheumatism in 1869 by the use of the Indian Spring, to which he was daily carried, the severity of the attack entirely precluding the use of his limbs.

One of our excursions was to some new and valuable quicksilver mines, in one of which the ' Rattlesnake ' pure quicksilver is found. The rock is crushed, and out rolls the quicksilver. It is the only mine in which the pure ore has been discovered, cinnabar being the mineral from which quicksilver is usually obtained.

The process of reducing the ore is very interesting and easy of comprehension. The object is to awaken the sleeping mercury, and this is accomplished by fire.

it is considered a disgrace by an Indian to have dunning-sticks thrown into his dwelling.

The cinnabar is put into furnaces, and after three or four days' heating the vapours are allowed to pass through small openings into condensing chambers, on whose walls the mercury globules form, and glide at once into small troughs, which conduct them to a large iron cauldron. They are then transferred to iron flasks, and are ready for the market.

On our way home we obtained some good specimens of the mountain and valley quails. Both are beautiful birds, about the size of a partridge; but the former has a long feather on its head, and the under part of its body is very distinctly marked in coloured bars, whereas the valley quail has a little top-knot, and is not so plainly striped. Its throat, too, is black, with a little white border, therein differing from the mountain-quail, whose throat is reddish-brown, and only white at the sides. The horse-shoe can be almost as plainly distinguished on these birds as on the male partridge. Both species afford capital sport, and are stronger in their flight than any other bird; but they are uncommonly difficult to find without dogs. As soon as flushed they are off with a rapid, wild flight, but seldom travel far, and soon pitch again in the thickest neighbouring coverts.

I am told mountain-quails are getting rare, and are being rapidly thinned off by the wild cats, which abound in California. But as these and other destructive animals have always existed, I do not see why the present scarcity of birds should be ascribed to them.

After a few days' sojourn in these 'lower regions,' our visit rendered none the less interesting and instructive by the Geyser Spring chicken-soup, and the appropriate sulphur and brimstone condiments with which our liberal host regaled us, we bade adieu to Pluto and Proserpine, and returned to San Francisco by Healdsburg and Petaluma.

This route was as picturesque as that which we took on our way to the Geysers, and possessed the advantage of only sixteen instead of seven-and-twenty miles' staging. The superb driving of Clarke Foss is missed on this road; but when the great 'whip' rests from his labours or has disappeared from the coach-box, I think the Healdsburg route will become the favourite one to the California Geysers.

A A

CHAPTER XXIV.

CONCLUDING REMARKS.

Healdsburg—Porters—Jewellery—An art—Rainy season—Catarrh—San Diego—The abalona hunter—Shooting—Hotel mania—Americans abroad—The West.

WE remained for the night at Healdsburg, and a more unpleasant one I never passed. The hotel was full of travellers, apparently all going in different directions, from the different hours at which the porter roused the whole house in his efforts to awaken the right man. In the room next to mine there was a man of the name of Brown, and the porter thumped at his door at intervals of about half-an-hour all through the night, in spite of the reiterated assurances of the unfortunate lodger that he was not going anywhere. The porter, however, said he knew better than that, as he had been told to call Mr. Brown at 2 A.M., and call him he would. Eventually, at about five o'clock, he once more came round to Mr. Brown to ask him what his initials were, and then found out that they did not correspond with those of the Mr. Brown he was in search of.

Travellers owning names that are not very uncommon would do well at hotels to leave their initials outside the door with their boots, for though the latter are seldom attended to in America, the former always command respect.

During our short journey by rail on the following day we saw nothing remarkable, except the enormous gold watchchain worn by the conductor. The masculine mind in America has a strong weakness (if there can be such a thing) for jewellery.

Railway conductors and attendants are considered very unbusiness-like if, after their first month, they have not secured sufficient means to purchase a handsome watch and chain. The sight of a diamond becomes quite distressing after a few weeks in America; diamond studs worn in the daytime, diamond pins stuck into neckties of the sailor-knot type or into the shirt between the studs, are so constantly seen, that these stones are conspicuous only by their absence.

'What kind of a chain would you like?' asks the jeweller. 'Well, I don't hardly know,' replies the young man. 'What kind of a chain do you think I ought to have; that is, what style do you think would be the most becoming for a young man who carries groceries to the best families in town?'

Such and similar conversations are not unfrequently heard, and an idea of the all-pervading love of adornment may be gathered from it. Bar-keepers, invariably, are splendid in their decorations, and their trade offers good opportunities for displaying their jewelled fingers.

America may not equal Europe in the cultivation of the arts and sciences, but it can point with pride to the nimble 'bar-keeper' as he manipulates 'a smash, a julep, or a corpse reviver.' Such dexterity and sleight-of-hand is seldom seen off the conjuror's stage; and it is no small accomplishment to be able to keep a six-foot liquid arc oscillating in the air from tumbler to tumbler.

A few days after our return to San Francisco a change in the weather betokened the approach of the rainy season. An abnormally high barometer was observed to be advancing on the Pacific coast and travelling eastward—a pretty sure sign that the annual 'November wave' was at hand. It is strange that of the many storms that yearly arise in the Rocky Mountain regions and sweep to the Eastern coast, this annual November storm is the only one which has its origin on the Pacific slope.

Predictions were soon verified; the many months of dust being followed by some weeks of constant rain, accompanied by mist and fog.

Fogs in California are not equal to the celebrated London species, which idle boys are said to cut up into thick pieces and throw at one another; but they are cold clammy concerns, and not to be encountered with impunity. They are apt to engender colds and sore-throats, of a more obstinate unconquerable kind than those of any other quarter of the globe. 'You may doctor and bandage your throat as you will, but the sense of its soreness will hang round you still.' Then is the time to hasten down to Southern California and enjoy the mild sunny winter climate of San Diego, which for invalids is said to be far superior to Nice, Mentone, and the Ribiera generally. Amusements of all kinds are to be found there, and plenty of occupation for sportsmen, botanists, and artists.

Conchologists, too, will find many beautiful shells on the coast near San Diego; amongst others the abalona, or California shell, the search after which is liable to end in a manner not altogether satisfactory.

The following casualty, which at the beginning of this year befell an abalona-hunter near San Diego, equals in horror Victor Hugo's account of the Devil-fish, in his 'Toilers of the Sea.' But first let me observe that the meat of the abalona, which is tougher than an old pair of leather gaiters, is esteemed a great delicacy by the Chinese.

The shells abound chiefly in the very south of Lower California, and two Chinese companies have been engaged there for several years in gathering them. They cleave the shells from the rocks at low tide, and after cutting the meat out they boil, salt, and dry it. It is then packed in bales and shipped to their own country.

In the neighbourhood of San Diego are precipitous rocks, sometimes quite abrupt in their formation, but occasionally broken. They are called the Coronades. To these rocks a Chinaman, a professional fisherman, known by the nickname of 'Chowder,' went out in his boat to hunt for abalonas.

His subsequent movements can only be surmised, and the supposition is, that after mooring his boat to begin his search he observed a large abalona in a cleft of the rock at a part covered with water at high tide. Throwing himself on his stomach, he reached over the ledge to wrench the delicacy from its fastness.

Abalonas are univalvular, and if in detaching one from the rock, to which it can fix itself almost immovably, it happens not to be wrenched away at once, it has the power of closing its single shell on the rock and imprisoning the hand, thus causing intense agony to the captive.

This was poor Chowder's fate.

The abalona was an unusually large one and the wretched man, unable to release himself, must soon have become conscious that he was doomed. From his position, leaning over the rock, he had not the power, even at the sacrifice of his hand if necessary, to tear himself free.

Imagine the agony of mind, as well as bodily pain, the unfortunate creature endured as he waited long hours for the rising of the tide which should end his misery by death.

The actual pain must have been excruciating, and there was no help within miles. The inexorable waters did their work at last, and when Chowder's body was recovered by a brother Chinaman, his dead hand was still clutched in the remorseless grasp of the abalona. The shell, which is in my possession, measures about thirty inches in circumference.

There is excellent wild-fowl shooting near San Diego, and at Kern-River and Tulare Lake, near Visalia; and game of all sorts, 'grizzlies' included, abounds there. But some of the best wild-fowl shooting I ever had was in the neighbourhood of San Francisco. I started off one morning with a man who made wild-fowl shooting his business, and a capital companion and thorough sportsman he proved to be.

We went up the Sacramento river, and at last arrived at his shooting-ground. For miles round nothing was to be seen but swamps, pools, and a wilderness of tules, or rushes, the haunts of thousands of wild-fowl.

After passing the night in his little sloop, early morn saw us astir and paddling off to our respective positions, which we reached before daybreak. At the first streak of dawn a sound of the fluttering and flapping of wings was heard, and over came the ducks, at first singly, then in flights.

So fast was the shooting that, although I had two guns, I had to wait now and then till they cooled sufficently to hold.

Splendid canvas-backs passed over with the velocity of a cannon-ball, and I think I must have missed a dozen of them in the first half-hour. Other ducks seemed hardly to move, so slow was their flight in comparison with that of the canvas-back.

This went on for about an hour, when the flights gradually ceased; so we gathered our ducks and returned to the sloop for breakfast. Afterwards my companion sculled me about the creeks, flushing endless ducks, and at one point where we landed making a good bag of snipe.

Towards evening we heard the well known 'Hawnk—Hawnk—Ee-awnk,' and presently the wild geese flew over us, but too high for a shot. This was only an advance flight, and before long endless strings of them were flying round and filling the air with their peculiar cry. One flight came so near us that we each bagged three, and as they fell it looked, as my companion observed, as if it snowed geese. There was no moon, so we were unable to continue our sport after five o'clock, although we heard, and could just distinguish, long streams of birds winging their way past us. Up to seven o'clock the flights continued —then all was silent. Our total bag for that day was twenty-three canvas-backs, thirty mallards, twenty teal, eight couple of snipe, nine geese, a few widgeon and pintails, and a bittern.

In comparison to the number often shot our bag was small. But I had never had such shooting before, and was therefore perfectly content, and returned to San Francisco with the hope of some time or other enjoying a few more days of such sport.

On returning from British Columbia I had been astonished to find that the buildings opposite my windows had all been pulled down, and on enquiry I learnt that another giant hotel was to occupy the site. There is a perfect mania for giant hotels in America. I hope in this new one they will study the art of boiling potatoes and roasting meat as well as that of profuse and useless decoration.

I believe that, in spite of the universal hotel-life in America, the discomfort of those dwellings has a great deal to do with driving Americans to Europe; but of course they would not confess so much.

I wonder whether Americans enjoying themselves

abroad are aware **of the abuse** heaped on them by their less fortunate brethren who are obliged to remain at home?

There is some reason for complaint too, **as thousands of** Americans who know every **corner of Paris** and every studio in **Rome** have **never seen** Niagara, much less California. Patriotic persons shake their heads and sigh **over** the enormous amount of money taken out of the country and **spent in** London, Paris, Switzerland, **and** Italy, whilst the magnificent scenery **of** their own country is neglected. But it must be remembered that—irrespective of the fact that travelling is much cheaper in Europe than in the United States, and that the **cost of** living at American watering-places and at all favourite resorts is so enormous that a whole family can enjoy some months of European travel for the same sum that a short sojourn **at any of these** fashionable places would entail—the Old World offers many attractions that **are** wanting in the New World.

In the first place, the social attractions afforded by the capitals of Europe are vastly superior to those of **America.** Then there are the charms of antiquity, of historical and **artistic** association; **the** wonderful picture-galleries, the museums, the sculpture; every**thing, in** short, to gratify the tastes of the merest tyro as **well as those of** the most cultivated connoisseur.

Can there be a **more** memorable era in the

life of anyone than **that of** the day **when** he first enters Rome? After having seen Rome, Naples, and Athens he **is** not likely **to** care for **Chicago** or San Francisco.

Ergo, **it would** be well for Americans first to **study** thoroughly their native land and afterwards to cross the Atlantic. The delights of European travel for ladies far outbid anything that can be offered in the New World. But for men, or rather for sportsmen, America **offers** an unrivalled field. After all, those who complain of American absenteeism must remember that the majority of their countrymen, having once seen Europe, are imbued with an irrepressible longing **to** return to their own land; firmly resolved not to leave **it** again.

To this **class** belong those who are always **craving** for change **of scene and fresh** excitement; **those who** rush through **grand** scenery, and who after **several** days' journey to some celebrated spot remain there two minutes, 'just to say they have been there.'

Not that this class is confined to America, though I think it thrives there in greater perfection than elsewhere.

Californians, above all, are eager to return to their country. But they have their unrivalled climate to urge as an excuse for hurried visits to less favoured lands. And truly the climate of California is marvellous. Fresh and exhilarating air, a clear blue sunny sky—equalled perhaps in Colorado and British Columbia, but in few other places—and a wonderful evenness of temperature, combine to make California a most charmingly attractive country to those who have once had experience of its delights.

The great, strong, and wildly rushing rivers, and the grand scenery of the West, seem to have imparted something of their freedom and character to the inhabitants. There is an absence among them of that narrowness, that mental tight-lacing, which squeezes all charity out of human nature, and which is so characteristic of the Old World; and there is the presence of an open-hearted fellowship between man and man, of a rare and generous kind.

With this tribute to the Far West I close the record of my 'Western Wanderings.' To those who have perused its pages, and have thus, as it were, wandered with me, I will only say—I shall be content if they lay it down with a better knowledge than they had before of the distant Evening Land.

www.ingramcontent.com/pod-product-compliance
Lightning Source LLC
Chambersburg PA
CBHW030430300426
44112CB00009B/928